THE JOURNAL OF THE ASSOCIATION OF MOVING IMAGE ARCHIVISTS

OVINGIMAGE THE MOVINGIMAGE THE MOVINGIMAGE THE MOVI

FALL 2017

The Moving Image (ISSN 1532-3978) is published twice a year in spring and fall by the University of Minnesota Press, 111 Third Avenue South, Suite 290, Minneapolis, MN 55401-2520. http://www.upress.umn.edu

Published in cooperation with the Association for Moving Image Archivists (AMIA). Members of AMIA receive the journal as one of the benefits of membership. For further information about membership, contact the Association of Moving Image Archivists, 1313 North Vine Street, Hollywood, CA 90028 (or e-mail amia@amianet.org or visit http://www.amianet.org).

Postmaster: Send address changes to *The Moving Image,* University of Minnesota Press, 111 Third Avenue South, Suite 290, Minneapolis, MN 55401-2520.

Inquiries and information about manuscript submissions should be sent to the editors, Susan Ohmer and Donald Crafton (movingimage@nd.edu). All manuscripts should be submitted as a Microsoft Word e-mail attachment, double-spaced throughout, using 12-point type with 1-inch margins, using the *Chicago Manual of Style,* 16th edition.

Review copies of books (no e-books, please) should be sent to Donald Crafton and Susan Ohmer, Department of Film, Television, and Theatre, DeBartolo Performing Arts Center, University of Notre Dame, Notre Dame, IN 46530. Review copies of Blu-rays and DVDs should be sent to Jen Bircher, Seahawk Mail, University of North Carolina Wilmington, 601 South College Road, Wilmington, NC 28403-5950.

Please allow a minimum of 4 months for editorial consideration.

Address subscription orders, changes of address, and business correspondence (including requests for permission and advertising orders) to *The Moving Image,* University of Minnesota Press, 111 Third Avenue South, Suite 290, Minneapolis, MN 55401-2520.

Subscriptions: Regular US rates: individuals, 1 year (2 issues) $30; libraries, 1 year $75. Other countries add $5 for each year's subscription. Checks should be made payable to the University of Minnesota Press. Back issues are $22.50 for individuals and $56.25 for institutions (plus $6 shipping for the first copy, $1.25 for each additional copy inside the United States; $9.50 shipping for the first copy, $6 for each additional copy outside the United States). *The Moving Image* is a benefit of membership in the Association of Moving Image Archivists.

Digital subscriptions to *The Moving Image* are available online through the JSTOR Current Scholarship Program at http://www.jstor.org/r/umnpress.

Most images reproduced in *The Moving Image* are available to view in color in the electronic edition of *The Moving Image,* accessible via JSTOR.

Founded in 1991, the **Association of Moving Image Archivists** is the world's largest professional association devoted to film, television, video, and digital image preservation. Dedicated to issues surrounding the safekeeping of visual history, this journal covers topics such as the role of moving image archives and collection in the writing of history, technical and practical articles on research and development in the field, in-depth examinations of specific preservation and restoration projects, and behind-the-scenes looks at the techniques used to preserve and restore our moving image heritage.

Jan-Christopher Horak *University of California, Los Angeles*

Priya Jaikumar *University of Southern California*

Martin Koerber *Deutsche Kinemathek*

Andrea Leigh *Library of Congress*

James Lindner *Media Matters*

Scott MacQueen *UCLA Film & Television Archive*

Mike Mashon *Library of Congress*

Annette Melville *National Film Preservation Foundation*

Anne Morra *Museum of Modern Art*

Charles Musser *Yale University*

Margaret Parsons *National Gallery of Art*

David Pierce *Media History Digital Library*

Rick Prelinger *Internet Archive*

David Robinson *Giornate del Cinema Muto*

Ralph Sargent *Film Technology*

Eric Schaefer *Emerson College*

Shelley Stamp *University of California, Santa Cruz*

Jacqueline Stewart *University of Chicago*

Sarah Street *University of Bristol*

Dan Streible *New York University*

Vanessa Toulmin *University of Sheffield/National Fairground Archive*

Gregory Waller *Indiana University*

Haidee Wasson *Concordia University*

Pamela Wintle *Smithsonian Institution*

Patricia Zimmermann *Ithaca College*

REVIEWS

BOOK

BLU-RAY

Editors' Foreword: Digital Tools and Networks

DONALD CRAFTON AND SUSAN OHMER

Media scholars, specialists, and those of us who engage with the materiality of film, television, and old and new media in our lives have been aware for a long time of the digitization of our endeavors. Some of us use rapidly evolving tools to teach and write; some of us use them mainly to access sources; some of us innovate those tools and curate the sources; some of us are still, figuratively speaking, trying to figure out the TV remote. This special issue of *The Moving Image* addresses all these constituencies.

We are fortunate to have two recognized specialists in the theory and practice of digital humanities (DH) to advise us. Dimitrios Latsis teaches at the School of Image Arts of Ryerson University in Toronto. He received his PhD in film studies from the University of Iowa and completed a postdoctoral fellowship in visual data curation at the Internet Archive. Grazia Ingravalle holds a PhD in film studies from the University of St. Andrews and has been awarded a Leverhulme Early Career Fellowship (2017–20) to work on her new research project about colonial archival films and contemporary archival exhibition practices. Currently she is working on a book, *Curating Film History: Film Museums and Archives in the Age of New Media*.

We commend our guest editors for achieving their goal of assembling "a primer on some of the most significant recent developments in the fields of film history, archiving, and preservation." It is an important contribution, especially because, at this early stage of what will be a vast transformation of a discipline, few of us can say with certainty what is coming. The experts they have selected give us a few glimpses of present and future possibilities. And it's an exciting, generally optimistic view.

We want to point out, though, as devil's advocate, that the discussions and debates will not stop here. Arguments and observations about the unfolding crises that digitization is triggering have been aired in this journal over the past five years and will no doubt continue. The present issue gives us a concentrated snapshot of the current situation. The rapid and pervasive shift to digital technologies, the conversion of stand-ard resources (such as trade journals and card catalogs) into searchable databases and scans, and the introduction of cutting-edge analytic tools and digital source materials described in several of our articles already have upended the field. Not only how we do our work but, moreover, the most fundamental ways of *thinking about and planning* how we go about doing our business have been altered.

Most of the writing on DH assumes, and several studies in this issue affirm, that these digital tools and networks are progressive and welcome additions to the archivist's and scholar's arsenal. That being said, in a couple contributions, we detect traces of a dystopian cloud that hangs over the conversation. Is digitization an improvement when the new tools make the old ones and their resources obsolete or inaccessible? Or do the machines displace something quintessentially personal and insightful about archiving and scholarship? Or are online networks substituting for the physical labor of hired staff and academic researchers? Now, these questions in various iterations have persisted since the Industrial Revolution to be sure, but the speed and pervasive nature of current changes have redrawn the critical discussion in sharp focus.

Technology is never pure, and the technological changes in our field predictably have an inescapable political context. Our digital world is shifting resources globally (boosting the economies of some nations and forcing reorganization in those of others). It is affecting young people's career choices and established workers' security. And it is changing the ways in which those institutions that produce, study, and present media are interacting with their constituencies, their publics, and—fundamentally—their revenue sources. In the United States—but our case is not unique—politically motivated deep cuts are being inflicted on the public funding of research, education, and cultural initiatives. Will the digitization tools and networks exemplified by the innovative and vital projects cited in this issue be nipped in the bud? Will private donors and corporations fill the funding gap, and what will they expect for doing so? Will the economies of digitization help the budget choppers, or will the digital redirection of energies save the day after all?

In academia, the digital humanities specifically referenced by many of our authors are a political lightning rod. An international conference, Scientification and Scientism in the Humanities, held in 2015, addressed the situation head-on.[1] Does the competition for precious funding force the professionalization of knowledge, and is that good or bad? Few would question that the availability of original resources (the Media

History Digital Library is the one most cited in this issue) raises the stakes of account-ability for scholarship. There is an expectation that opinion and speculation ultimately must be verifiable with sound empirical support. However, to what extent does creat-ing or curating the resources become an end in itself? And would that be good or bad?

A major, provocative work that was published just as this issue of the journal was being assembled is Acland and Hoyt's *The Arclight Guidebook to Media History and the Digital Humanities* (reviewed in this issue by Bregt Lameris).[2] There Eric Hoyt made a strong case for

> the need to count digital collection building and software development as legitimate forms of scholarship. The question of what counts as scholarship is about more than tenure; it's about the ways graduate students are advised, the ways jobs are constructed, the prestige economy that nudges academics to take up one project instead of another, and the ripple effects of all of those decisions.[3]

His observations, of course, apply beyond academia to media institutions in general. And while his appeal makes sense and finds echoes in our articles, it also invites criticism of digitization as evidence of the encroaching scientification of the field.

Scientism and numeratization are terms that humanists have used pejoratively to criticize the reductive positivism of empiricist concepts. Likewise, the scientification to which Liliana Melgar Estrada and her collaborators allude in their article refers to the efforts by humanists to add a "provable" dimension to their work through statistics, graphs, and "hard science" analyses. Several of the arguments put forth in this issue implicitly respond to these criticisms. They indirectly engage with the following topics (among others) that were debated at the 2015 conference:

- extortive use of statistics, scales, and prognostics
- mathematization of humanities
- digitization as a strategy to make topics more "scientific"
- application of technological methods and the mechanical worldview
- traditional crafts and its "modern" technologies[4]

Despite digital initiatives' alleged threat to the old-style practice of the humanities, our special issue as a whole makes it clear that scientific and humanistic approaches are not binary opposites. They are productive companions, in practice, as collaborating coworkers and, in theory, as symbiotic concepts. The wide-ranging understanding of the cultural, political, and intellectual ramifications of the digital world as outlined here is, more and more, an absolutely necessary component of research. Going digital is an opportunity, but we should be aware that getting there may mean making difficult changes.

Donald Crafton is a professor emeritus. He taught in the Department of Film, Television, and Theatre at the University of Notre Dame.

Susan Ohmer is the William Carey and Helen Kuhn Carey Associate Professor of Modern Communications. She teaches in the Department of Film, Television, and Theatre at the University of Notre Dame.

NOTES

1. Christoph Wulf, Harish Naraindas, Axel Michaels, and Sundar Sarukkai, "Concept Note," Scientification and Scientism in the Humanities International Conference, New Delhi, November 25–26, 2015, 2–4, http://www.jnu .ac.in/Conference/CSSS_prog.pdf. The conference topic ostensibly addressed the humanities in India and Europe, but we consider its topics and questions to be generalizable.

2. Charles R. Acland and Eric Hoyt, eds., *The Arclight Guidebook to Media History and the Digital Humanities* (Falmer, U.K.: REFRAME Books, 2016), http://reframe.sussex.ac.uk/reframebooks/archive2016/the-arclight-guidebook-to -media-history-and-the-digital-humanities/.

3. Eric Hoyt, "Curating, Coding, Writing: Expanded Forms of Scholarly Production," ibid., 348.

4. Wulf et al., "Concept Note," 3.

Guest Editors' Foreword:
Digital Humanities and/in Film Archives

DIMITRIOS LATSIS AND GRAZIA INGRAVALLE

The continuous redefinition of the role and purview of archivists and curators of moving image media has been driven, in no small measure, by the development of digital tools and networks. To better understand this shift and start mapping its current impact on archives and film preservation, this special issue of *The Moving Image* assembles perspectives from leading curators, archivists, academics, and digital humanists who have developed innovative platforms to disseminate the work done in moving image archival collections. They provide new tools and resources for both research and pedagogy, share best practices, discuss opportunities for collaboration, and address challenges from leading digital humanities (DH) projects in the audiovisual archival field.

Most of these projects are still in progress, so the reader will find that this collection of feature articles and Forum pieces signals the current developing status—or "iterative" nature, to quote Charles Tepperman—of the digital humanities. The contributions compellingly reflect the state of the field, while still leaving open critical questions for future discussion. One such question is certainly whether DH methodologies and tools advance new epistemologies and practices for research in film and media studies and in archival moving image collections. While our contributors reject the idea that by incorporating (partially) automated tasks, DH methodologies lend increased scientific credibility to media analyses and histories, they all highlight the heuristic value of its applications. As the articles in this special issue emphasize, many of the tasks involved in DH projects (creating a database, segmenting a film sequence, annotating, selecting variables, etc.) in fact force us to interrogate established vocabularies, prompting us once more to (re)define, for instance, "race film," a film "shot," or an "archival record." The digital humanities, as these examples show, encourage interinstitutional and interdisciplinary collaborations among scholars and archivists, inviting them to open up the results of their work to awareness, criticism, and debate.

Particular focus is placed on outreach initiatives that give access and visibility to nonfiction, amateur, and nontheatrical film: programming, platforms for user-contributed content, crowdsourcing, and original ways of annotating, sharing, and cross-referencing time-based media. We also address pedagogy that utilizes primary sources, facilitates (under)graduate research, and encourages broader stakeholders, such as K–12 instruction and local and community-based organizations.

Shane O'Sullivan approaches these goals by exploring institutional projects that in the last fifteen years have granted access to British audiovisual archival materials for education. O'Sullivan particularly concentrates on the pioneering work of current British Film Institute (BFI) head of education Paul Gerhardt and the collaboration between the BFI and Kingston University on a pedagogical project teaching students to reuse moving image archive material in video essays.

Philipp Dominik Keidl expands a thorough consideration of the exhibition strategies of the Australian Centre for the Moving Image in Melbourne into a broader consideration of what media archaeological thinking and practices can mean outside the purview of academia, specifically as enabled by digital technologies and environments. An expanded and crucially public iteration of media archeology can stand as an equal partner and generator of discourse that leads to more conceptual contributions to film and media history.

Liliana Melgar Estrada, Eva Hielscher, Marijn Koolen, Christian Gosvig Olesen, Julia Noordegraaf, and **Jaap Blom** collaboratively survey different video annotation and editing tools widely used in media studies and production. The authors examine two kinds of video software, ELAN and NVivo, to analyze a sequence from *People on Sunday* (Robert Siodmak et al., 1930). They assess the advantages and drawbacks of each, along with the larger implications for moving image scholars, professionals, and archivists.

What would a digital humanities approach to film colors look like? In answering this question, **Barbara Flueckiger** reflects on the ERC Advanced Grant FilmColors project at the University of Zurich, an extension of one of the best-known DH projects to deal with film history, the Timeline of Historical Film Colors. With computer-assisted tools, such as video annotation and a database of color patterns from a wide array of films, FilmColors aims to merge quantitative and qualitative approaches to demonstrate what a highly technical methodology can make possible for the study of style and aesthetics, while also facilitating film archives' restoration workflows.

With "(Micro)film Studies," **María Antonia Vélez-Serna** challenges archivists and historians to reconsider their definitions of preservation-worthy materials while tackling one of the most significant providers of paratexts for film and media histories: microfilm. She argues that widespread, systematic digitization (as evidenced in projects like the British Newspaper Archive and the Media History Digital Library) has revolutionized our methodologies and behavior as historians. These resources, though, bring about their own medium-specific challenges.

We move, then, to the University of California, Los Angeles–based DH project Early African American Film. **Marika Cifor, Hanna Girma, William Lam, Shanya Norman, Miriam Posner, Karla Contreras,** and **Aya Grace Yoshioka** discuss the methodological, historical, and epistemological questions they faced in building a comprehensive database of the African American race film industry between 1905 and 1930.

Charles Tepperman introduces readers to the newly launched Amateur Movie Database (AMDB), a digital resource that aims to advance knowledge about the history of amateur cinema. Using carefully researched metadata, visual and historical materials from a range of online and archival sources, and specially commissioned essays, AMDB is an excellent example of a DH project that can help catalyze preservation and recovery efforts for the enormously important category of nontheatrical cinema. The questions Tepperman poses (Whom should these projects, researchers, and archives address? How should they be organized and presented? What are the most effective digital tools and interfaces for our users?) are the same ones that film scholars and technologists are increasingly asking daily.

Paolo Simoni discusses the use of geodatabases and geolocation apps that help users interact with the growing collections of the Italian Amateur Film Archive in Bologna. These tools enable users to explore the changing landscape of the two Italian cities of Bologna and Reggio Emilia through the eyes of amateur filmmakers, advancing what Simoni defines as an urban "media stratigraphy."

The next article distances itself from traditional historians' concerns with archival films' textual dimension and investigates instead the archival traces of the activities of the makers, distributors, exhibitors, and audiences involved in the Media Arts Center Movement. **Lindsay Kistler Mattock** discusses Mapping the Independent Media Community, a DH project based at the University of Iowa that maps the global entanglements between independent moving image artists, distributors, museums, governmental bodies, and local communities in the late 1970s.

Simona Monizza shares the perspective of a large-scale digitization and access project initiated by the EYE Filmmuseum in the Netherlands to preserve and make available short films, an often neglected but valuable mode of filmmaking. By discussing internal workflows and the process of dealing with exhibitors, and by providing an online platform for the project, Monizza demonstrates that film heritage dissemination does not compete but in fact can be synergetic with an investment in digital infrastructure and an engagement of the theatrical sector, along national and transnational lines.

In her report on the timely and highly innovative conference Transformations I: Cinema and Media Studies Research Meets Digital Humanities Tools (organized by New York University's Cinema Studies department on April 15–16, 2016), **Marina Hassapopoulou** considers the convergence of these two fields as evidenced by the work of the academics and technologists who participated in an atmosphere of exchange and collaboration. Out of the multiplicity of the participants' approaches, a consensus emerged that "the creation of tools, online research initiatives, and multimodal pedagogy should be considered as important humanities work" in its own right. The editors and contributors to the present issue of *The Moving Image* share this sentiment.

A review of a book that might well prove to be a pioneering starting point for the "institutionalization" of DH within the field of cinema studies rounds out our issue. *The Arclight Guidebook to Media History and the Digital Humanities* is arguably the first collection of essays specifically dedicated to the theory and practice of DH in moving image media. The book is part of the larger Project Arclight, which is a collaboration between Concordia University and the University of Wisconsin–Madison. As our reviewer, **Bregt Lameris,** surmises, the application behind it, the symposium in which this collection of essays originated, and the book provide very important new initiatives and possibilities for the use of digital tools in media historical research.

Finally, **Jeremy Carr** supplies an engaging review of Flicker Alley's recent Blu-ray release *3-D Rarities*. We have distributors like Flicker Alley to thank for quietly restoring and making accessible films that might otherwise be forever confined to the archive or lost for the lay audience. Their new and back catalog releases (https://www.flickeralley .com/)—such as *Early Women Filmmakers: An International Anthology, Masterworks of American Avant-Garde Experimental Film 1920–1970,* and *Chaplin's Mutual Comedies,* to name a few—are equal parts entertaining and inspirational, setting a standard for quality and substance.

Our hope as editors is that this issue will act as a primer on some of the most significant recent developments in the fields of film history, archiving, and preservation. It should offer a tool kit for archivists and researchers looking for ideas and partners in implementing DH methodologies in their own work. We also hope that it will provoke a rethinking of the purposes, stakeholders, and ethical considerations of caring for and disseminating our audiovisual heritage in the twenty-first century.

Grazia Ingravalle holds a PhD in film studies from the University of St. Andrews and recently was awarded a Leverhulme Early Career Fellowship (2017–20) to work on her new research project about colonial archival films and contemporary archival exhibition practices. She is currently working on a book manuscript, titled *Curating Film History: Film Museums and Archives in the Age of New Media*, which is based on her dissertation.

Dimitrios Latsis is assistant professor of film studies at the School of Image Arts of Ryerson University in Toronto. He received his PhD in film studies from the University of Iowa and completed a postdoctoral fellowship in visual data curation at the Internet Archive, where he served as film curator. His work has been funded by the Smithsonian Institution, CLIR, and the Mellon Foundation, among others. He is currently coediting an anthology on documentaries about the visual arts produced in the 1950s and 1960s.

ARCHIVES FOR EDUCATION

SHANE O'SULLIVAN

The Creative Reuse of Moving

Images in the United Kingdom

In a recent report on film education in Europe, the British Film Institute

(BFI) defines *film literacy* as "the level of understanding of a film,

the ability to be conscious and curious in the choice of films; the

competence to critically watch a film and to analyse its content, cinematography and

technical aspects; and the ability to manipulate its language and technical resources

in creative moving image production."[1] This article explores the liberalization of mov-

ing image archive materials for educational use in higher education and the pedagogic

use of archive content in video essays—a new form of film scholarship made possible

by digital technology that hones film literacy and bridges the theory–practice divide

between film studies and film practice for both students and academics. By remix-

ing and recontextualizing found image and sound, how can "video writing" enhance students' critical engagement with film studies, develop a more sophisticated use of film language in their practice, and make scholarly research in film more accessible to the YouTube generation?

The article expands on an interview with BFI director of education Paul Gerhardt and his pioneering work on film literacy and educational access to archives—from his BBC Creative Archive pilot to a new initiative using BFI archive material to make student video essays at Kingston University, where I teach filmmaking. The BFI report recognizes that negotiating access to archive content for educational use is a core element of its education strategy. Gerhardt argues that our ease of access to the printed word should also be applied to the moving image: "If we start off with the premise that we live in the age of the word and the picture, and that both are indispensable for our roles as citizens and our experience as learners and our careers... how do we apply the same access to both?"[2]

In the United Kingdom, we take it for granted that, no matter who owns the rights, we can access and read in a public library almost any book that's ever been published, because of the "public lending right" model, which remunerates authors and publishers for books borrowed. Gerhardt proposes a similar "public lending right" for the moving image—"in the new digital landscape, the moving image should be acknowledged as having the same educational value as the printed text."[3]

With a new model of access to this underused audiovisual source of public knowledge, Gerhardt could then ask, "What kind of tools, what kind of skills and what kind of assets do we [the BFI] need to make available for people to be active participants in [education and society]?"[4]

THE BBC CREATIVE ARCHIVE

At the Edinburgh International Television Festival in 2003, BBC director general Greg Dyke placed public access to the corporation's rich archive at the heart of his argument for the renewal of its charter. Digital technology and broadband delivery have made it possible for the BBC, as a publicly owned broadcaster, to share its "treasure trove" of content with the British people—"[they] have paid for it and our role should be to help them use it."

Dyke imagined a child downloading free BBC clips to use in a homework presentation "on lions, or dinosaurs, or Argentina or the industrial revolution . . . a dream which we will soon be able to turn into reality": "We intend to allow parts of our programmes, where we own the rights, to be available to anyone in the UK to download so long as they don't use them for commercial purposes. Under a simple licensing system, we will allow users to adapt BBC content for their own use. We are calling this the BBC Creative Archive."[5] The subsequent *Building Public Value* charter renewal document set out the plan for the Creative Archive, promising "free access to BBC content for learning, for creativity, for pleasure": "The BBC's programme archive is owned by the British people. Until now it has remained largely inaccessible as there has been no cost-effective mechanism for distribution. Digital technology removes this barrier." Newly commissioned research has indicated that "53% of internet users download content for their own compilations," so BBC-owned archive content would now be opened up for educational and community use, offering "new learning opportunities and fresh ways for people to participate and contribute as citizens": "Our goal is to turn the BBC into an open cultural and creative resource for the nation . . . and where exciting new works and products are made using this material, we will showcase them on BBC services."[6]

In 2005, Mark Thompson replaced Dyke and supported the Creative Archive idea. He commissioned a pilot from Paul Gerhardt, then BBC controller of adult learning and head of commissioning for the BBC/Open University. In April, a few weeks before the birth of YouTube, the BBC, the BFI, Channel 4, and the Open University founded the Creative Archive Licence Group, making five hundred clips of factual content available to UK users for downloading and remixing under a single noncommercial, shared attribution license. The license was "heavily inspired" by Creative Commons, whose cofounder, Lawrence Lessig, heralded the scheme as "the single most important event in getting people to understand the potential for digital [and artistic] creativity."[7] The clips included news, natural history, and local content. Rights clearance was acknowledged as "one of the biggest challenges" facing the project, and remixed films could only be republished within the United Kingdom.

Two artists who specialized in found footage films were given full access to the BBC archives through Creative Archive placements. Chris Dorley-Brown produced a three-hour DVD compilation, *The BBC in the East End 1958–1973,* for a public library in East London. He located the original participants in BBC footage and remade three episodes with them and some of the original filmmakers, "unraveling" how the programs were made.[8]

One of the BBC's biggest anxieties, says Gerhardt, was "how to handle user-generated content"—how far could it go in "working with its audience" like this? He remembers debates with colleagues about nightmare scenarios and the level of policing, monitoring, and moderating that would be required—as, say, if BBC footage were co-opted for anti–fox hunting campaigns. As a result, the license carried "no endorsement" and "no derogatory use" provisions intended to protect BBC footage from being used "for campaigning or promotional purposes" or in defamatory or derogatory ways.[9]

Gerhardt's long-term ambition was to create a single portal aggregating archive material from broadcasters and cultural organizations, which could be used by the public "under the same licence terms, from a range of different suppliers . . . a common resource which will extend the public's access while protecting the commercial rights of intellectual property owners."[10]

ITN Source later joined the scheme, but only after this commercial news provider voiced concerns about the potential market impact of free public access to the BBC archives on its own commercial archive business. ITN advocated low-resolution watermarked clips only and sought assurances that digitization funded by the license fee would not provide a commercial advantage to its direct competitor, BBC Worldwide.[11]

The successful fifteen-month pilot generated one hundred thousand registered users, five hundred thousand downloads, and an award for "interactive innovation" in the British Academy Television Craft Awards. Lord David Puttnam spoke of the power of public service initiatives like the Creative Archive to realize the full educational, cultural, and creative benefits of film heritage collections, empowering people to "enhance their cultural awareness, their critical faculty and their creative skills" while making them "much more aware of the way in which the media shapes the way in which they view the world." Two of the cornerstones of the renewed BBC charter were "promoting education and learning" through accessible specialist content and "stimulating creativity and cultural excellence."[12]

The next step was to license the Creative Archive scheme through a Public Value Test and market impact assessment, but this never happened. As Gerhardt explains, Mark Thompson had two other very costly projects in development at the time—the much-delayed iPlayer catch-up service and a new "digital version of the education curriculum," which ultimately was scrapped at a cost of £200 million when the commercial children's TV sector complained it was infringing on the free market. Thompson later told Gerhardt he should have backed the cheaper Creative Archive project, but in attempting to maximize public value and access while protecting commercial value for archives and rights owners, it would have faced similar hurdles.[13]

The BBC iPlayer successfully launched in 2007 and allows users to stream and download BBC programs for a limited period. Except for occasional Adam Curtis commissions and the fascinating Artists' Moving Image at the BBC initiative in 2014, opportunities to creatively remix and reuse BBC content in a nonbroadcast environment have all but disappeared. In retrospect, Gerhardt feels the Creative Archive was ambitious but "way before its time," as the BBC slowly transitions "from being a broad-caster to a content provider, where its users have a much greater relationship to what it does and feel they own it more."[14]

After Gerhardt's departure, BBC Archives worked with Simon Popple (University of Leeds) on two research projects (The Open Archive and Fusion) from 2007 to 2009 through an Arts and Humanities Research Council/BBC Knowledge Exchange Partnership. Popple reexamined the BBC's historical representation of the 1984–85 miners' strike by screening BBC archival footage of the strike to former miners and retired police officers on both sides of the dispute:

> The research explored how communities might take ownership of cultural and historical materials in which they are represented, and how they could use archi-val sources to give voice to their own stories and construct their own histories. The research resulted in . . . a series of films, under the title Strike Stories that told participants' own stories and offered new perspectives on the strike.[15]

In the Netherlands, the EYE Filmmuseum's Celluloid Remix initiative challenged "young creatives" to creatively reuse orphan film fragments from the Bits and Pieces Collection to create short remixes as part of the Images for the Future project. Annelies Termeer reflected on the lessons learned from the first contest before it ran again in 2012, recommending shorter films, higher-resolution footage, "enough time to select footage and theme . . . the right balance between informing and stimulating the audience," and scheduling it outside student exam periods.[16]

Paul Gerhardt continued to work with artists and filmmakers through his consultancy Archives for Creativity, negotiating access to BBC archives for John Akomf-rah's essay films *The Nine Muses* (2010) and *The Stuart Hall Project* (2013). He found it "very, very hard work . . . even though there was no commercial advantage to using that material whatsoever." He feels the BBC will open up educational rights to its collection eventually but that doing so is impossible under the current model of rights clearance, where each hour of archive content can take six hours to clear:[17] "What the BBC could do—and I think at some point, it must do—is to work with the BFI and other organizations to make the case that educational access to the BBC's archives is a national right rather than a copyright exception."[18]

The Educational Recording Agency licenses educational institutions to capture off-air broadcasts and stream TV and radio programs for teaching and research purposes, in "walled gardens" like Learning on Screen's Box of Broadcasts (BoB) service. Rights holders are compensated under a blanket agreement, which Gerhardt would like to extend to include remixing and reuse of content. He estimates that 3 percent of the BBC archives have been digitized, so there would be major costs involved, but "a digitization priority process could be put in place" to respond to the curriculum demands of teachers.[19]

Since 2013, the BBC Archive Development has partnered with Learning on Screen on the Research Education Space (RES) platform, a catalog of nine hundred thousand BBC titles available on the BoB service, dating back to 2007. Like the larger Digital Public Space the BBC has been developing with the BFI and other cultural partners, this is "a unified online space" for screening only. As Gerhardt notes, the focus is on searchability, discoverability, and metadata rather than on empowering people to "generate their own stories" and bring "a new sensibility and a new form of digital creativity" to archive material.[20]

In 2013, Paul Gerhardt was appointed as the BFI's first director of education. He inherited Film Forever, the institute's five-year plan for 2012–17. Two of its key strategic priorities were "expanding education and learning opportunities" and "unlocking film heritage . . . by investing in preservation, digitisation, interpretation and access." BFI chair Greg Dyke—the initial champion of the Creative Archive at the BBC—identified one of the key barriers to access as "the changing framework for intellectual property affecting rights-holders, citizens and educational users."

As part of a "new education offer targeted at 5–19 year olds across the UK to promote watching, making and understanding film," Film Forever imagined "a compelling new online platform . . . [including] online tools for making and editing films, downloading films to watch and re-use (linking into our film heritage strategy)." Dyke and Gerhardt had another chance to enable creative access to archives for the education sector but still faced several challenges: "Of the BFI's vast collections, only a tiny proportion is wholly owned by the BFI—and therefore available to exploit without requiring further permission. No more than half of this has been digitised. . . A further important challenge for the BFI is to develop a policy on creative expression, on how archive content can be creatively reused."[21]

Among the fifteen recommendations of Gerhardt's subsequent strategy paper (2014) were proposals for "a nationwide initiative around 'Identity and Provocation,' where diverse communities are provided access to archive film . . . to provide opportunities for debate, analysis and the re-working of content," and "'BFI bundles' of downloadable educational resources, available through the BFI Player . . . for educators to incorporate and use in their own delivery."[22]

A free-to-access educational channel would be developed for the BFI Player—the recently launched commercial video on demand (VOD) platform—and build on earlier VOD initiatives for education, BFI Screenonline, InView, and the existing BoB service. But, crucially, the channel would enable reuse of content, embodying the BFI as "a cultural programme provider, a knowledge institution, and an educational resource . . . developing a moving image literacy . . . shaped by issues of representation (does it reflect who we are?), access . . . and democratisation (learners becoming practitioners)."[23]

The BFI pledged to work with rights holders and archives "to extend the current licensing arrangements to include historic broadcasting and audio-visual collections for educational use, both inside and outside the classroom," and to "widen [copyright] exceptions . . . to offer much broader and deeper access to collections for both educators and learners."

THE VIDEO ESSAY AND THE ESSAY FILM

Alongside Paul Gerhardt's pioneering work on educational access to archives, the last ten years have also seen the emergence of the video essay as a new mode of film scholarship. As Eric Faden notes, "for over 100 years, film theory and criticism has run on a parallel but distinctly different track from its object of study. Scholarship lived in a literary, textual world that operated according to a firmly established intellectual practice of argumentation and analysis."[24]

Faden cites Walter Ong's *Orality and Literacy* (1982) in describing "two historical shifts in human communication" when new technology transformed the way we produce and inscribe knowledge—"the move from an oral culture to an alphabetic culture . . . and from an alphabetic culture to an electronic culture." He notes how traditional film scholarship "swims upstream against Ong's historical trajectory": "We are interested in film, video, and new media (electronic culture) but publish essays (alphabetic culture) and, even worse, we take these essays to conferences and *read them aloud* (oral culture). Formally, we are going backwards."[25]

Since the advent of DVDs in the late 1990s, "the unattainable text" described in Raymond Bellour's seminal 1975 essay can now be examined frame by frame and shot by shot, repeatedly. Digital access to the "object of study" has "opened up new ways of seeing old movies" and a new mode of film scholarship.[26]

In 1948, Alexandre Astruc, inspired by the evolving cinematic language of Jean Renoir, Orson Welles, and Robert Bresson, called for cinema to "break free from . . . the immediate and concrete demands of the narrative, to become a means of writing just as flexible and subtle as written language." He called "this new age of cinema the age of *caméra-stylo* (camera-pen). . . . The film-maker/author writes with his camera as a writer writes with his pen."[27]

Astruc's auteurist manifesto inspired the critics-turned-filmmakers of the French New Wave to experiment with the essay film. Faden notes that video essays are rooted in the long tradition of that form and the work of directors like Chris Marker, Agnès Varda, and Jean-Luc Godard. Astruc also inspired Faden to begin "making short films and videos in lieu of academic conference papers"—what he called "media stylos," now more commonly called the "audiovisual essay" or "video essay," the latter of which terms I use here.[28]

As Keathley and Grant note, this ability to legally rip and remix found image and sound in video essays means "film scholars can 'write' using the same tools that constitute their objects of study . . . and [play] with a source text as a way to think about it." Video essays illustrate "ideas and concepts difficult to convey through text alone."[29] Scholars can show rather than describe films to illustrate their arguments, quoting "fragments of the work as a shared frame of reference" rather than taxing "the reader's visual memory" of a film.[30]

As Lavik notes, the essay film sits between avant-garde and documentary practice, less experimental than one, less assertive than the other. It's an elastic term, and a precise definition is elusive.[31]

Faden notes two distinctions between the video essay and the essay film—essay films are primarily made by filmmakers addressing "scholarly or intellectual topics" for a theatrical or film festival audience, whereas video essays are made by "scholars who become filmmakers" and are cross-platform digital works that can be screened in the classroom, at a conference, or online. This formulation feels increasingly outdated, as many of the leading video essayists online today are freelance filmmakers and editors, and my own journey from filmmaker to video essayist confirms my point.[32]

Essay films often draw on the literary essay, defined by Phillip Lopate as a personal, subjective reflection on a single subject, "a continual asking of questions—not necessarily finding 'solutions,' but enacting the struggle for truth in full view."[33] As Faden notes, the academic essay strives to be definitive, structuring its argument around a "fixed rhetorical mode" of thesis, supporting evidence, and conclusion. In contrast, the video essay "suggests possibilities—it is not the end of scholarly inquiry; it is the beginning": "It explores and experiments and is designed just as much to inspire as to convince. . . . [It] moves scholarship beyond just creating knowledge and takes on an aesthetic, poetic function . . . [evoking] the same pleasure, mystery, allure, and seduction as the very movies that initiated our scholarly inquiry."[34] As Faden notes, this mixed and fluid rhetorical mode makes both essayist and spectator consider form in a way the traditional scholar does not:

The scholar must consider ideas of image, voice, pacing, text, sound, music, montage, rhythm, etc. In effect, we have to deal with the very same problems that our subjects deal with. And by grappling with these problems first hand, scholars instantly improve their critical and teaching skills. Quite simply, once you make a movie (or attempt to do so), you never look at another film the same way again.[35]

FROM EXPLANATORY TO POETIC

"The essential question faced in the production of the scholarly video is not technologi-cal, but conceptual . . . how to develop a rhetoric that 'matches' a mode of presentation consisting of moving images and sounds—a mode that is therefore as much poetic as it is explanatory."[36] Keathley compares many video essays to audiovisual adaptations of traditional written essays, using argumentation and analysis and "rendered primarily in the explanatory mode": "Short critical essays on a given film or filmmaker, typically read in voice-over by the author and supplemented with carefully chosen and organised film clips . . . subordinated to explanatory language."[37] He argues that video essays demand "a mode of 'writing' that supplements analysis and explanation with a more expressive, poetical discourse. . . . To paraphrase Jean-Luc Godard, film scholars can now answer images not only with words, but also with other images."[38] Keathley calls this the poetic mode: "Instead of explaining some critical insight about a film, these videos, at their most effective and inventive, perform it," resisting written or spoken explanation. The challenge, he claims, is to blend "the explanatory authority of one and the poetical power of the other."[39]

Lopate's definition of the essay film prizes "rational thought" and the explana-tory, insisting that "an essay-film must have words, in the form of a text either spoken, subtitled or intertitled. . . . The text must represent a single voice . . . have a strong, personal point of view . . . [and] represent an attempt to work out some reasoned line of discourse on a problem."[40]

Video essayist Kevin B. Lee attributes Chris Marker and Agnès Varda with this widespread presumption that "a subjective voiceover narration is essential." For Lee, essay films can "express the process of subjective thought" through montage of image, sound, and text alone. He argues that "moving images . . . contain tremendous as-yet-untapped potential to shed critical light on themselves." Faden agrees that "the language and techniques of cinema can make an argument and present evidence," highlighting patterns and details in and between films "without any traditional voiceover or guiding 'essay.'"[41]

TEACHING VIDEO ESSAYS

As Faden notes, there are "few incentives" for academics to undertake time-consuming video essays and overcome the "considerable practical and legal obstacles on the path to the brave new world of audiovisual film criticism": "The technical challenges of mastering . . . editing software (not to mention, the aesthetic skills of mixing text, image, and sound together in a visually exciting and intellectually effective way) proves [sic] daunting to many."[42] While many of his students have "experimented with moving images to create or critique meaning," he sees "a gap between technique and aesthetics." As more students gain the technical skills to create video essays, "fewer are learning the aesthetic sensibilities to create *interesting* works." He emphasizes, therefore, "critical innovation over technical skills."[43]

In assessing student remix assignments, Lauren Berliner focuses on "critical thinking" and "the conceptual" rather than production value—how students "critically examine choices of representation, audience, and the relationship between form and content." She prizes creativity and collaboration, a clear argument, a strong unifying concept or theme, and a thoughtful justification for "each audio and visual choice."[44]

Film scholars and students must understand the provisions of fair use (in the United States) or fair dealing (in Canada and the United Kingdom) within the evolving landscape of copyright law. American scholar Suzanne Scott uses video essays to engage students with copyright issues, teaching them to justify the "transformative scholarly impact" of their use of found footage in their work within fair use doctrine.[45]

Scholarly video essays are yet to gain widespread acceptance in the academy in research or assessment, despite a small but growing number of peer-reviewed publications offering professional validation. The most prominent of these is *[in]Transition*—"the first peer-reviewed academic journal of videographic film and moving image studies," launched in 2014 by Catherine Grant, Drew Morton, and Christian Keathley and sponsored by Media Commons and *Cinema Journal*. Video essays are accompanied by a supporting statement and open peer review.[46]

Irene Gustafson acknowledges the enormous power the academy wields "in authorizing modes of knowledge production," citing Victor Burgin's 2009 essay on the traditional academic separation "between thinking and making, between scholarship and craft"—a distinction that still governs practice-based research today, within conservative and "powerful structures of assessment and citation, accepted methodologies and ways of rhetoric—demanding 'new knowledge' and innovation before legitimising new digital modes of analysis."[47]

The "rhetorical performativity" of the video essay presents a new mode of scholarship whose claims to knowledge production in research and assessment are not as clear-cut as those of conventional written essays. According to Gustafson,

> thinking with and through images/sounds is different from thinking with and through words. . . . We want innovation but we also expect a certain level of discourse from a scholarly treatise, we want a certain clear and *recognizable* performance of precision and rigor. Sometimes, we can assess based on what a person needs to know in order to produce an object, rather than what is immediately recognizable from the object itself.[48]

Catherine Grant describes the process as "working through practice to produce new knowledge . . . [without knowing] in advance the processes and forms that will help produce new knowledge. We need to have a notion that what we do is not just research but it's *experimental*."[49]

As a filmmaker fairly new to academia, it's interesting to read the reflections of film studies scholars making their first films and describing the process of "finding a film in the edit." Shaping a narrative and structuring an argument within a documentary are similar processes, but without the predetermined form of traditional scholarship. Grant describes the joy of not just writing *about* but also working *with* the material and the discoveries that experiments in montage can reveal for scholars, students, and filmmakers.

THE KINGSTON UNIVERSITY PILOT

After interviewing Paul Gerhardt about his work, I pitched him a proposal around the educational use of BFI archive material in undergraduate video essays at Kingston University. Although the BFI's film literacy strategy targets primary and secondary education, Gerhardt is keen to support initiatives that extend this into higher education. The BFI's *Sight and Sound* magazine has been commissioning video essays from the likes of Kogonada, Robert Greene, and Kevin B. Lee since 2012.[50]

My interest in video essays stems from my own practice as a maker of archive-driven historical feature documentaries who has recently entered academia. I have written extensively about access to archive content and recently started making video essays myself.[51]

My proposal for Kingston University was inspired by a recent BFI collaboration with BBC Learning, which used BBC talent and BFI archive material to "help children aged 7–11 make their own short documentaries exploring the lives of British people . . . [during] the Second World War." The project developed as a spin-off from *Britain's Greatest Generation* (2015), a four-part BBC social history series directed by Steve Humphries (Testimony Films). Interviewers of survivors of World War II used BFI archival footage to illustrate their stories. The BFI's Into Film, the young filmmakers' engagement program, replicated the project for teachers and children in primary schools:[52] "So you have an interview between a ten-year-old and a 95-year-old, and the ten-year-old is part of a crew making a documentary . . . [with] a set of downloadable [BFI and British Council] archive materials from that period . . . wonderful footage of the 1945 election or the early days of the Health Service, veterans coming home."[53] Dormant film from the archive was transformed into "living material that young people [could] fall in love with and engage with" while making dozens of films.[54]

The BFI's Future Film program also partnered with the European Cultural Foundation's Remapping Europe, a Remix Project. Fifty "migrant media-makers" from the United Kingdom, Poland, Turkey, and Spain created remixes deconstructing "prevailing imagery of migrants" in Europe.[55]

In September 2016, I met Gerhardt again with BFI director of digital Edward Humphrey. They discussed their plans for a new digital platform like the BFI Player for educational use—a research and learning environment in which academic researchers and students from all disciplines can download and remix BFI content under an educational license to create their own films. In the meantime, they agreed to provide access to BFI-owned film heritage materials for the production of video essays by first-year filmmaking students on Kingston's BA film degree—"the first time the BFI has licensed its archive for reuse by university students on a course-related project in the United Kingdom."[56]

The twelve nonfiction films I selected from the BFI National Archive are mainly set in London and loosely themed around youth culture and immigration, from the Free Cinema movement of the late 1950s (*Nice Time,* Claude Goretta, Alain Tanner, 1957; *We Are the Lambeth Boys,* Karel Reisz, 1959) to the films of John Krish (*Return to Life,* 1959; *Mr. Marsh Comes to School,* 1961; and *Divide and Rule—Never!,* 1978, a "punk-infused documentary by the Newsreel Collective [that] invites young working class Londoners to discuss their experiences of racism").[57] Eight are owned by the BFI or are under Crown copyright, and four were approved by third-party rights holders, including Kodak and BP.

Figure 1. Filming *We Are the Lambeth Boys* (directed by Karel Reisz), Graphic Films, 1959. One of the films from the BFI National Archive available for reuse on the Kingston University pilot scheme. Copyright Graphic Films/Estate of Leon Clore. Courtesy of the BFI.

My initial playlist included fascinating material from regional film archives, but agreements are not yet in place to reuse this material for educational purposes.

The pilot ran from January to March 2017, in the second semester of our new documentary production module. In the first semester, students make a short documentary on people and places in an assigned Central London borough. We then introduce representation and time by asking them to make a video essay as a critical and creative response to one of the short documentaries from the BFI collection. By integrating up to two minutes of archive footage into ten-minute films, students go beyond a poetic video essay based solely on found footage to quoting and responding to archive content with their own original material. End-of-semester assessed presentations chart their research process and the aesthetic choices they make, integrating archival representations of London into their own stories of life in the city today.

If successful, the BFI hopes to extend the pilot to second- and third-level institutions across the country. The planned digital platform for education promises finally to deliver on the work started with the BBC Creative Archive. It also presents

Figure 2. Still frame from *Divide and Rule—Never!*, Newsreel Collective, 1978. Another of the films reused on the BFI/Kingston University pilot. Copyright British Film Institute.

an opportunity to build a transnational community of practice around the use of the video essay and archive-driven essay films in film studies and practice, creating a diverse, asset-rich research and learning environment for this new mode of film scholarship.

CONCLUSION

The new BFI2022 five-year plan promises support for cross-platform work expanding "the possibilities of storytelling and form" and targets "the engagement of 16–30 year olds with British independent and specialised film" as they form "their film tastes for a lifetime." It promises to "develop a well-evidenced manifesto for film in the classroom" but is noticeably more reticent than its predecessor on plans for the reuse of archive material.[58]

Since 2003, Gerhardt has been trying to develop a portal for the download and reuse of precleared moving image material from publicly owned collections at the BFI and BBC. In an age when video essays on YouTube and in academia are capturing the imagination of students, access to moving image archive materials has not yet been liberalized for educational reuse. Public broadcasters and cultural organizations are missing a critical opportunity to engage sixteen- to thirty-year-olds using the language of film itself.

In April 2016, Tony Ageh, controller of archive development, cocreator of the iPlayer, and champion of the Digital Public Space, left the BBC to become chief digital officer at the New York Public Library: "Everything I told the BBC to do they didn't understand or do.... The library is the one memory institution that lets you take the artists' work home. That means you can come back with your own ideas."[59]

At the 2016 Learning on Screen conference, Bill Thompson, head of partnerships for BBC Archive Development, summarized the key obstacles to the reuse of archive content as complicated rights clearance, which are that (1) reuse was never conceived or explicitly consented to with older material, (2) there is potential for reputational damage in how such material might be used, and (3) seemingly innocuous licensed material might later prove highly controversial—like footage of Jimmy Savile, the BBC children's program presenter later discovered to have been a pedophile.[60]

Though the utopian aims of Greg Dyke are unworkable under the current clearance model, plenty of BBC-owned material could be cleared and withdrawn if later found to be contentious. The proof is in the Chronicle project that Thompson launched with BUFVC (now Learning on Screen) in 2012, a collection of thousands of videos from BBC Northern Ireland's television news output from 1963 to 1976. Digitized access was provided to educational users who signed a sublicense agreement. The document clearly sets out the limited streaming and metadata use allowed, places restrictions safeguarding reputational damage, and prohibits fair dealing and reuse of any kind.[61]

I asked Thompson if, in a "walled garden" like the BoB service, reuse could be allowed on such low-risk curated material through the same licensing process. "Possibly," he said. The existing rights clearance covers classroom use but not public screening, even in a "walled garden," so new mechanisms are needed to address this. It seems to me the elitist "reputational damage" argument is simply a means to deny the public—the underlying rights owners who have paid for and own the archive—access to represent their communities and "construct their own histories."[62] As Jaimie Baron notes, "history is not the texts produced about the past. Rather, it is the experience of history that is generated by the reader's encounter with those texts, the historical consciousness that people incorporate into their everyday lives.... History is our creation ... continually co-constituted in our encounters with traces of the past."[63] Baron describes the "archive effect" produced by our "experience of the archival document within a given text" and

the fresh insight imbued by its appropriation in a different temporal and narrative context. This effect is multiplied when student filmmakers work with archive footage and
explore how to mobilize traces of the past in their films, bringing a new sensibility and
voice to the material.[64]

As well as learning *about* film history as passive viewers, students should
be able to actively work *with* moving image archive materials, using recontextualized
historical materials as creative expression, a way to refine their aesthetic choices and
their political ideas and to represent their communities. Digital technology can activate
multiple voices in the writing of our cultural memory, but only if our public broadcasters
and cultural organizations collectively cede control of the digital assets needed to do so.

Shane O'Sullivan is a lecturer and documentary filmmaker at Kingston
University, London. He is the author of *Who Killed Bobby? The Unsolved
Murder of Robert F. Kennedy* (2008) and contributed a chapter to *Screening
the Tortured Body: The Cinema as Scaffold* (2016).

NOTES

1. British Film Institute, "Screening Literacy: Film Education in Europe,"
2013, http://www.bfi.org.uk/screening-literacy-film-education-europe.
2. Paul Gerhardt, personal interview with the author, June 26, 2015.
3. British Film Institute, *Impact, Relevance, and Excellence: A New Stage for
Film Education,* 2014, http://www.bfi.org.uk/sites/bfi.org.uk/files/down
loads/bfi-film-education-strategy-impact-relevance-and-excellence-2014-03.
pdf, 14; in the United States, the "first sale doctrine" applies and no royalties
are payable (17 U.S.C. § 109).
4. Gerhardt interview.
5. "BBC Plans to Open Up Its Archive to the Public," August 24, 2003, http://
www.bbc.co.uk/pressoffice/pressreleases/stories/2003/08_august/24/dyke
_dunn_lecture.shtml.
6. British Broadcasting Corporation, *Building Public Value, Renewing the
BBC for a Digital World,* 2004, http://downloads.bbc.co.uk/aboutthebbc
/policies/pdf/bpv.pdf, 60–63.
7. BBC Creative Archive License Group, http://www.bbc.co.uk/creative
archive/.
8. "BBC Creative Archive Licence Group," http://www.interact.mmu.ac.uk
/placements/host/bbc; "BBC News Opens Its Archives for First Time," January 3, 2006, http://www.bbc.co.uk/pressoffice/pressreleases/stories/2006/01
_january/03/; Paul Ganley, "Copyright and IPTV," *Computer Law and
Security Report* 23 (2007): 250; "Interview with BBC Creative Archive Project

Leader," *Wikinews*, June 22, 2006, https://en.wikinews.org/wiki/Interview
_with_BBC_Creative_Archive_project_leader.

9. Gerhardt interview; "The Licence," BBC Creative Archive License Group,
http://www.bbc.co.uk/creativearchive/licence/index.shtml.

10. "BBC Creative Archive Pioneers New Approach to Public Access Rights
in Digital Age," May 26, 2004, http://www.bbc.co.uk/pressoffice/press
releases/stories/2004/05_may/26/; "Interview with BBC Creative Archive
Project Leader."

11. "House of Lords Select Committee on BBC Charter Review—Minutes of
Evidence and ITN Memoranda," July 6, 2005, http://www.publications
.parliament.uk/pa/ld200506/ldselect/ldbbc/50/5070601.htm.

12. Paul Gerhardt, "Broadcast Archives and the Digital Public Domain," presentation, 2009, http://www.communia-project.eu/node/210.html, 21; Department for Culture, Media, and Sport (DCMS), *Draft Broadcasting Agreement
with the BBC*, Cm 6872, 2006, www.bbc.co.uk/bbctrust/governance
/regulatory_framework/charter_agreement.html, 3; DCMS, *Royal Charter for
the Continuance of the British Broadcasting Corporation*, Cm 6925, 2006,
www.bbc.co.uk/bbctrust/governance/regulatory_framework/charter
_agreement.html, 2.

13. Gerhardt interview.

14. Six artists were given access to the BBC archives to make six films for the
iPlayer, http://www.bbc.co.uk/programmes/articles/8d3c4R4rT0DVt4RzyZY
6KN/artists-moving-image-at-the-bbc; Gerhardt interview.

15. "The Pararchive Project—Background," http://pararchive.com/about
/background/; "Strike Stories—Films," http://media.leeds.ac.uk/research
/research-projects/strike-stories-films/.

16. Celluloid Remix, https://celluloidremix.openbeelden.nl; "Celluloid
Remix—Lessons Learned," http://beeldenvoordetoekomst.nl/en/research
/celluloid-remix-lessons-learned.html.

17. *Knowledge Is*, 2011, https://vimeo.com/29667387; Archives for Creativity,
http://www.archivesforcreativity.com/; Gerhardt interview.

18. Ibid.

19. In 2016, the British Universities Film and Video Council (BUFVC) was
rebranded as Learning on Screen.

20. Gerhardt interview.

21. "The Artist in the Archive," http://www.bfi.org.uk/archive-collections
/archive-projects/artist-archive.

22. British Film Institute, *Impact, Relevance, and Excellence*, 17–18.

23. Ibid.; Screenonline, http://www.screenonline.org.uk/; BFI InView, http://
www.bfi.org.uk/inview.

24. Eric Faden, "Strangers X: A Proof of Concept," *The Cine-Files* 7 (Fall
2014), http://www.thecine-files.com/faden/.

25. Walter Ong, *Orality and Literacy* (New York: Methuen, 1982); Eric Faden,
"A Manifesto for Critical Media," *Mediascape*, Spring 2008, 1, http://www
.tft.ucla.edu/mediascape/Spring08_ManifestoForCriticalMedia.html.

26. Raymond Bellour, "The Unattainable Text," *Screen* 16, no. 3 (1975): 19–
28; Laura Mulvey, *Death 24× a Second* (London: Reaktion Books, 2006), 8,
160.

27. Alexandre Astruc, "The Birth of a New Avant-Garde: La Caméra-Stylo," in *The New Wave*, ed. Peter Graham (New York: Doubleday, 1968), 18, 22. See also "La Camera Stylo-Alexandre Astruc," http://www.newwavefilm .com/about/camera-stylo-astruc.shtml.

28. Christian Keathley, "La Caméra-stylo: Notes on Video Criticism and Cinephilia," in *The Language and Style of Film Criticism*, ed. Alex Clayton and Andrew Klevan (New York: Routledge, 2011), 179; Faden, "A Manifesto for Critical Media."

29. Catherine Grant and Christian Keathley, "The Use of an Illusion: Child-hood Cinephilia, Object Relations, and Videographic Film Studies," *Photogenie* (2014), http://www.photogenie.be/photogenie_blog/article/use-illusion; Faden, "A Manifesto for Critical Media."

30. Erlend Lavik, "The Video Essay: The Future of Academic Film and Television Criticism?," *Frames Cinema Journal* 1 (July 2012), http://framescinema journal.com/article/the-video-essay-the-future/.

31. Ibid.

32. Faden, "A Manifesto for Critical Media," 2.

33. Phillip Lopate, "In Search of the Centaur: The Essay-Film," in *Beyond Document: Essays on Nonfiction Film*, ed. Charles Warren (Middletown, Conn.: Wesleyan University Press, 1996), 244–45.

34. Faden, "A Manifesto for Critical Media," 2; Lopate, "In Search of the Centaur."

35. Faden, "A Manifesto for Critical Media," 4.

36. Christian Keathley, "Teaching the Scholarly Video," *Frames Cinema Journal* 1 (2012), http://framescinemajournal.com/article/teaching-the -scholarly-video/.

37. Keathley, "La Caméra-stylo," 180.

38. Ibid., 179.

39. Ibid., 190; Keathley, "Teaching the Scholarly Video."

40. Lopate, "In Search of the Centaur," 245–46, 268.

41. Kevin B. Lee, "Video Essay: The Essay Film—Some Thoughts of Discontent," *Sight and Sound*, August 2013, http://www.bfi.org.uk/news-opinion /sight-sound-magazine/features/deep-focus/video-essay-essay-film-some -thoughts; Faden, "Strangers X."

42. Ibid.

43. Faden, "A Manifesto for Critical Media."

44. Lauren Berliner, "The Paradox of Ubiquitous Production," *Cinema Journal Teaching Dossier* 4, no. 1 (2016), http://www.teachingmedia.org /the-paradox-of-ubiquitous-production.

45. Suzanne Scott, "Teaching Transformativity/Transformative Teaching: Fair Use and the Video Essay," *Cinema Journal Teaching Dossier* 1, no. 2 (2013), http://www.teachingmedia.org/teaching-transformativitytransfor mative-teaching-fair-use-and-the-video-essay/.

46. "About *[in]Transition*," http://mediacommons.futureofthebook.org /intransition/about-intransition.

47. Irene Gustafson, "On the Importance of Being Two-Faced: Production in the Classroom," *Cinema Journal Teaching Dossier* 4, no. 1 (2016), http:// www.teachingmedia.org/integrating-production-in-film-and-media-courses

-cinema-journal-teaching-dossier-vol-4-1/; Victor Burgin, "Thoughts on 'Research' Degrees in Visual Arts Departments," in *Artists with PhDs: On the New Doctoral Degree in Studio Art,* ed. James Elkins, 71–80 (Washington, DC: New Academia, 2009).

48. Gustafson, "On the Importance of Being Two-Faced."

49. Catherine Grant, "How Long Is a Piece of String? The Audiovisual Essay," presentation, Frankfurt, 2013, http://reframe.sussex.ac.uk/audiovisual essay/frankfurt-papers/catherine-grant/.

50. "Sight and Sound Videos," http://www.bfi.org.uk/sight-sound-magazine /videos.

51. My first video essay, *Anatomy of a Murder: Sirhan Sirhan and Robert Kennedy,* was shortlisted for Best Research Film of the Year in the AHRC Film Awards 2016; Shane O'Sullivan, "The Economy of Memory: Archive-Driven Documentaries in the Digital Age," *Journal of Media Practice* 14, no. 3 (2013): 231–48.

52. "Archive Film Inspires a New Generation," March 19, 2015, http://www .bfi.org.uk/news-opinion/news-bfi/announcements/new-childrens-film making-project-commemorates-life-britain-1930.

53. Gerhardt interview.

54. Ibid.

55. Doc Next Network, http://www.docnextnetwork.org/remappingeurope/.

56. Kingston University, http://www.kingston.ac.uk/news/article/1797/23 -feb-2017-kingston-universitys-new-creative-partnership-with-british-film -institute-bfi-gives-film-students-access-to/.

57. *Divide and Rule—Never!,* BFI Player, https://player.bfi.org.uk/film/watch -divide-and-rule-never-1978/.

58. British Film Institute, *BFI2022,* 2016, 6–7, http://www.bfi.org.uk/2022/.

59. Jemima Kiss, "BBC Digital Expert Tony Ageh Poached by New York Public Library," April 6, 2016, https://www.theguardian.com/media/2016/apr/06 /bbc-tony-ageh-new-york-public-library.

60. "RES FAQ," https://bbcarchdev.github.io/res/faq#faq-archive; "The Research and Education Space," http://bufvc.ac.uk/projects-research/projects timeline/res-bob.

61. "Chronicle Website and Sub-license Agreement," http://bufvc.ac.uk /chronicle.

62. "The Pararchive Project—Background."

63. Jaimie Baron, *The Archive Effect* (New York: Routledge, 2014), 7, 173, 177.

64. Ibid.

TOWARD A PUBLIC MEDIA ARCHAEOLOGY

PHILIPP DOMINIK KEIDL

Museums, Media, and Historiography

WHAT, WHEN, AND WHERE IS MEDIA ARCHAEOLOGY?

Although media archaeology has developed into a widespread re-

search framework since the 1990s, scholars still struggle to find a

generally accepted answer to the question of *what* it is. Media archaeologists as well

as their critics are still debating whether the term refers to "an approach, a model, a

project, an exercise, a perspective, or a discipline."[1] Indeed, media archaeologists are

loosely bound together by a shared interest in new historiographical methods based

on the study and reevaluation of media temporality and materiality. Wanda Strauven

divides this shared research agenda into four dominant research inquiries that seek

the old in the new, the new in the old, recurring topoi, and ruptures and discontinuity.[2]

However, while media archaeologists have continued to debate what media archaeology is or could be, the related questions of *when* and *where* media archaeology is practiced have attracted considerably less attention.

Given that "the history of media archaeology has been a history of discourse-oriented analysis,"[3] scholars have located media archaeological ideas largely within the realm of academia. Media archaeologists might venture to various archives, collections, museums, attics, and basements to study media technologies neglected by teleological historiographies. Although scholars have turned to artifacts typically outside of the academy, they have rarely scrutinized how media archaeological thinking materializes outside the institutional and intellectual frameworks of the university complex. Until now, the only nonscholarly practices that have garnered considerable attention are media archaeological art and media archeology as a curatorial practice for art and large-scale projections.[4] Thus, despite its reputation as a "nomadic enterprise" and a "traveling concept" that easily crosses disciplinary boundaries,[5] it appears that media archaeology does not travel outside of academia or the art world. Consequently, we know relatively little about how the technological, cultural, social, and political effects that have shaped university-based and artistic media archaeology might have led to media archaeological thinking and practices outside these two institutional contexts.

Thomas Elsaesser describes media archaeology as a symptom of new film history, the vast and fast adaptation of digital technologies, and the increasing display of cinematic and other moving images in art museums and galleries beginning in the 1970s and 1980s.[6] While new film history might have emerged in the relatively enclosed space of academia, the two other symptoms Elsaesser lists have had substantial impact on conceptions of media technologies and histories in the public realm. Smaller, lighter, and handier media technologies were advertised to consumers, who then had to adapt and use them in everyday practices, either replacing or combining them with older media forms. Museum exhibitions on film and media reached vast audiences through advertisements, reviews, and public debates about film and media as heritage. Scholars and artists might be the most prominent and visible media archaeologists, but if media archaeology indeed represents a "historiographic 'perspective correction'" in the changing mediascape of the late twentieth and early twenty-first centuries,[7] it also becomes necessary to investigate participants in these debates who are neither scholars nor artists.

A certain indifference to nonscholarly historiography is not an exclusive characteristic of media archaeology. Historians and archaeologists have a long history of marginalizing public engagements with the past and often see them as superficial, nostalgic, commercial, and ultimately inferior to their own work.[8] Studies on everyday experiences of and in history making have been limited to the subfield of public history and archaeology, respectively, in which scholars champion the participatory nature of the making of history.[9] Consequently, public history and archaeology do not engage with scholars employed outside academia or scholars' creation of an accessible history in public spaces such as the museum. Public history and archaeology refer to historiography as an inclusive activity and engagement with a diverse range of objects, places, and practices deeply embedded in everyday life. If we apply the inclusive notion of "participatory historical culture" to media archaeology,[10] it becomes possible to think about the notion of public media archaeology as a framework to study involvement in the production of history beyond scholarly and textual production.

Of course, it might seem counterproductive to expand the already open definition of media archaeology and to further dilute it by association with a broad concept like the "public." Indeed, public media archaeology does not intend to fix media archaeology's unfixed character within academic discourses. Furthermore, the notion of public media archaeology should not represent a straightforward validation of marginalized approaches and practices. Rather, public media archaeology offers an opportunity to investigate how media archaeological thinking is practiced outside scholarly frameworks and the art world. The concept is not interested in how media users engage with old or new technologies but rather in how perceived historical connections and ruptures result in alternative conceptualizations of past, present, and potential future media as well as how these practices result in extra-academic historical speculation.

Consequently, the notion of public media archaeology urges us to expand our examination to objects, sources, and sites outside archival collections and libraries that are less likely to be collected or make the transition from private to institutionalized collections. The inclusion of ephemeral, short-lived, or unrealized media technologies has been at the core of media archeological scholarship, but the proposed investigation outside academia intends to do more than find new additions to a long list of neglected technologies. The concept is also meant to enable a more concrete study of the knowledge these practices create and mediate independently from scholarly intervention. In other words, individuals and groups collecting, displaying, and working with media technology outside academia and the art world do not just provide the hardware for examination. Instead, their work with media technologies mediates ideas about media history that do not necessarily adapt scholarly sources but function and circulate independently in more vernacular discourses. If, up to this moment, media archaeology has focused mainly on scholarly and artistic practices, public media archaeology is dedicated to more vernacular modes of production by acknowledging and examining how knowledge is created and disseminated.

As will be elaborated in this article, *ephemeral, short-lived,* and *unrealized* are adjectives that should not be applied only to individuals, groups, and practices outside institutional frameworks and networks. They also describe media technologies and practices that museums and archives developed for the communication of knowledge about their collections, which in recent years have displayed previously neglected technologies in their galleries. Part of the curatorial process of such exhibitions has been the development of installations to present the material objects and contextual information that go beyond the mere arrangement of displays and labels. Yet, while archival collections have migrated into exhibition spaces, educational museum installations rarely make it into their institutions' archives. Once the exhibitions finish, they are dismantled or repurposed and at best documented in the form of production notes and photographs that might not be considered worth archiving. The result is the loss of media objects as well as the erasure of how curators intended to mediate historical knowledge and, in turn, how visitors engaged and worked with this knowledge. In this way, museums and their archives fail to collect, document, preserve, and evaluate their own shifting roles, methods, and technologies in the making of history. A dual loss therefore becomes particularly evident when we look at film and media museums whose visualizations of history are as much forgotten as the history of visualizing film and media history itself.

This article discusses the concept of public media archaeology as it pertains to the practices of the Australian Centre for the Moving Image (ACMI) in Melbourne and argues that ACMI is a media archeological laboratory where curators and visitors engage with media archeological thinking and knowledge production through the development of and engagement with media installations respectively. The article outlines the potential of film and media museums to act as historiographical workshops where speculations about film and media's past are encouraged. However, rather than framing these modes of thinking as direct forms of applied media archeological theory to the museum, I argue that public media archeology is defined through the process of defamiliarizing common historical narratives and institutional parameters. While media in the museum have been previously defined as expanded cinema, othered cinema, museum media, and useful cinema,[11] public media archaeology is used in this article to describe the creation of what can be called defamiliar cinema and media.

WHAT, WHEN, AND WHERE IS PUBLIC MEDIA ARCHAEOLOGY?

The museum can be approached as a media archaeological laboratory from the perspective of both curators and visitors. The former requires an examination of the development and production of the exhibition narrative, whereas the latter demands an examination of how visitors engage with the exhibition content and activities. In other words, we must understand how curators mediate media archaeological thinking through the act of curating as well as how visitors can and do participate in these debates throughout their visit. This requires an understanding of the media archaeological modes of thinking implied in the exhibition narrative. It also encourages the study of the preproduction of these exhibitions as much as how visitors contribute their own knowledge and perspectives. Accordingly, it requires the analysis of how particular historical contexts are placed into a multimedia narrative that guides visitors in their exploration, while it also depends on an understanding of visitors' spontaneous and unscripted interactions with the exhibition. Both approaches are complicated, because curatorial notes are hard to access—if they have been created at all—while visitor engagement rarely leaves visible traces in the exhibition space. If documented, however, public media archaeology can be used as a conceptual tool to understand these two processes.

The notion of public media archaeology draws from recent research projects that take a more hands-on, experimental, and playful approach to discourse-oriented media archaeology. Wanda Strauven and Alexandra Schneider's research project, Kinderspiel, examines how children engage with media's different temporal and historical layers through their free play "with home video tools to the bricolage of old and new media devices, from repurposing existing media objects to drawing or designing their own toys."[12] Their project stresses alternative localities for media archaeology, including playgrounds, kindergartens, schools, living rooms, and bedrooms, among others. It also frames media archaeology as a spontaneous, improvised, and ephemeral undertaking that emerges in everyday life without a theoretical background or interests in mind. Indeed, objects and ideas are as quickly constructed and used to produce media as they are dismantled and erased. Media archaeological play is therefore an important reminder that official collection and preservation policies exclude many processes and practices that thereby are irretrievably lost. It also points to the fact that family homes and estates might be the most diverse archives for the study of public media archaeology. In many ways, the spontaneous, improvised, and ephemeral—not to mention undocumented—undertakings associated with children's play can also be linked to the contemporary practices of museums that ask their visitors to engage in play, and produce content and knowledge, during their stay. But the playful character of media archeology as practice also relates to curatorial moments of brainstorming and free-associated planning, before budgetary, technological, legal, and spatial restrictions limit plans and vision.

Although more closely positioned within traditional academic environments, Andreas Fickers and Annie van den Oever place a similar emphasis on hands-on engagement with their concept of experimental media archaeology. They argue that media archaeologists should focus less on discursive reconstructions of remembered usages and configured, expert, and amateur users and engage more through historical reenactments with media's materiality and past.[13] They argue that this form of experimental approach will provide

> new insights in the sense of time and temporality inscribed in the materiality of media technologies ... enhance awareness of the spatial and topographical information inscribed in media practices ... enable a better understanding of the "constructivist nature" of media technology products [and] make scholars of past media technologies "experience" rather than intellectually appropriate the acts of making and screening film as social and cultural practices.[14]

Their experimental study of media technologies is particularly relevant for museums as their exhibitions depend on historical reenactment and participation. Of course, museums often present history to their visitors through aural presentations, and the direct, haptic handling of original displays is rare. This complicates the hands-on approach the authors describe. Yet, interactive workstations and workshops within the museum space offer hands-on engagement, which fosters experimentation and thus a better understanding of cultural practice. In turn, for curators, the planning and production of exhibitions and their media installations and displays entail collaboration with archivists, engineers, and the millions of media amateurs, collectors, and other technical experts that van den Oever and Fickers deem so important.[15] Museums therefore relate to experimental media archaeology and its emphasis on knowledge creation outside academia, although they emphasize the evaluation and interpretation of this knowledge without the direct interference of university-trained scholars. Thus public media archaeology draws from experimental media archaeology but simultaneously aims to expand it. It is less interested in collecting data for media archaeologists to analyze than in providing a conceptual tool to understand where, how, and when media archaeological thinking has become part of a wider public culture that deals with the history of a constantly altering mediascape.

The ideological connotations of "public" are not unproblematic, particularly in relation to the institution of the museum. Nick Merriman explains the inherent tension between the institutional and intellectual connotations of the term as follows:

> The first [meaning] is the association of the word "public" with the state and its institutions (public bodies, public buildings, public office, the public interest), which emerges in the era of intensive state formation from the Early Modern

period onwards. . . . The second is the concept of "the public" as a group of individuals who debate issues and consume cultural products, and whose reactions inform "public opinion." . . . On the one hand, therefore, we have a notion in which the state assumes the role of speaking on behalf of the public and of acting "in the public interest." . . . On the other hand, the second notion of "the public" encompasses debate and opinion, and is inherently unpredictable and conflictual. . . . So, the two notions of "the public"—the state and the people—have always been potentially in tension.[16]

Public media archaeology refers neither to the state nor to a homogenized conceptualization of a unified public sphere; rather, it refers to notions of public history and archaeology and functions as a "shorthand term to describe the huge diversity of the population, who do not earn their living" as professional media archaeologists. Furthermore, it acknowledges that "those who are not professional archaeologists [are] a shifting set of cross-cutting interest groups which sometimes have a great deal in common, but often have little in common at all."[17] In other words, public media archaeology refers to all those agents and practices engaged with media archaeological thinking outside direct academic organizations and infrastructures.

How, then, could one respond to the questions of "what, when, and where is public media archaeology?" Answers to the first two parts of the question do not differ from those debated among scholars. Media archaeology as practiced in public engages with different layers of media temporality and materiality and participates in parallel readings of old and new media. Consequently, public media archaeology is not a new or recent phenomenon but emerged parallel to academic discourses, if not earlier in the form of private collections, analyses, and speculations. As such, the concept acknowledges the diverse contexts, approaches, and results of media archaeological thinking. It functions as an umbrella term that encompasses play, historical reenactments, and other everyday practices in public and private environments. The museum is only one site of many, and the work of private collectors who preserve, restore, and build media technologies is as much a form of public media archaeology as practices of such professional and amateur preservation and restoration projects of private photography, film and media technologies, merchandise collections, steampunk, and archaeogaming.[18]

Another pressing question is how public media archaeology represents a historiographic perspective correction. Is it even possible to present alternative historiographies beyond monographs, anthologies, seminars, or lectures that will convince readers, listeners, and spectators? Instead of approaching public media archaeology as the production of alternative histories to replace established narratives, it might be more fruitful to describe it as a defamiliarization of established historical knowledge that forces one to see common history in an unfamiliar way, enhancing perception and contemplation of historiography. Russian Formalist Viktor Shklovsky, when he introduced the concept of defamiliarization to literary theory, intended to counteract brief perception, insufficient attentiveness, and a lack of responsiveness to objects and texts. As Shklovsky explains, after several encounters with an object, it becomes so familiar that "we do not see it—hence we cannot say anything significant about it."[19] Shklovsky's observations pertain to art, but they have a similar impact on public media archeology and its products. They reject or defy linear narratives of the past and force us to look at film and media history in complex terms. In other words, public media archaeology does not provide new histories but instead encourages a heightened awareness of historiography itself. It insists that a certain narrative structure is a choice that could have taken other forms. Media archaeological thinking within the institutional context of the museum results in the defamiliarization of film history as much as the defamiliarization of the institution of the museum.

ACMI AND THE DEFAMILIARIZATION OF THE (FILM AND MEDIA) MUSEUM

ACMI's decision to promote itself as a center instead of a museum is a form of institutional defamiliarization. Founded on the desire to "position itself as a pioneering new media institution [which would] engage in the production of alternative forms of cultural citizenship,"[20] ACMI was simultaneously associated with and distanced from familiar frameworks of museums, archives, and libraries. As John Smithies, the center's inaugural CEO, explained after the opening in 2002,

> it is possible to include ACMI in the family of a museum, library or gallery but this too easily ignores the differences. [ACMI] is an example of a new generation of cultural institutions—one that will move beyond the limitation of a physical site and that fully embraces and celebrates the dominant pervasive mediums of the past 100 years and the future.[21]

Indeed, the desire to distance ACMI from traditional notions of cultural institutions has been a common thread in the development of the center from the 1980s to its opening. ACMI was supposed to become a central space to learn about and foster participation among different agents in the production of media. Early briefing papers, curatorial statements, and production notes written in the 1990s indicate that curators never envisioned ACMI as a site where visitors would learn solely about film and media history; rather, they conceived of it as a space where the public and the industry would not only experience all forms of moving image media but also engage in the conception of future media forms.

The idea that ACMI was a center rather than a museum, archive, or library certainly was supposed to place it in an increasingly national and international competitive heritage market.[22] But the idea of a center also indicated the desire to at least partially replace overarching narratives that address all visitors with more open, fluid, and diverse content. This would, in turn, encourage an engagement with media temporality that traditional, object-focused approaches would not be able to offer. ACMI's embrace of flexibility is not a single example but forms part of a landscape of museological reform, in which, according to Jennie Morgan, museums become "flexible." As she explains, "the flexible museum does not seek to express narratives [but instead draws] on new kinds of ordering categories" that are "rooted less in chronology and traditional subject-disciplines and more in the social, experiential and emotional."[23] Consequently, the flexible museum embraces the impossibility of comprehensiveness and the partial and evolving nature of knowledge. It does this by following broader museological trends that replace notions of objectivity and fixity with more attentiveness to visitor interest and expectations.[24]

ACMI's desire for quick change and more topical gallery and visitor experiences—as well as an increased contemplation about moving images and their past and future—is evident in descriptions about possible exhibition technologies and display strategies. The team behind the center aimed to push the boundaries of presentation methods used by film and media museums in Frankfurt, London, and New York.[25] ACMI's curators wanted the moving image and immersive screen experiences, rather than the materials used to produce, distribute, and promote them, to take center stage. Early planning phases were defined by an emphasis on new digital technologies that promised to simplify the inclusion of screens and projections into exhibition spaces. This would enable more complex constructions of media installations, allowing for changing programs and display arrangements. Various documents written in the 1990s also express ACMI's curators' desire not only to excavate machines for display but also to develop and work with state-of-the-art technologies. This reveals how important it was for the curators to engage with the future of media rather than with the past.

Many of the notes indicate how the curators experimented with innovative displays.[26] One of these includes a description of an elevator video lift with liquid crystal displays that would offer a short but memorable journey to the main exhibition.

As visitors were fully surrounded by moving images, the lift ride was supposed to play with visitors' perceptions of movement and speed. Each section of the center was to be structured around a different screen environment, which ranged from relatively familiar cinematic projection spaces to screen panoramas and virtual reality booths. As was repeatedly stated in the documents, a screen-based exhibition design offered flexibility, as it would enable ACMI to show different programs throughout the day. In other words, the center could meet the needs and expectations of different visitor groups, targeting schools in the morning and early afternoon and adults in the late afternoon and evening. In addition to fast content changes, the exhibition space itself was supposed to be flexible and mobile. Robots would move with the visitors or follow them through certain parts of the exhibition. Handheld devices were supposed to provide extra information and individual interaction with screens, offering a selection of exhibition guides and digital extensions of the physical exhibition space. Furthermore, online visitors from all over the world could explore a digital extension of the gallery from home.[27] While the documents and notes available at the Public Record Office Victoria in Melbourne are brief and reveal little about how far these ideas progressed in the preproduction process, they nonetheless demonstrate the creativity and motivation to use digital technologies for the conceptualization of timely exhibition frameworks that would create new forms of public interaction with and production of moving image histories.

The reviewed documents do not indicate specific reasons for the change in direction, and it would be mere speculation to determine what was impossible or too expensive to build. The materials do not include concrete construction sketches, budget plans, or any other form of production notes indicating how advanced the planning was for the individual installations. But the ideas outlined in the documents point toward the need to develop a more general understanding of curators as media producers whose work is not limited to the selection, arrangement, and description of cameras, costumes, set designs, props, merchandise, and memorabilia, among other things. Curators are also involved in selecting scenes, conducting and recording interviews, and conceptualizing and producing montages, compilations, collages, split-screen sequences, and animations.[28] This creation of screen content comes with the task of developing and constructing media installations that display the produced content. Screens and projections need to be integrated into complex architectural arrangements in the overall exhibition designs. Scale, portability, mobility, flexibility, and durability therefore become concrete questions curators need to engage with when planning where and how to place and arrange screens. Each placement raises questions for curators about the site specificity of the screen and the experience it offers in terms of time, space, and exhibition content. Ultimately, these imaginary media indicate the desires and aspirations projected onto communication technologies. They also position ACMI as an active space of collaborative media production rather than merely an institution. ACMI did not realize many of these exhibition features, which is why they can be best described as imaginary media for an imaginary institution.

As Eric Kluitenberg explains, imaginary media are more than metaphors or contemporary claims about technological possibilities.[29] They are connected to the lineages of tangible media. They raise hopes, impact developments, disappoint, and sometimes even become realized. Imaginary media research, then, is an alternative to apparatus historiography. It provides insights into how imaginary media are also shaping the representation of real machines and technologies.[30] In the case of ACMI, such research helps us to understand how media transform the museum in terms of content production and invites us to rethink its institutional boundaries. It is possible to connect this to a longer tradition of museums that use media to establish firm historiographies. However, the center's proposals urge us to develop a more concrete understanding of how these media installations create an (imaginary) exhibition space that is no longer simply a place to experience the past of cinema but a space where future media are produced and experienced.

When ACMI opened its Screen Gallery, it was celebrated as a state-of the-art exhibition venue. This initial excitement, however, was followed by large-scale public disenchantment. Critics expressed skepticism regarding the high maintenance costs and subsidies necessary to maintain the complex technological infrastructure of the exhibition spaces. The institution was hard to find and harder to navigate once inside. Others argued that the programming of the exhibitions was too intellectual and inaccessible for nonexpert visitors. Soon, ACMI's exhibition space had acquired a cold and clinical reputation. Visitors experienced a sense of emptiness as they explored its fragmented spaces. For some, the focus on digital technology was too heavy and left them wondering why the center had no permanent exhibition with cinematic artifacts.[31]

Although ACMI's aspirations remained unfilled, the now-closed Screen Gallery suggests the potential of museum media for institutional defamiliarization. Visitors' contemplation was redirected from exhibition content to the exhibition framework itself. As a completely screen-based exhibition, the Screen Gallery provided interactive and immersive media experiences that favored chronological media histories. The content-flexible gallery generated debate about what kind of institution ACMI should be. The curators had not anticipated, though, the public's desire for traditional exhibition models. Only a few years after its opening, ACMI struggled with financial, management, and image problems. When Tony Sweeney was appointed director in 2004, the center embarked on redevelopment and turned to more accessible exhibition formats. The 2009 opening of Screen Worlds, its current permanent exhibition, pushed ACMI closer to traditional, linear exhibition models.

SCREEN WORLDS AND THE DEFAMILIARIZATION OF FILM AND MEDIA HISTORY

Imaginary media are only one of several heuristic categories that can be used to describe museum installations. Screen environments and educational media installations can also be approached through Jussi Parikka's categories of media archaeological art that include imaginary media but also (1) visually engage with historical themes, (2) invoke alternative histories, (3) use obsolete materials and solutions to engage with emerging media cultures, (4) draw from concrete archives, and (5) engage with the materiality of technology.[32] Many of the media machines imagined and produced for film and media museums fall into at least one of these heuristic categories. The work with media technologies to present old and obsolete forms as well as to re-create old ones with new technologies is an inherent challenge in curating these exhibition formats. The resulting new assemblages represent media histories' multiple temporalities and materialities. Although these installations may offer visitors the chance to visualize historical information that shapes and supports a predominant narrative chosen by the exhibitions in ACMI's Screen Worlds, they have an opposite effect when they scrutinize the narrative on display.

Screen Worlds contains several installations that draw from archival resources to present and engage with the materiality of film technologies and other production materials. These installations' visualization of film and media history defamiliarizes the historical narrative that unfolds in the rest of the exhibition. In many regards, Screen Worlds is a compromise between ACMI's original curatorial vision and public demand for more accessible, if not traditional, programming. At first sight, an abundance of screens and photographs seems to dominate the space and overshadow the many costumes, scripts, concept art, merchandise, and other production materials or memorabilia that are placed between the different moving and unmoving images. Screen Worlds approximates an object-centered exhibition, the approach that the original plans for the museum tried to avoid. In fact, the exhibition does follow on first sight what David Bordwell has called the "basic story"[33] and Thomas Elsaesser the "telos" of film history: "greater and greater realism, evolutionary schemes from silent to sound and from black and white to color, from flat, two-dimensional screen surfaces to 3D, and from the peephole to the IMAX screen."[34]

Several media installations, however, break with the deterministic narratives of technological progress, canonical masterpieces, and the achievements and inventions of a few masters and pioneers. They encourage visitors to ask why certain objects and topics are featured more prominently than others. This becomes evident in at least two of the exhibition's three units. Whereas the interactive playground *Sensation* resembles a science center more than a traditional museum, the *Emergence* and *Voices* units follow patterns of technological progress, artistic innovation, and the canonization of groundbreaking inventions and production. While *Voices* introduces Australian talent working in media industries, *Emergence* covers the technological development of moving images, introducing them one at a time: film, sound, television, broadcasting, video games, and then the internet. Yet a closer examination of the digital and analog media on display indicates that the installations at times rupture the conventional historical narrative, forcing visitors to think about the process of historiography itself. In other words, they defamiliarize film history.

This is particularly the case in the unit *Emergence,* which is arranged in a circle and leaves it to the visitor to decide whether to follow a path from the seventeenth century to the future or the other way around. While this form of arrangement enables visitors to jump nonchronologically between different sections and periods, the main rifts that might encourage media archaeological thinking come in the form of different digital installations featured in the exhibition. The first rupture—or the last, depending on where a visitor begins her walk through the exhibition—is the section *The Future*. It is introduced with three quotes that highlight the unpredictable success and expansion of media. Charlie Chaplin's claim that cinema is "little more than a fad" is as much quoted as Lee de Forest's judgment of television as an "impossibility." These perspectives are complemented by *Popular Science* magazine's prediction that computers in the future may weigh no more than 1.5 tons. With its question, "Where do you go next?" the museum provides visitors with the agency to speculate what kinds of media may or may not be successful in the future, what kinds of qualities media should have, and what qualities that are irrelevant today will be of importance tomorrow. The three incorrect forecasts, thus, jeopardize the trajectory and claims proposed by the exhibition and question the truth claims of the museum's proposed history.

The arrangement of media history along the old-to-new continuum is further problematized with an installation named *Genealogy,* within *The Future* exhibition. The installation label states that it is impossible to define a clear origin of moving images and therefore declares the previously or forthcoming strict and uninterrupted periodization invalid. *Genealogy*'s label emphasizes that the history of media is not "the product of predictable and necessary advance[s] from primitive to . . . complex apparatus." Instead, the visitor is reminded that moving image technologies never die, always rematerializing in another form, and that innovation does not proceed in a straight line but instead is always looping back on itself. The installation ends with a quote from James Burke that asks whether we "can consider the past and see the future." The visitors have not arrived in the future per se; rather, they are asked to look at media history as a cyclical, not linear, development, in which phenomena appear, disappear, and reappear.

A dynamic chart visualizes the many origins of modern media. It outlines the multiple historical affiliations and resonances of different moving images without ever reproducing the rhetoric of straightforward genealogies. The visitors can touch an image projected on a table to access information about different devices. Each box connects to various others, connecting several audiovisual media and highlighting the unstable categories of old and new. Every time the visitor touches a reference point, alternative options and paths pop up across the table that offer various opportunities to dig up new influences and connections. The installations send the visitor deeper and deeper into a labyrinth of numerous pasts and possible futures. The vast web of possibilities confronts the visitor with seemingly endless options that slowly move across the table and from the background to the foreground, thereby making it nearly impossible for the visitor to keep track of his own path. The installation also includes devices absent in the rest of the exhibition, such as the microscope or shadow cards, which expand the historical range of media from modernity to far beyond the Renaissance. These always-emerging connections dismantle narrative modes of media history within and beyond the exhibition. Depending on which section the visitors start with, they are reminded that the selection of apparatus, objects, and moving images on display forms only a snapshot of media history. Furthermore, the exhibition stresses that contemporary mass entertainment is much younger than other techniques of seeing and hearing. *Emergence*'s display of the chronological path of media development over the last 120 years transforms it into a multitemporal window revealing alternative advances that could have been, and still are, plausible. In other words, the installation implies that cinema's future might not be exhausted; other directions are still possible.

The introduction of imaginary media in some installations further denies the notion of a singular origin story for moving image media. A compilation of science fiction movies, for example, introduces the genre as one of the most fruitful grounds for the study of imaginary media. There are scenes from *eXistenZ* (David Cronenberg, 1999) and *Minority Report* (Steven Spielberg, 2002), among other films. While the former shows an imagined video game system plugged into a player's body to immerse him in virtual reality, the latter shows a video wallpaper displaying individually tailored advertising messages for each passerby. Another exhibit juxtaposes these fictional accounts of possible future technologies with actual media currently in development in various technical laboratories. A label directly addresses the uncertainty of these media's future and their role in production, distribution, and consumption. In fact, the exhibition highlights the possibility that these media will never make it into mainstream production and therefore would be absent from media history.

One workstation offers a glimpse of how visitors react to these media archaeological ideas and what ideas they might bring to the museum space themselves. ACMI invites visitors to draw and describe their own visions of future media with a pen on a piece of paper. A selection of previous predictions that were posted online on the museum's Flickr account is projected on a large screen, appearing in different variations each time.[35] What unfolds on-screen is a range of ideas about media as a means of transcending space and time. Moreover, the sketches mix reality and virtual reality, foresee the increasing convergence of the body with technology, and introduce new connections between currently existing and past media. These idiosyncratic sketches of futuristic media, which oscillate between utopian and dystopian visions, document unrealized possibilities, the reinvention of obsolete media, policies for possible archives of the future, and connections of the old to the new in unfamiliar ways. Consequently, they undermine the trajectories of progress that the museum otherwise puts on display.

CONCLUSION

Public media archaeology encourages further studies of media archeological practices and processes outside academia. In the case of the museum, this includes the imagination, development, and presentation of media technologies and installations as well as visitor engagement with these machines. By looking at ACMI through the lens of public media archaeology, it has become possible to explore how media archeological ideas can surface even in environments that seem to rely on teleological models of film and media history. ACMI's Screen Worlds does not follow a cohesive media archaeological approach. Nonetheless, the installations imply that ideas about the old in the new, the new in the old, continuities and ruptures, and other recurring topoi are part of the curatorial process of producing media content and objects. Moreover, the visitors' sketches signal that they do engage in these debates within the exhibition space and, most likely, before and after their visit.

The analysis of ACMI also shows that any conclusions can only be preliminary, especially if museums and archives do not systematically collect and make available data about the installations. The documents underlying this research on public media archaeology were often incomplete and unfinished. As such, this argument is only the first step toward a more comprehensive investigation into ACMI's curatorial philosophy and methods. To gain a better understanding of public media archaeology and its role in the museum, it would be necessary to gain further access to documents outlining the production, display, and reception of exhibitions on moving image history. This would include curatorial statements, advertising, budget plans, construction sketches and plans, and correspondence between curators, filmmakers, and archivists. Until these data become accessible, it will be difficult to advance research on film and media histories in the museum and how these exhibitions engage visitors in debates regarding the past, present, and future of media.

This article, then, is also a plea for a media archaeology of film and media museums. Research on these museums needs to be extended to the materiality of the media installations they build. Inspection of how media installations are integrated into an overall exhibition design is complicated because, once the exhibition is dismantled, documentation is rarely kept, and if it is, it is often only available as images. As this study of ACMI has shown, however, media installations form a considerable part of the curatorial process. We can only understand film and media museums' history and their modes of historical production if we acknowledge that they are both media exhibitors and media producers that actively engage in contemporary discourses.

In terms of visitor participation within the space of the museum, these modes of thinking are considerably mediated by the exhibition environment. The ACMI, however, is only one site where public media archaeology appears. While the center's history and its current exhibition have been active sites for media archaeological thinking, further investigations into other film and media museums would delineate how this thinking emerges in other curatorial endeavors. Public media archaeology can help to foster a better understanding of these practices, not as mere case studies for scholars, but as contributions to seemingly common and propagated understandings of film and media history.

Philipp Dominik Keidl is a PhD candidate in film and moving image studies at Concordia University in Montreal.

NOTES

1. Wanda Strauven, "Media Archaeology: Where Film History, Media Art and New Media (Can) Meet," in *Preserving and Exhibiting Media Art: Challenges and Perspectives*, ed. Julia Noordegraaf, Cosetta G. Saba, Barbara Le Maître, and Vinzenz Hediger (Amsterdam: Amsterdam University Press, 2013), 63.

2. Ibid., 68.

3. Andreas Fickers and Annie van den Oever, "Experimental Media Archaeology: A Plea for New Directions," in *Techné/Technology: Researching Cinema and Media Technologies, Their Development, Use, and Impact*, ed. Annie van den Oever (Amsterdam: Amsterdam University Press, 2014), 272.

4. For a more detailed discussion of media archaeology and art, see Garnet Hertz and Jussi Parikka, "Zombie Media: Circuit Bending Media Archaeology into an Art Method," *Leonardo* 45, no. 5 (2012): 424–30; Garnet Hertz and Jussi Parikka, "CTheory Interview: Archaeologies of Media Art," *CTheory*, 2010, http://www.ctheory.net/; Erkki Huhtamo, "Resurrecting the Technological Past: An Introduction to the Archaeology of Media Art," *Intercommunication* 14, 1995, http://www.ntticc.or.jp/; Jussi Parikka, *What Is Media Archaeology?* (Cambridge: Polity Press, 2012), 136–58; Strauven, "Media Archaeology," 73–74. For a discussion of media archaeology as a curatorial practice, see Andrew Hoskins and Amy Holdsworth, "Media Archaeology of/ in the Museum," in *The International Handbooks of Museum Studies*, vol. 3, *Museum Media*, ed. Michelle Henning, 23–41 (Chichester, U.K.: Wiley-Blackwell, 2015). For a general discussion of museums' relationship to media archaeology, see Michelle Henning, "Museums and Media Archaeology: An Interview with Wolfgang Ernst," ibid., 3:3–22.

5. Parikka, *What Is Media Archaeology?*, 167.

6. Thomas Elsaesser, "Media Archaeology as Symptom," *New Review of Film and Television Studies* 14, no. 2 (2016): 183–84.

7. Ibid., 183.

8. In 2015, the *Journal of Contemporary Archaeology* dedicated its forum section to the relationship between archeology and media archeology. See *Journal of Contemporary Archaeology* 2, no. 1 (2015). Jerome de Groot, *Consuming History: Historians and Heritage in Contemporary Culture* (London: Routledge, 2009), 1–6.

9. See Raphael Samuel, *Theatres of Memory* (London: Verso, 1996); Paul Ashton and Hilda Kean, eds., *People and Their Pasts: Public History Today* (Basingstoke, U.K.: Palgrave Macmillan, 2009); Hilda Kean and Paul Martin, *The Public History Reader* (Abingdon, U.K.: Routledge, 2013); Keith Jenkins, *Re-thinking History* (London: Routledge, 2003); Nick Merriman, *Public Archaeology* (London: Routledge, 2004).

10. Roy Rosenzweig and David Thelen, *The Presence of the Past: Popular Uses of History in American Life* (New York: Columbia University Press, 1998), 190–208.

11. For a detailed discussion of these concepts, see Andrew V. Uroskie, *Between the Black Box and the White Cube: Expanded Cinema and Postwar Art* (Chicago: University of Chicago Press, 2014); Erika Balsom, *Exhibiting*

Cinema in Contemporary Art (Amsterdam: Amsterdam University Press, 2013); Michelle Henning, *Museums, Media, and Cultural Theory* (Maidenhead, U.K.: Open University Press, 2006); Haidee Wasson, "Big, Fast Museums/Small, Slow Movies: Film, Scale, and the Art Museum," in *Useful Cinema,* ed. Charles Acland and Haidee Wasson, 178–204 (Durham, N.C.: Duke University Press, 2011); Alison Griffiths, *Wondrous Difference: Cinema, Anthropology, and Turn-of-the-Century Visual Culture* (New York: Columbia University Press, 2002).

12. Wanda Strauven and Alexandra Schneider, "Kinderspiel: A Project on Children as Media Archaeologists, Media Makers and Media Players," http://www.kinderspielproject.com/.

13. Fickers and van den Oever, "Experimental Media Archaeology," 276–77.

14. Ibid., 277.

15. Ibid., 278.

16. Merriman, *Public Archaeology,* 1–2.

17. Ibid., 2.

18. These practices are connected to media archaeological thinking in Parikka, *What Is Media Archaeology?,* 1–2; Roger Whitson, *Steampunk and Nineteenth-Century Digital Humanities Literary Retrofuturisms, Media Archaeologies, Alternate Histories* (New York: Routledge, 2017); Andrew Reinhard, "Excavating Atari: Where the Media Was the Archaeology," *Journal of Contemporary Archaeology* 2, no. 1 (2015): 86–93; Raiford Guins, *Game After: A Cultural Study of Video Game Afterlife* (Cambridge, Mass.: MIT Press, 2014); Lincoln Geraghty, *Cult Collectors: Nostalgia, Fandom, and Collecting Popular Culture* (London: Routledge, 2014), 183–85. Giovanna Fossati and Annie van den Oever, *Exposing the Film Apparatus: The Film Archive as a Research Laboratory* (Amsterdam: Amsterdam University Press, 2016).

19. Viktor Shklovsky, "Art as Technique," in *Literary Theory: An Anthology,* ed. Julie Rivkin and Michael Ryan, 8–14 (Malden, Mass.: Wiley-Blackwell, 2017).

20. Natalia Radywyl, Amelia Barikin, Nikos Papastergiadis, and Scott McQuire, "Ambient Aesthetics: Altered Subjectivities in the New Museum," in Henning, *International Handbooks of Museum Studies,* 3:421–23, 417.

21. John Smithies, qtd. ibid., 3:422.

22. For a detailed analysis of museums' role in tourism and heritage markets, see Barbara Kirshenblatt-Gimblett, *Destination Culture: Tourism, Museums, and Heritage* (Berkeley: University of California Press, 1998).

23. Jennie Morgan, "Examining the 'Flexible Museum': Exhibition Process, a Project-Approach, and the Creative Element," *Museum and Society* 11, no. 2 (2013): 160.

24. Ibid.

25. Peter Griffin, president of Film Victoria, visited several museums in Europe and the United States to conduct research on contemporary exhibition trends. See Griffin, *Trip Report: London, Cannes, Dusseldorf, Berlin, London,* May 1996, General Correspondence Subject Files, Public Record Office Victoria, VPRS 11855/P0002/7.

26. Unfortunately, what can be found at the Public Record Office Victoria in Melbourne cannot give a complete picture of the imagined media technologies envisioned for the museum. In fact, many descriptions are of a rather short nature and speak more to a desire to develop something newer than concrete information on preproduction.

27. The most coherent summaries of these ideas can be found in *Building an Australian Centre for the Moving Image 1995,* Draft Proposal, May 1993, General Correspondence Subject Files, Public Record Office Victoria, VPRS 11855/P0002/2; *Australian Centre for the Moving Image Melbourne,* Report to Office of Major Projects, Department of Planning and Development, Victoria, September 1993, General Correspondence Subject File, Public Record Office Victoria, VPRS 11855/P0002/2; *Future Realities Gallery—An Exhibition of Screen Culture,* General Correspondence Subject Files, Public Record Office Victoria, VPRS 11855/P0002/7; *Cinemedia Screen Gallery Online,* General Correspondence Subject Files, Public Record Office Victoria, VPRS 11855/P0002/20; *Tomorrow's Picture: The Future of the Proving Image at Federation Square,* August 1998; John Smithies, *Screen Exhibition: Exhibiting the Present and the Future of the Moving Image on the Cinema Screen, Television Screen, Interactive Screen,* January 1998, General Correspondence Subject Files, Public Record Office Victoria, VPRS 11855/P0002/20.

28. For a detailed analysis of contemporary museums as media producers, see Jenny Kidd, *Museums in the New Mediascape: Transmedia, Participation, Ethics* (Farnham, U.K.: Ashgate, 2014).

29. Eric Kluitenberg, "On the Archaeology of Imaginary Media," in *Media Archaeology: Approaches, Applications, Implications,* ed. Erkki Huhtamo and Jussi Parikka (Berkeley: University of California Press, 2011), 48.

30. Ibid. Also see Eric Kluitenberg, "Second Introduction to an Archaeology of Imaginary Media," in *The Book of Imaginary Media: Excavating the Dream of the Ultimate Communication Medium,* ed. Eric Kluitenberg, 7–26 (Rotterdam: Debalie and NAi, 2006).

31. The AFI Research Collection at RMIT University holds an extensive collection of press clippings on ACMI. For the aforementioned criticism, see, among others, Ron Lowe, "My Say," *Herald Sun,* February 9, 2007; Corrie Perkin, "Centre Opts for Surround Screen," *Australian,* June 4, 2007; Greg Burchall, "Filmic Underdog Bites Image," *Age,* August 15, 2007.

32. Parikka, *What Is Media Archaeology?,* 138–141.

33. David Bordwell, *On the History of Film Style* (Cambridge, Mass.: Harvard University Press, 1997), 12–45. For an analysis of how the basic story was adapted by museums, see Alison Trope, *Stardust Monuments: The Saving and Selling of Hollywood* (Hanover, N.H.: Dartmouth College Press, 2012), 13.

34. Thomas Elsaesser, "The New Film History as Media Archaeology," *Cinémas* 14, no. 2–3 (2005): 90.

35. See "In the Future... What Do You Think Film, Television and All the Other Media We Enjoy Will Be Like in the Future?," https://www.flickr.com /photos/acmi/sets/72157623926405033/.

FILM ANALYSIS AS ANNOTATION

LILIANA MELGAR ESTRADA,
EVA HIELSCHER, MARIJN
KOOLEN, CHRISTIAN GOSVIG
OLESEN, JULIA NOORDEGRAAF,
AND JAAP BLOM

Exploring Current Tools

00:05:26.881   Selection: 00:00:00.000 - 00:00:

00:05:10.000   00:05:15.000   00:05:20.000   00:05:25.000   00:

Shots [44]	Wolfgang and Christl sitting on table, waiter brings coffee	Christl drinkin	Wo
Scenes [13]	Wolfgang and Christl in street café drinking coffee and talking		
Characters [17]	Wolfgang, Christl	Christl	W
re activities [2]	drinking coffee		
eet scenes [1]	street café		
hniques/ae [14]	dissolv medium close-up	close-up	cl

With the VCR's increasingly widespread use in the 1980s and 1990s,

film scholars and historians acquired new techniques for doing film

analysis. Whereas previously, analysis performed on celluloid films

had been restricted to on-site research in film archives,[1] the VCR technology's playback

mode allowed scholars to fast-forward, rewind, pause, and segment films in settings

outside of the archive.

Also, since the 1990s, the rise of the internet and the appearance of a great

variety of computational tools have spawned scholarly practices for segmenting and

annotating films. Digitization also has allowed linking digitized films to contextual film-

related materials in CD-ROM and DVD editions as well as presenting them on curated

websites. In the past twenty years, the possibilities of hypermedia and enhanced CD-ROM editions of films have resulted in groundbreaking projects such as Lauren Rabinovitz and Greg Easley's *Rebecca Project* (1995) and Yuri Tsivian's CD-ROM *Immaterial Bodies* (2000)—also called a Cine Disc—released through Marsha Kinder's Labyrinth project,[2] and, more recently, DVD editions like *Digital Formalism* (2007–10), based on the digitized collection of Soviet filmmaker Dziga Vertov's films at the Austrian Filmmuseum, which originated from experiments with automated semantic content analysis of big data. The tool kits were developed by media theorist Lev Manovich, with software for multimedia annotation such as ANVIL.[3]

Although film analysis and audiovisual publication formats that relied on video annotation and hyperlinking in past decades may have seemed somewhat exotic and offered a limited range of choices,[4] now, though, annotation and editing are becoming increasingly accepted in scholarly research projects allowing scholars to annotate larger corpora of films and to produce increasingly personal interpretations. There is a wide range of software to choose from, not only for presentations or publication but also as research tools in their own right. From being what film scholar Raymond Bellour in the 1970s famously bemoaned an "unattainable text," film—in its electronic avatar—became attainable.[5]

This article describes a study of the information systems (so-called tools) that have made this possible. We begin with the assumption that it is important that scholars discover and use these tools to understand and critically discuss how the systems influence the process of analysis and its results. This closer approach will, as Olesen claims, "elucidate the epistemological underpinnings of digital film history's methods."[6]

Because not much is presently known about the implications of using these computational tools for film scholarship, this article aims to contribute to the initial effort to understand these implications. We focus on one side of the problem, which is the lack of an overview of existing tools and a description of their conceptual models and affordances[7] (i.e., easy replaying, segmenting, annotating, or collaborating) based on empirical experiments. Reporting about the connection between the characteristics and functionalities of the tools with research goals will help in comprehending the implications of their use.[8] This work is the result of a collaborative effort between media scholars and information scientists. We are motivated by the need to codevelop systems and information services for audiovisual media-centered research within the Dutch National Digital Humanities infrastructure.[9]

This article evaluates two types of video annotation tools that can be used during the analysis phase of the research process, to demonstrate their affordances and pitfalls. The following section presents an inventory of the different types of existing tools. The next section describes a case study wherein we tested these tools in a small film analysis project. Specifically, we evaluated the tools ELAN and NVivo for analyzing an excerpt of a 1930 film. The third section synthesizes the main methodological implications of the use of these systems in media scholarship. In the conclusion of the article, we evaluate the implications of using these tools for film analysis.

DIGITAL TOOLS FOR MOVING IMAGE ANNOTATION

The digital humanities community uses the word *tool* to refer to any software component, application, or information processing system that supports the analysis process or the creation (authoring) of digital content. Tools are "whatever we can get our hands on, annotate, collate, interoperate . . . repeat and stir."[10] Word processors or spreadsheets, which have been used by media scholars for decades,[11] can be considered the most basic types of analysis tools. The sophisticated stand-alone audiovisual analysis tools in media studies date from the 1990s, from the moment digital video could be played back on personal computers.[12]

The proliferation of digital audiovisual media presents new opportunities and challenges for information scientists and professionals as well as for film scholars. From their perspective, time-based media are perceived as a "blind medium" for retrieval,[13] which means that it is not possible to access the content in the same way as it is possible for text. There are different ways to solve the problems of accessing audiovisual data, such as adding manual, automatic, or semiautomatic (crowd-driven) annotations. Thus communities create their own notations for different purposes and in different contexts.

Scholarly annotations are often created manually during the research process. Previous research has shown that the scholarly research process consists of several iterative phases,[14] along which annotation activities frequently occur. Thus the "analysis" phase consists of both a series of activities for preparing and enriching the data via annotations and "that part of research where the results of annotation and transcription are subject to the judgement and intervention of the scholar who seeks to extract useful information, draw lessons, and form conclusions."[15] In the case of using audiovisual sources, these activities tend to occur more iteratively, that is, by "repeatedly accessing, searching, marking-up (annotating), transcribing, analyzing, and presenting materials."[16] Annotation is an important part of this process, not only in media studies but in all humanities disciplines, which is why it is considered to be one of the "scholarly cross-cutting primitives."[17]

New annotation prototypes are regularly implemented in the context of individual research projects, after which they are abandoned. In general, the abundance of tools is a challenge for new users, who must identify which tools exist, get acquainted with their capabilities, and decide which one is most suitable for a given research endeavor. These factors create what Julia Noordegraaf called "a gap . . . between the affordances of digital data and computational tools, and their application in media studies, despite the growing number of successful experiments in this area."[18]

We have created a comprehensive (but not exhaustive) list of existing systems that support annotation of audiovisual media. First, we conducted a literature review and consulted experts to identify the most widely used annotation tools. Second, we extended this overview by using existing academic publications or websites that explicitly state the purpose of inventorying existing tools. We also analyzed several scholarly publications in which film and media scholars report on the use of digital tools in their research.

Important surveys that we selected included the proceedings from one of the first workshops on this topic held in Siegen, Germany, at the Media Upheavals Research Center, Digital Tools in Media Studies.[19] It provided a first overview of advances in computationally supported media studies research. More recently, documentary filmmaker and film scholar Livia Giunti has examined four applications for film analysis and annotation (Cinemetrics, Advene, Lignes de temps, and the Digital Cinema Project) and compared how these "active reading" tools encourage researchers to explore new approaches.[20] Barbara Flueckiger used an online social network platform to ask participants of a film studies group about their experiences working with video annotation tools.[21] *The Arclight Guidebook to Media History and the Digital Humanities,*[22] although not intended as a survey, offered a comprehensive landscape of the tools used by media scholars in the context of their projects. We also selected several surveys of multimedia annotation tools that have been applied in the past years in the field of information science.[23] In addition, we chose surveys accounting for computer software that assists qualitative data analysis (QDA) (which we detail in the section "Qualitative Data Analysis Software").[24] Finally, several large-scale projects are starting to create "tool registries" to keep inventories widely available and up to date. Examples include the registries maintained by the linguistics infrastructure CLARIN,[25] the Digital Research Tools Directory (DiRT),[26] and the European Digital Infrastructure for the Arts and the Humanities (DARIAH).[27] We did not systematically analyze all the tools registered there for video annotation, but we did select those currently available. We also added to the DARIAH registry the tools that we found in our own literature review.[28]

In the surveys, we identified more than fifty existing tools suitable for time-based media annotation and access. We focused on the ones used for digital video annotation, which we grouped into six categories:

1. *Professional time-based media annotation tools* (described further in a subsequent section). These support different manual (or semiautomatic) annotation tasks in a single stand-alone platform or more dedicated tools for performing specific tasks, for example, shot division and tagging.

2. *Qualitative data analysis software (QDA)* (described further in a subsequent section). QDA software offers features that correspond to qualitative analysis principles, for instance, from grounded theory (Pickard and Childs, 2013) to discourse analysis (Paulus and Lester, 2015), as is typical in the social sciences.

3. *Nonlinear editing systems.* These are professional systems that are used for editing digital video in a nondestructive way, as opposed to analog methods of editing. Although they are designed for editing digital video footage, they can also be used for "reversing" the editing process via semiautomatic annotation.

4. *Automatic image/video analysis tools.* These tools originate in research areas known as content-based image retrieval (CBIR), content-based video retrieval (CBVR), visual information retrieval,[29] and multimedia information retrieval.[30] These techniques combine aspects of pattern recognition, artificial intelligence, signal processing, and computer vision[31] to detect basic patterns of low-level visual features (e.g., colors or shapes) in images or video. As this "low-level approach"[32] is rarely done manually, content-based annotations are usually understood to be automatic.

5. *Audiovisual collection–specific browsers or web publishing platforms.* These are search engines or exploratory search systems that use web content management systems by collection providers or researchers to publish their own collections. They currently offer basic support for corpus creation and preliminary annotation during the exploratory phase of the research. These annotation facilities are useful for doing preanalysis via segmentation, classification, and linking. The tendency to support analysis during browsing (for media fragment creation and classification) will increase in the coming years.[33]

6. *Customized applications for crowdsourcing projects.* These include

systems that are tailored to specific data collection needs via crowd or niche contributions. These systems fall outside of the scope of our study, because scholars do not use them to perform their analyses but only to collect annotations by external actors. They are relevant, however, because they support annotation tasks, which could be guided and structured as well.

Table 1 shows that video annotation tools are used in many disciplines, with actively maintained tools in each group (the latter indicated by an asterisk). In the following, we focus on the first two groups, because the tools in these groups were designed mainly to support annotation as analysis and to be used in research. For the case study in the next section, we selected one tool from each of these two groups, considering as positive factors for our selection whether the tools are currently and actively maintained, the extent to which they are reported in scholarly publications, whether they are widely recognized or used, and the extent to which the authors of this article are familiar with them. We considered it a positive factor if a tool was free and open source, a criterion that most tools in the second group did not meet. On the basis of these criteria, we selected ELAN from group 1 and NVivo from group 2.

Table 1. Available tools for video annotation

Type	Domain in which the tool originated	Tools[a]	Film/TV studies reporting use of these tools
Professional video annotation tool	Communication studies/linguistics	ANVIL,* ELAN,* EXMARaLDA*	[b,c]
	Computer science (discipline agnostic)	YUMA	Not found
	Education/research (several domains)	Advene, Clipper*	Not found
	Film/media studies	Cinemetrics,* Lignes de temps, Videana	[d,e]
	Oral history	OHMS: Oral History Metadata Synchronizer*	Not found
	Performative arts	Rekall,* PM2Go*	Not found
QDA software	Social sciences	Atlas.ti,* MaxQDA,* NVivo,* Transana*	[f]
Nonlinear editing systems	Media production	Adobe Premiere ProCC*[g]	[h]
Automatic image and video analysis tools	Information and computer science, media studies, scientific domain	ImageJ,* MATLAB*	[i,j,k,l]
Audiovisual collection–specific browsers and/or web publishing platforms[m]	Film/media studies	YouTube,* LinkedTV Editor Tool,* MyEUscreen,* Semantic Annotation Tool (SAT),* MediaThread,[n] INA Video Dataset for Research,* CLARIAH MediaSuite*	[o,p]
Customized applications for crowdsourcing projects	Information sciences, cultural heritage	Waisda	[q,r]

[a]An asterisk indicates that the tool is actively maintained.

[b]Stefan Hahn, "Filmprotokoll Revisited: Ground Truth in Digital Formalism," *Maske und Kothurn* 55, no. 3 (2009): 129–35.

[c]See Adelheid Heftberger, Michael Loebenstein, and Georg Wasner, "Auf Spurensuche im Archiv: Ein Arbeitsbericht," *Maske und Kothurn* 55, no. 3 (2009): 137–48. See also Christian Gosvig Olesen, "Formalising Digital Formalism: An Interview with Adelheid Heftberger and Matthias Zeppelzauer about the Vienna Vertov Project," in *Shifting Layers: New Perspectives in Media Archaeology across Digital Media and Audiovisual Arts,* ed. Miriam De Rosa and Ludovica Fales (Milan: Mimesis International,

forthcoming), and Adelheid Heftberger, Yuri Tsivian, and Matteo Lepore, "Man with a Movie Camera (SU 1929) under the Lens of Cinemetrics," *Maske und Kothurn* 55, no. 3 (2009): 31–50.

[d]Yuri Tsivian, "Cinemetrics: Part of the Humanities' Cyberinfrastructure," in *Digital Tools in Media Studies: Analysis and Research: An Overview*, ed. Michael Ross, Manfred Grauer, and Bernd Freisleben, 93–100 (Bielfeld, Germany: Transcript Verlag, 2009). See also Matthias Stork, "On Cinemetrics, Video Essays, and Digital Scholarship—An Interview with Dr. Yuri Tsivian and Dr. Daria Khitrova," *Journal of Cinema and Media Studies* 9 (Fall 2015).

[e]Livia Giunti, "L'analyse du film à l'ère numérique: Annotation, geste analytique et lecture active," *Cinéma & Cie* 14, no. 22/23 (2014): 127–43.

[f]For examples from several disciplines, see Graham R. Gibbs, "Using Software in Qualitative Analysis," in *Sage Handbook of Qualitative Data Analysis*, 277–94 (Los Angeles, Calif.: Sage, 2014).

[g]This and/or other desktop video editors are used to create video essays (scholars such as Drew Morton, Jason Mittell, and Christian Keathley have all discussed the topic of videographic scholarship and criticism). The creation of video essays highly depends on fine-grained annotations of the nonedited video content.

[h]Lea Jacobs and Kaitlin Fyfe, "Digital Tools for Film Analysis: Small Data," in *The Arclight Guidebook to Media History and the Digital Humanities*, ed. Charles R. Acland and Eric Hoyt, 249–69 (Falmer, U.K.: REFRAME Books, 2016).

[i]Adelheid Heftberger, Michael Loebenstein, and Georg Wasner, "Auf Spurensuche im Archiv. Ein Arbeitsbericht," *Maske und Kothurn* 55, no. 3 (2009): 137–48.

[j]Kevin L. Ferguson, "The Slices of Cinema: Digital Surrealism as Research Strategy," in *The Arclight Guidebook to Media History and the Digital Humanities*, ed. Charles R. Acland and Eric Hoyt, 270–99 (Falmer, U.K.: REFRAME Books, 2016).

[k]Tony Tran, "Coding and Visualizing the Beauty in Hating Michelle Phan: Exploratory Experiments with YouTube, Images, and Discussion Boards," in *The Arclight Guidebook to Media History and the Digital Humanities*, ed. Charles R. Acland and Eric Hoyt, 196–215 (Falmer, U.K.: REFRAME Books, 2016).

[l]Christian Gosvig Olesen, Eef Masson, Jasmijn van Gorp, Giovanna Fossati, and Julia Noordegraaf, "Data-Driven Research for Film History: Exploring the Jean Desmet Collection," *The Moving Image* 16, no. 1 (2016): 82–105.

[m]These could also be considered as distinct tools. For example, YouTube is a "collection" browser that enables different types of user-generated annotations (e.g., creating a corpus via bookmarks and tags, or subtitling), whereas Scalar and Omeka are web content management systems that enable publication and organization of digital content, based also on a wide variety of annotations, assigned mostly by content administrators or curators in this case. About the implications of using YouTube as a "database," see Frank Kessler and Mirko Tobias Schäfer, "Navigating YouTube: Constituting a Hybrid Information Management System," in *The YouTube Reader*, ed. Pelle Snickars and Patrick Vonderau, 275–91 (Stockholm: National Library of Sweden, 2009).

[n]This tool is web based, works as a module compliant with semantic web standards, and uses the W3C Open Annotation data model. See https://sites.dartmouth.edu/mediaecology/.

[o]Mark Williams, "Networking Moving Image History: Archives, Scholars, and the

Media Ecology Project," in *The Arclight Guidebook to Media History and the Digital Humanities*, ed. Charles R. Acland and Eric Hoyt, 335–46 (Falmer, U.K.: REFRAME Books, 2016).

[p]Willemien Sanders, "EUscreen at the SITIS Conference in Bangkok," *EUScreenXL: Official Blog*, January 14, 2016, http://blog.euscreen.eu/archives/8604.

[q]Gary Geisler, Geoff Willard, and Eryn Whitworth, "Crowdsourcing the Indexing of Film and Television Media," in *Proceedings of the 73rd ASIS&T Annual Meeting on Navigating Streams in an Information Ecosystem*, 82:1–82:10 (Silver Spring, Md.: American Society for Information Science, 2010).

[r]Liliana Melgar Estrada, Michiel Hildebrand, Victor de Boer, and Jacco van Ossenbruggen, "Time-Based Tags for Fiction Movies: Comparing Experts to Novices Using a Video Labeling Game," *Journal of the Association for Information Science and Technology* 68, no. 2 (2017): 348–64.

PEOPLE ON SUNDAY THROUGH THE LENS OF DIFFERENT TYPES OF TOOLS

We used both ELAN and NVivo to analyze a digitized film fragment from *People on Sunday* (Robert Siodmak et al., 1930).[34] In selecting this case, we considered criteria such as the film's archival history, its historical significance, and its aesthetic appeal (rich in visual information and content). In this way, the film would allow us to explore a wide range of the tools' functionalities. We attended to the specific ways in which the tools configure the relations among the media artifacts, the levels of analysis, and the types and methods of annotation. We also considered it an advantage if the scholars were familiar with the title in advance, because it would allow for focusing on the tool rather than on getting familiar with the film.

The silent semidocumentary *People on Sunday* is a German, black-and-white film that tells the story of five people and the Sunday they spend outdoors as a respite from the working week, like others in the city of Berlin. It was widely lauded by critics at the time. Following World War II, however, the film was regarded less favorably by German critical theorists. Most prominently, Siegfried Kracauer interpreted it as a display of the petty-bourgeois vacuity that explained how the Nazi regime could have come into power.[35]

The film remains striking today because of its maverick approach to filmmaking, which involved using untrained actors and natural settings. It offers a fascinating, candid portrait of city life and youth culture that encapsulates a modern society not yet clouded by the prospects of war. Historically, the film is significant in that it shares numerous features with the city symphony films of the 1920s and 1930s—in fact, it has often been described as a city symphony and cross section film—because of its focus on city life. The daily reality of young urban dwellers has positioned it as a precursor to later New Wave films.[36] For these reasons, *People on Sunday* was, in terms of both content and style, a rich source to explore in this exercise. Because our principal purpose was to evaluate and compare the ELAN and NVivo video annotation tools, we did not conduct a full film analysis but instead limited ourselves to analyzing the eighteen-minute first sequence.

A title card explains the restoration process. The opening sequence starts with the credits of the film, followed by an introduction of the five protagonists: taxi driver Erwin Splettstößer, sales clerk Brigitte Borchert, hedonist and wine merchant Wolfgang von Waltershausen, film extra Christl Ehlers, and a fashion model, Annie Schreyer, who is Erwin's girlfriend. The sequence consists of two main parts. The first one introduces the city of Berlin. We see Wolfgang and Christl, who, on a Saturday evening, accidentally meet in front of the Berlin Zoo railway station. They talk, go for a drink, and agree to meet again the next day at a nearby lake. The second part portrays the domestic struggles of Erwin and Annie, whose plan to go out is foiled by the appearance of Wolfgang, who has come to play cards and drink with Erwin. The opening sequence ends at 00:18:46,[37] when a title card introduces the start of the next day: "Sonntag" (Sunday).

Each of the three media scholars in our team focused his or her research by analyzing the fragment with two different tools, from the perspective of two specific themes. First, we focused on the way the film represents the city of Berlin—arguably one of the protagonists of the film. Second, we looked at the ways in which the film's style and content represent 1929–30 urban youth culture. The following sections outline the ways in which the ELAN and NVivo tools facilitated this analysis, each starting with the motivation for the tool, followed by a discussion of its main characteristics and a short example of its application in the analysis.

Professional Tools for the Complex Annotation of Video and Audio

From the inventory of tools described in the previous section, we observed that a group of them specialize in supporting semiautomatic, complex video analysis. These tools are offered as stand-alone desktop applications and/or web-based applications. Among others, this group contains tools such as Advene and Lignes de temps (for video), Synote (for audio), and OHMS (for audio or video interviews). These tools have all been created in the context of information science experiments or within domain-specific projects. In the area of film studies, besides Lignes de temps, examples of domain-specific tools include Videana (for a wide range of annotation tasks) and the Cinemetrics "frame accurate tool"[38] (for very specific annotation tasks, such as segmentation and tagging of segment types).

For the analysis of the opening sequence of *People on Sunday*, we selected

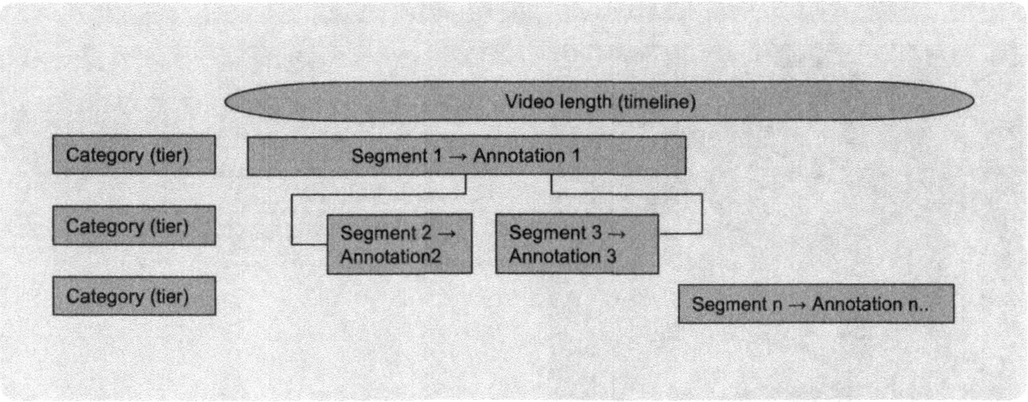

Figure 1. Schematic of the tiered approach in ELAN, showing how annotations are related to video segments. Drawing created by the authors.

ELAN, which was created at the Language Archive of the Max Planck Institute for Psycholinguistics (Nijmegen, Netherlands). It was developed by and for a community of linguists and communication scholars. Because it supports multimodal annotations, it can also be used in film studies and other disciplines. One motive for choosing ELAN was that it is currently used in at least two film-related projects: in doctoral research on city symphonies by one of the authors of this article and in an ERC project on the analysis of color in film by Flueckiger and her team.[39] It also offers complete and detailed documentation; several publications discuss it; and it is a free and open-source tool that is actively supported and maintained. The latter is a condition for a smooth working process and the reason for preferring ELAN over Lignes de temps, a tool designed specifically for film analysis but that is not currently maintained or properly documented.[40] Another tool initially created in the linguistic domain, ANVIL, was used in the Digital Formalism project,[41] but it is not open source. (We discuss some of the implications of this trait in the last section.)

ELAN, as is the case with most of the tools in this group, provides a "tiered" or "layered" approach to segmentation and annotation. The media stream, therefore, can be divided into multiple segments and grouped into categories (called tiers). ELAN facilitates this via vertical rows, each corresponding to an annotation type or tier (e.g., motifs) and a horizontal, temporally based distribution of segments per row. Segments can vary in length in each layer. There is the option to create dependencies between segments (hierarchical relations and constraints for the dependencies). Figure 1 shows an abstract schematic of this structure.

To analyze a movie with ELAN, at least one tier and segmentation along that tier are required. In contrast to Lignes de temps, which includes automatic shot boundary

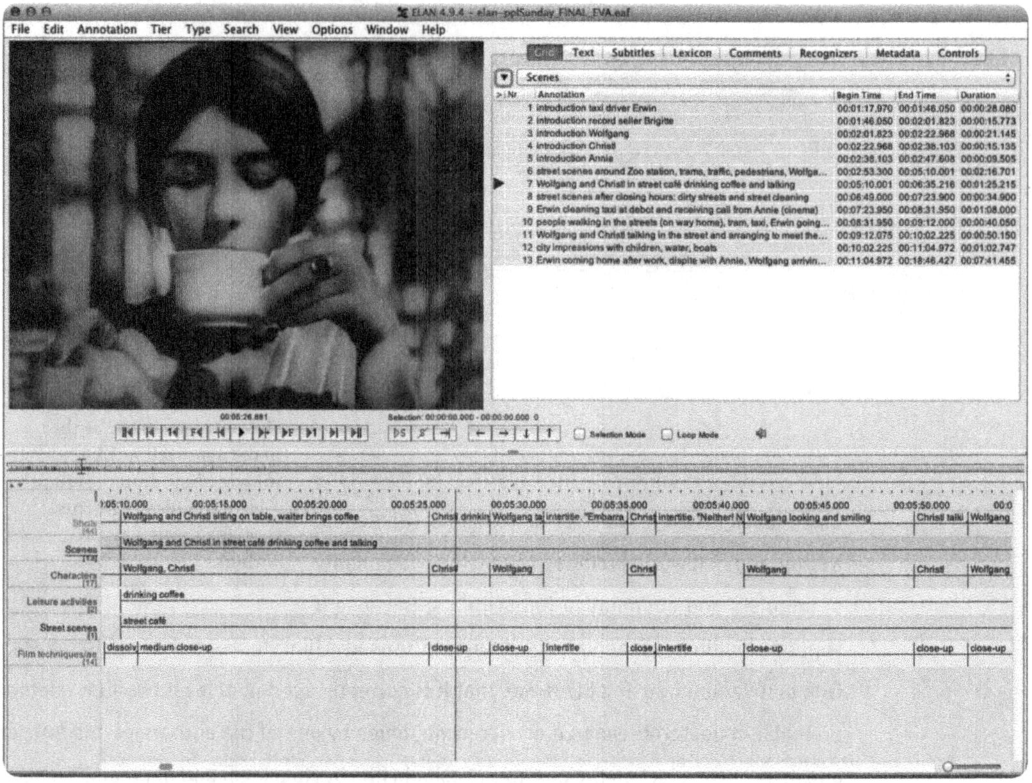

Figure 2. Tiered approach offered by the tool ELAN applied to the analysis of *People on Sunday.* ELAN screenshot courtesy of the ELAN developers.

detection for automatic segmentation at the level of shots, ELAN requires the researcher to indicate segments manually.[42] Creating annotations is considered a "manual process consisting of repeated close inspection of segments of the audio and or video signals. . . . Determination of begin and end time of each unit is the first step in this process, followed by the assignment of a value to each unit."[43]

In our study, the scholars working with ELAN made a very fine-grained segmentation of the film at the level of shot change. Among the various aspects of the film were items like characters, editing, camera angles, mise-en-scène, markers of space and time, and props. These aspects were either decided in advance or discovered during the segmentation process. For example, when creating a tier for identifying the appearance of each character, the scholar realized she needed a more fine-grained segmentation that would allow her to annotate all the shots that have the characters in them as shown from different camera angles. It was possible to create three subsegmentations on separate tiers for this purpose (i.e., shots, characters, and film techniques) using the possibilities the tool provides to interrelate the different fragments. These different layers are shown on the left side in Figure 2.

Because ELAN offers different working modes (segmenting, annotating, transcribing, synchronizing), it is possible to decide in which order these tasks could be performed. For example, we may segment first and then annotate or do this at the same time. Thus another possibility is first to decide which aspects (or tiers) need to be annotated and then to create the segments for each tier along the timeline. Thus segmentation granularity may change depending on the type of tier. Finally, we may then add the annotations to each segment box. The annotations must be inserted into the segment boxes and can be one of three types: a free word (tag or keyword), a controlled word (using a predefined list of terms, such as a vocabulary list or thesaurus), or a longer text or comment. Therefore, when creating annotations, researchers choose between a bottom-up approach, entering noncontrolled terms or open descriptions, or a top-down approach, whereby the elements to be identified are known in advance (such as camera angles or editing techniques). In the top-down approach, it is possible to integrate "externally defined" vocabularies, for example, the "Film Language Glossary."[44] For this exercise, we opted for the free-words bottom-up option.

Figure 2 illustrates the result of our exercise with ELAN. The first tier represents a shot-by-shot segmentation. In the second tier, these are combined into scenes. The third layer (characters) and the fourth (aesthetic techniques) were created to support the analysis of editing style in combination with each character's appearance. Finally, the fifth (leisure activities) and the sixth (street life) layers permitted us to analyze in detail the main elements related to our two research questions (Berlin street life and youth culture).

Presenting the different layers in a simultaneous visualization allowed us to demonstrate empirically the various aspects of the film that normally are perceived intuitively. In particular, the detailed analysis the tool facilitates made it possible to externalize the observations that normally take place inside the scholar's mind during close analysis.

Using ELAN, the fine-grained segmentation and annotation of the scene in which Wolfgang and Christl encounter each other in front of the entrance to the Berlin Zoo railway station yielded insight into the way in which the film style thematizes the characters through their encounter. First, Wolfgang and Christl are portrayed in separate, single shots. Christl is shown in medium static shots that portray her as passively waiting, while Wolfgang is shown in medium panning or tracking shots that stress his dynamism or restlessness. The latter is further emphasized by the fact that he is portrayed against (shots of) passing cars, trams, and trains and that, in the first shot in which Wolfgang and Christl are seen together (from 00:03:50 onward), Wolfgang approaches Christl, who is still waiting on the pavement, by walking around her in circles. This close analysis provided insight into the classic use of space to narrate the first encounter of two young urban dwellers. There is a general movement from two spaces and single frames to the characters' union in one space (the pavement in front of the kiosk) and their eventual coming together in a single frame. The pattern is repeated at the terrace: after an establishing shot, we encounter them in shot–countershot sequence (through close-ups of their faces), and then at the end, they are portrayed in a single frame, emphasizing their growing intimacy. Many of these analytic findings could also have been reached through traditional analyses done on paper. We will comment on this in the "reflection" section that follows.

The ELAN segmentation of this scene also directed our attention to the scene's rhythmic editing, which is used to suggest a narrative and largely replaces the need for intertitles. In addition, we could identify and pinpoint in the timeline all scenes displaying street life and traffic in Berlin as well as the different leisure activities of the four main characters (drinking coffee in a street café, going to the movies, listening to music, smoking, etc.) that support the analysis of the portrayal of youth culture in the film. The main advantage of this tool proved to be its search functions, which allow different combinations of queries, for instance, pairing all the shots that relate to transportation or to themes like "work," or using patterns of terms from different layers to facilitate deeper thematic or formal analysis. We did not use dependencies between tiers, but this could also be a powerful feature for further querying the annotations. A further evaluation of the implications of using professional, complex video annotation tools such as ELAN for film analysis is provided in the discussion section.

Qualitative Data Analysis Software

The second tool we evaluated, NVivo, belongs to the software group computer-assisted qualitative data analysis (CAQDAS) or simply QDA.[45] This type of software was developed in the 1980s and was first released commercially in the 1990s. These tools originated in the social sciences, where they were developed for supporting QDA using grounded-theory principles and methods.[46] Even though they were primarily designed to analyze textual sources, most packages include the possibility to investigate audiovisual sources as well. QDA methods that are supported by these tools include, for instance, the use of "coding" techniques (bottom-up, or top-down by using controlled vocabularies), thematic analysis, discourse analysis, and content analysis, as well as memoing and commenting during the interpretation process.

In the case of audio and video, transcripts can be imported and synchronized.

The tools include basic controls for facilitating the annotation activity during visualization, such as adding time stamps, real-time summaries or transcripts, keywords, and playing back, forward, pausing, and controlling speed. These programs are often used to help researchers keep their documents in a single location. For example, the much-used package Atlas.ti calls these environments *hermeneutic units*. Most packages are now starting to offer support for mixed-method analysis, whereby structured data (e.g., via "cases," as in NVivo) can be combined with manually coded annotations.

Applying our selection criteria for picking one package in this group was not easy, because the most used programs are being updated constantly and offer similar facilities. We selected NVivo for our exercise with this group of tools based on a previous analysis[47] that showed it has a more robust model for creating textual representations of videos than does Atlas.ti, the next immediate competitor. Another important tool in this group is Transana, developed at the University of Wisconsin in 2001. It is the main QDA package developed exclusively for video annotation. However, because its interface and structure are rather complex, we decided not to use it for this exercise.[48]

NVivo offers only manual segmentation facilities. As in most QDA packages supporting video annotation, a segment can be created for any time span. Every segment can have a start time, end time, and "transcript," which is also called a "content field." In NVivo, in addition, a column can be added to the content field for entering a "speaker's" name. In the Windows version of NVivo, the column "Speaker" can be changed to another variable, and more columns or custom fields can be added after it, which can be used flexibly to enter unique values describing the segments.

The content field can be used to enter any type of free description or natural language representation of the segment. The user can add a single word, a sentence, or a longer text and choose its relation to the segment (e.g., a label for an object, a speech-to-text transcript, a summary, a personal observation). The so-called nodes or codes can be assigned to the entire content field or to parts of it (to any minimum level: words or parts of words). Any text within the transcript field can be coded, using existing or new codes. Those codes become locators (or index terms) to the content of the transcript, which is, in turn, linked to the time-coded segment.

When using NVivo, similarly to the exercise with ELAN, the first decision concerned the question of how to segment the film. The creation of segments in NVivo and in most other QDA packages is done in a single (vertical) list of rows. These segments can only be typed by using the "content field" mentioned earlier (Figure 3). Thus the decision about which segments to create is even more open and left to the scholar. We identified at least three ways of doing segmentation using NVivo. First, one can segment

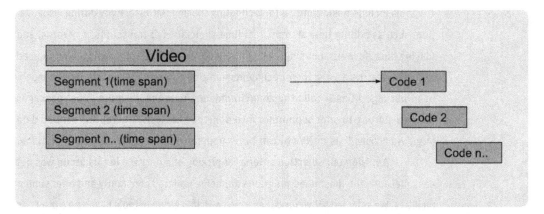

directly, via the timeline, which is useful when coding objects or camera movements, for example (see Figure 4, top right).

Figure 3. Schematic of the segmentation and annotation facilities in NVivo, showing the types of annotations that can be added to video segments.

Second, it is possible to create broader segments and add longer textual descriptions to the content field, making using bigger blocks of units for the analysis possible, for example, setting a specific number of scenes or sequences where city life or leisure activities are shown or specifying the basis of the broader narrative structure. In this case, it is possible to analyze the different aspects, such as motifs (the representation of youth), and locations and the cityscape in the film by coding the text directly (not via the timeline). After this is done, different top-level codes for motifs and locations/cityscape can be created. In ELAN, the user would create two separate tiers (see Figure 4, second panel from the left).

Third, one can create segments by using a combination of both approaches, via the linking facilities between the timeline and the content field offered by NVivo. In this case, codes assigned directly to the timeline can be linked to each content field where they belong, allowing for combining broader descriptions and longer time frames with more specific time-coded objects in the timeline. Figure 4 shows this third approach.

When we tried to mirror the same method that we used in ELAN to create different tiers, in NVivo, we ended up with a flat list of segments with undifferentiated typologies (Figure 4, bottom right). When we tried to use the custom field entry option for adding the type of segment (equivalent to the tier name in ELAN), and then used the filtering options for displaying the code stripes along the timeline, the visualization of these different aspects in an overview as individual categorized tracks with their nested elements was limited.

NVivo's limitations in creating layers of segments and of search results not

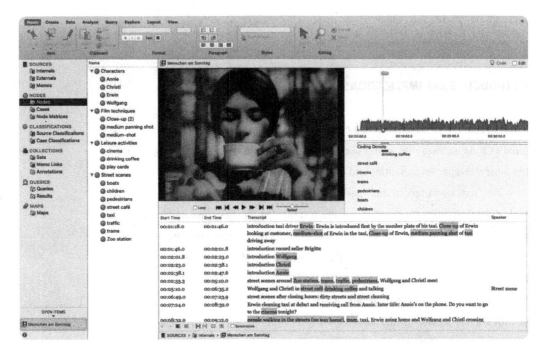

Figure 4. Coding via the timeline and the content field in NVivo. Screenshot courtesy of the software company.

showing the context of the segment meant that, when analyzing *People on Sunday,* we could not identify, as easily as in ELAN, the use of space in the scene in which Wolfgang and Christl meet for the first time. Identifying groups of motifs and places, however, was significantly more efficient and flexible than with ELAN. This was especially apparent during the task of rearranging the terms (or codes) that appear after a bottom-up identification and the resulting taxonomy.

A clear advantage of QDA packages is that more than one film can be integrated into the same project. This facilitates the constant exploration and simultaneous comparison of different films based on their shared codes. For example, if a motif is assigned to two or more films, it is always possible to get a list of fragments (and links to the segments) where those codes or motifs occur. Taking the scene with the still photographer at the beach that occurs later in *People on Sunday* and defining the integration of still photographs into the moving images as a code make it possible to identify other scenes in a corpus of films that also contain this aspect. An obvious example would be *Man with a Movie Camera* (Dziga Vertov, 1929), in which film frames are integrated in the film-editing sequence with Elizaveta Svilova working at the montage table. Or it is possible to identify all scenes taking place at the Berlin Zoo station in Berlin films from the 1920s, including the early scene in *People on Sunday.* This manual comparison function is especially productive with larger corpora of films, but it also requires very precise coding and use of identical vocabularies and descriptions. We comment about the implications of this in the conclusion.

METHODOLOGICAL IMPLICATIONS FOR FILM ANALYSIS

In this section, we describe the main elements that make the connection of tool characteristics and functionalities with research goals more obvious, focusing on highlighting the most relevant commonalities and differences between the two groups of tools.

First, we observed that, perhaps due to the small scale of our analysis, the tools did not significantly change the manual or analog practices involved in the close analysis. Nonetheless, there were obvious advantages to using the tools. Their affordances made the task easier by providing visual annotation support and possibility of going back and forth between annotation and analysis and by facilitating search and advanced retrieval of the annotations. We believe that the latter may increase the possibilities of finding unexpected connections when films are analyzed in their entirety or when the corpus is bigger.

Second, what we find to be the most significant added methodological value of these tools is that they allow the scholars to reproduce previous manual visual analysis practices in a more systematic way. This enhanced self-awareness during the analysis makes the process explicit to the researchers and facilitates communicating procedural decisions or findings to others.

We found that the most thought-provoking analyses inspiring self-reflection and methodological discussion were related to segmenting and defining what is a "unit of analysis." Issues include the potential for integrating automatic segmentation support in the "manual" annotation tools, the categorization of these fragments together with the creation of analysis protocols, the need for visual support of the annotations being created during the analysis, and the linking to external sources. We summarize our evaluation of these issues next.

Segmentation and Selection of a "Unit of Analysis"

Both types of tools are agnostic in relation to segmenting the video stream (which is to say, the segments or analytical units can have any length). Scholars tend to highlight that there is no single way of segmenting a film and that segmentation is the very first level where subjective interpretations of a film's style and content begin. As Bellour noted in his groundbreaking work on analysis of film form and narration, "segmentation is a *mise-en-abîme*, a 'plumbing of depths,' a process that has no end theoretically—which does not mean that it has no meaning, in fact, that is its whole meaning."[49]

Professional tools, including editing tools, are designed to enable meticulous, fine-grained segmentations with the frame-by-frame precision of microseconds.[50] While this could be an advantage of digital tools over manual analyses done on paper (of the sort that Bellour advocated), it could also be a disadvantage. They enable full accuracy, but this may not always be needed.[51]

In our discussions, the authors considered that the most "interpretively agnostic" way to segment was at the level of shot. The interpretations of the other tiers are based on it, and in film studies, it is common to claim the "shot" as the basic unit.[52] But there are exceptions. For example, according to Miriam Posner, "writing on Rossellini's *Paisà,* André Bazin observed that the film's essential unit is not the shot but the 'fact,' one slice of time and space, itself worthy of interpretation and filled with meaning."[53] Because both tools in our case study can arbitrarily set the boundaries of segment selection, any nonstandard units of analysis could potentially be chosen. Digital tools invite just this kind of methodological and conceptual experimentation. They also reaffirm the need to maintain an interdisciplinary perspective. The annotation tools and units of analysis developed for specific disciplines may trigger innovative conceptualizations in other, perhaps unexpected, fields.

In practice, the choice of the level of granularity for the unit of analysis is not trivial. When scholars apply an annotation tool, the parameters must be decided in advance because those selections significantly affect the amount of time that the annotation tasks will require and will influence the results. Requiring a precise time-coded segment analysis versus a less rigorous one depends on the type of film(s) being analyzed and on the type of research questions being asked. Professional tools invite more formalist analyses. QDA packages, however, afford a wider range of possibilities, including analyzing themes and content, studying the socioeconomic history of the media, or tracing formalist historiography. Neither approach is yet optimal for enabling precise formal analyses, which we discuss in the conclusion.

Semiautomatic Annotation Support

Annotating manually is a time-consuming process.[54] Thus there are high expectations that annotation could eventually be automated or that digital technologies could be combined with manual annotation. "Shots," because they are a fundamental unit for many film analyses, could be integrated into state-of-the-art automatic analytic systems. Presumably these would be offshoots of pattern-recognition routines used in language research projects that detect speaker turns in an audio recording. These multimodal annotation tools seem to be applied rarely to video.[55] Two film studies examples are Lignes de temps and the tool kit Videana, which are no longer maintained.[56] In these two cases, shot boundary detection algorithms were used as an extension of the annotation programs running locally. Another tool kit, ACTION, developed in the framework of the Media Ecology Project, utilizes independent web services to identify shot boundaries.[57] It remains to be seen whether these techniques might be too restrictive. And the question remains whether taking the shot as the default unit of analysis still allows for the potentially rich and controversial theoretical issues this assumption entails. This is one of the reasons why techniques that replace certain manual annotation tasks should be carefully judged on their theoretical and methodological consequences.

Annotation Protocols

The coding techniques used by digital tools we evaluated can integrate highly structured annotation and systematic annotation protocols into the same software to become part of the "hermeneutic markup."[58] Because semiotic film theories are central analytic frameworks,[59] the different types of tools should support this protocol construction. We observe that ELAN is more conducive to having a predefined coding protocol, because it is more practical to define in advance its tiers and encoding vocabularies. This is because the annotations are contained within the segment blocks and not created as extra layers, as in the QDA software, which limits the facilities for the constant rearranging of codes/annotations as they are being created. Instead, the QDA tools have been built around the principle of bottom-up "code books," a concept in qualitative research equivalent to "protocol." These emerge and evolve during the analysis. The most flexible approach is offered by the QDA package, where the three-step process of transcribing,[60] coding, and then classifying the codes of the transcript facilitates the creation of ampler segments, while still enabling fine-grained identification of specific elements.

Finally, the integration of protocols within the tools, combined with the qualitative registration of commentary during analysis,[61] may encourage online collaboration, with the added value of grounding the controlled vocabularies in the source materials.

Multilayer Annotation, Time-Based Structure, and Visualization

Because film scholars (as well as linguists and communication scholars) often think in terms of timelines and segmentations with layers of annotation, the way this is supported has methodological implications.

Tiers are useful if one is interested in detecting the co-occurrence of certain events, props, or techniques, for example, to support the systematic analysis of various aspects of the film, such as the types of shots and the treatment of space.[62] The downside is that doing this systematically is very time consuming and that switching between recording all relevant details on the timeline and annotating that information requires a highly efficient tool to make the task fast and smooth.

In practice, although we found that both groups of tools can enable the multi-level categorization of segments, display the annotations along the timeline, and search on types of segments, the QDA package does not offer this approach in a straightforward way. Nor does it support a simultaneous visualization based on layers. Both groups of tools offer the freedom of linking the segments to the timeline via specific time stamps; the ELAN tool more naturally accommodates this, since segments and annotations have a one-to-one relationship because the segment "box" is the container for the annotation. In the QDA package, two options exist: coding directly via the timeline and assigning codes to specific points of time, or coding via the content field, where this is possible. Visualization as tiers is not supported in these packages.[63] Film is a time-based, linear medium, and visualizing and analyzing a horizontal timeline ruler together with the tiered approach (as in ELAN) imitate this linearity.[64] The tiered approach, though, seems less suited to nonlinear analyses of films or other media objects.

Linking to Contextual Materials

A significant difference between the two groups of tools is that in the QDA packages, other noncollateral texts in addition to the "transcripts" can be incorporated into the same project. For example, these texts could be previous analyses, reviews of the film, the film script, or a list of intertitles. Coding allows the texts (entire or selected passages) to be linked to specific segments of the film, and vice versa. One may overview the complete project and tag text passages that refer to a certain scene or passage in an article. Or one can detect scenes that are frequently cited in the literature and have become canonical in film history. Given the claims that writing media history is often based on "surviving print discourse" and that media are always conceived in relation to other texts,[65] using the tool to annotate texts and video simultaneously affords a contextual approach to film and other media analysis. Most QDA packages, though, are restricted, because the ones that offer video annotation are released as commercially licensed, closed systems, making it difficult to combine their capabilities with those of other tools.

CONCLUSION: CHALLENGES, LESSONS LEARNED, AND FUTURE WORK

The digital turn has forced a shift in humanities research in the past decades. Scholars face the fact that the annotation continues to be a meticulous and laborious process. Vast amounts of audiovisual media research depend on manual annotation, the building blocks for interpretation, synthesis, and narrative description.[66] Little is known, however, about the extent of system support available for this scholarly task. As Silver and

Patashnick have commented on film analysis, "whether researchers are not using technology to facilitate the analysis of audiovisual data or simply not reporting their use is unclear."[67]

This overview compared available tools and summarized our hands-on tests of two types. Because they are first generation, these tools reproduce results that could have been obtained manually.[68] We found that, at this stage, the most significant methodological impact is the option of making the analytic procedures more explicit. Consequently, the tools ask users to conceptualize more precisely the methods they employ. For example, the criteria for segmenting and selecting a unit of analysis or the definition of the terminology used for coding may be preselected.

While this capability might be disparaged as the "scientification" of a scholarly practice, we argue that the new digital tools encourage more self-reflection about scholarly work.[69] As Michael Ross has pointed out, "in this respect it is not a question of replacing the spectator's subjectivity by means of automatic digital tools, but rather to support it, to make it more profound, and—most importantly—to make it intersubjectively accessible and comprehensible for others."[70] Indeed, the categories and procedures we used in our analyses can be referenced to specific fragments, segments, and texts, thus multiplying the levels of communication possible with peers, both informally and through scholarly publication.[71]

Future experiments will reveal further the potential of these technologies. Aggregated and—most importantly—collaborative annotations will be available for bigger corpora, all the better to reveal patterns and investigate correlations. We also consider the combination of manual annotations with automatic annotations, which we mentioned in the previous section, as a future direction. Furthermore, the annotation outputs created in these tools can be exported to be visualized or combined easily with the results from other tools. The outputs also may be mixed with other media, opening the path to experiment with the transtextual and performative nature of digital segmentation and annotation.[72]

Digital tools that support moving image annotation and analysis may "emancipate" the critical analysis of film and other audiovisual media. The more these tools become available, however, the greater is the need to test them in actual research projects, because only then can we detail their design and data models and see how their applications enhance and constrain methods for annotation and analysis.

Computer scientists and developers collaborating with scholars in the building of tools, as was the case in the development of Lignes de temps and Digital Formalism, is the most productive working relationship. The implications for the education of current digital scholars are clear. They will need to increase their collaboration with information system designers, to be more proficient in using source code and to be able to customize existing tools to reach their goals.[73] It is also important that scholars influence commercial developers in creating software and that they urge them to aim for the interoperability of the new systems.[74] This would mean that scholars have some responsibility to learn how to do more advanced data processing and to recognize the importance of using open formats so that annotations can be used across different tools. The rewards include reduced dependency on singular tools from commercial providers and the possibility for scholars to choose their own research questions and to tailor the tools for specific tasks. With such an approach, digital annotation tools would enable scholars to be explicit, critical, collaborative, and open about the assumptions underlying their analyses, which ultimately may be the real value of moving to digital.

Liliana Melgar Estrada has a doctorate in information science from the University Carlos III in Madrid. She currently works as a postdoctoral researcher at the University of Amsterdam, conducting user studies and requirement analysis for the development of the media studies section of the Dutch Infrastructure for Digital Humanities and Social Sciences (CLARIAH).

Eva Hielscher is a PhD candidate at Ghent University, a film researcher, and a moving image archivist. She holds an MA degree in preservation and presentation of the moving image from the University of Amsterdam. In 2007, she was awarded the Kodak Fellowship in Film Preservation for exceptional archival interests and studies by the Association of Moving Image Archivists. Most recently, she worked as a film archivist and curator at the Netherlands Institute for Sound and Vision.

Marijn Koolen is a digital humanities researcher and scientific developer at the Huygens Institute for the History of the Netherlands. Before that, he was assistant professor of digital humanities at the University of Amsterdam and senior scientific engineer at the Netherlands Institute for Sound and Vision, working on the Dutch CLARIAH project, which is developing a large-scale research infrastructure for humanities research.

Christian Gosvig Olesen is a postdoctoral researcher at the University of Amsterdam in the research project The Sensory Moving Image Archive: Boosting Creative Reuse for Artistic Practice and Research (2017–19) led by professor of film heritage and digital film culture Giovanna Fossati. Currently he is also principal investigator in the research project MIMEHIST: Annotating EYE's Jean Desmet Collection (2017–18) funded by the Netherlands Organization for Scientific Research and has been invited by the EYE Filmmuseum as researcher-in-residence in the academic year 2017–18. His research has been published in journals such as *The Moving Image* and *NECSUS*.

Julia Noordegraaf is professor of digital heritage at the University of Amsterdam, where she leads the digital humanities project Creative Amsterdam: An E-Humanities Perspective. She is also board member for media studies in CLARIAH, the Dutch national infrastructure for digital humanities research, funded by the Netherlands Organization for Scientific Research.

Jaap Blom is a software engineer specializing in the field of cultural heritage and online media. Working at the Netherlands Institute for Sound and Vision, he has participated in various (European) research projects related to utilizing audiovisual and textual content analysis technologies for the benefit of archivists, media professionals, and the general public. He is currently working on the development of the media studies section of CLARIAH.

NOTES

1. The VCR is but one of the several technologies that significantly influenced scholarly practices. See, e.g., Stephen Bottomore, "Scholarly Research, Then and Now," *Early Popular Visual Culture* 14, no. 4 (2016): 302–18.

2. An example is the international conference Celluloid Goes Digital, which is perhaps the first one on the topic of how to design digital editions of films and link contextual data or information to the films and their content. See Martin Loiperdinger, ed., *Celluloid Goes Digital: Historical-Critical Editions of Films on DVD and the Internet. Proceedings of the First International Trier Conference on Film and New Media, Trier, Germany, October 2002* (Trier: WVT Wissenschaftlicher Verlag, 2003). Yuri Tsivian, *Immaterial Bodies: A Cultural Anatomy of Early Russian Films,* produced by Barry Schneider, edited by Marsha Kinder (Los Angeles, Calif.: Annenberg Center for Communication and University of Southern California, 2000), CD-ROM.

3. Michael Kipp, "ANVIL: The Video Annotation Reseach Tool," in *The Oxford Handbook of Corpus Phonology,* edited by Jackes Durand, Ulrike Gut, and Gjert Kristoffersen, 420–36 (Oxford: Oxford University Press, 2014).

4. Closed-edition formats, such as DVD, still have widespread utilization among film historians, for instance, at the important archival film festival Il Cinema Ritrovato in Bologna.

5. See Raymond Bellour, "The Unattainable Text," *Screen* 16, no. 3 (1975): 19–28; Michael Witt, *Jean-Luc Godard: Cinema Historian* (Bloomington: Indiana University Press, 2013); Mark Parker and Deborah Parker, *The DVD and the Study of Film: The Attainable Text* (Basingstoke, U.K.: Palgrave Macmillan, 2012).

6. Christian Gosvig Olesen, "Formalising Digital Formalism: An Interview with Adelheid Heftberger and Matthias Zeppelzauer about the Vienna Vertov Project," in *Shifting Layers: New Perspectives in Media Archaeology across Digital Media and Audiovisual Arts,* ed. Miriam de Rosa and Ludovica Fales (Milan: Mimesis International, 2016).

7. The concept of affordance was introduced by psychologist James Gibson to explain visual perception. Gibson, "The Theory of Affordances," in *Perceiv-*

ing, Acting, and Knowing, ed. R. E. Shaw and J. Bransford, 67–82 (Hillsdale, N.J.: Lawrence Erlbaum Associates, 1977). The term has been adapted by the human–computer interaction community to explain the principles of interface design.

8. For a comparable example that provides an overview of tools for geospatial analysis (GIS) and examples of their application in film studies, see Laura Horak, "Using Digital Maps to Investigate Cinema History," in *The Arclight Guidebook to Media History and the Digital Humanities,* ed. Charles R. Acland and Eric Hoyt, 65–102 (Falmer, U.K.: REFRAME Books, 2016), http://projectarclight.org/book/.

9. For CLARIAH, the Dutch research infrastructure for Digital Humanities, see http://www.clariah.nl/.

10. "Remix the Manuscript: A Chronicle of Digital Experiments," http://sites.dartmouth.edu/RemixBrut/.

11. Michael Ross, M. Grauer, and Bernd Freisleben, eds., *Digital Tools in Media Studies: Analysis and Research—An Overview* (Bielefeld, Germany: Transcript Verlag, 2009), 9.

12. *The Computer Chronicles,* Desktop Video 720, dir. Peter Nichols, 1990, https://archive.org/details/desktopvideo.

13. About the annotation processes of scholars using audiovisual media, see Liliana Melgar, Marijn Koolen, Hugo Huurdeman, and Jaap Blom, "A Process Model of Scholarly Media Annotation," presented at the ACM Conference on Human Information Interaction and Retrieval, Oslo, Norway, March 7–11, 2017; Christine Sandom and Peter Enser, "VIRAMI: Visual Information Retrieval for Archival Moving Imagery," in *International Cultural Heritage Informatics Meeting: Proceedings from ICHIM01,* ed. David Bearman and Franca Garzotto, 141–52 (Pittsburgh, Pa.: Archives and Museum Informatics, 2001).

14. The research process of several groups of media scholars is described in Marc Bron, Jasmijn Van Gorp, and Maarten de Rijke, "Media Studies Research in the Data-Driven Age: How Research Questions Evolve," *Journal of the Association for Information Science and Technology* 67, no. 7 (2015): 1535–54.

15. Alan Marsden, Adrian Mackenzie, and Adam Lindsay, "Tools for Searching, Annotation and Analysis of Speech, Music, Film and Video: A Survey," *Literary and Linguistic Computing* 22, no. 4 (2007): 469–88.

16. Ibid., 470.

17. John Unsworth, "Scholarly Primitives: What Methods Do Humanities Researchers Have in Common, and How Might Our Tools Reflect This?," presented at Humanities Computing: Formal Methods, Experimental Practice, King's College, London, May 13, 2000; Ciaran B. Trace and Unmil P. Karadkar, "Information Management in the Humanities: Scholarly Processes, Tools, and the Construction of Personal Collections," *Journal of the American Society for Information Science and Technology* 68, no. 2 (2017): 491–507.

18. Julia Noordegraaf, "Computational Research in Media Studies: Methodological Implications," *Kwalon* 21, no. 1 (2016): 52–59.

19. Ross et al., *Digital Tools.*

20. Livia Giunti, "L'analyse du film à l'ère numérique: Annotation, geste analytique et lecture active," *Cinéma & Cie* 14, no. 22/23 (2014): 127–43.

21. Barbara Flueckiger, Filmwissenschaft/Film Studies Facebook page, May 27, 2016, https://www.facebook.com/groups/175716329122592/permalink /1287478024613078/.

22. Acland and Hoyt, *Arclight Guidebook.*

23. We identified three surveys in the past five years: Stamatia Dasiopou-lou, Eirini Giannakidou, Georgios Litos, Polyxeni Malasioti, and Yiannis Kompatsiaris, "A Survey of Semantic Image and Video Annotation Tools," in *Knowledge-Driven Multimedia Information Extraction and Ontology Evolution: Bridging the Semantic Gap,* ed. Georgios Paliouras, Constantine D. Spyropoulos, and George Tsatsaronis, 196–239 (Berlin: Springer Science + Business Media Deutschland, 2011); Carsten Saathoff, Krishna Chandram-ouli, Werner Bailer, Peter Schallauer, and Raphaël Troncy, "Multimedia Annotation Tools," in *Multimedia Semantics: Metadata, Analysis and In-teraction,* ed. Raphaël Troncy, Benoit Huet, and Simon Schenk, 223–39 (West Sussex, U.K.: John Wiley, 2011); Lyndon Nixon and Raphaël Troncy, "Survey of Semantic Media Annotation Tools for the Web: Towards New Media Ap-plications with Linked Media," in *The Semantic Web: ESWC 2014 Satellite Events,* ed. Valentina Presutti, Eva Blomqvist, Raphael Troncy, Harald Sack, Ioannis Papadakis, and Anna Tordai, 100–114 (Berlin: Springer International, 2014).

24. There are several surveys of QDA packages. We selected two: Graham R. Gibbs, "Using Software in Qualitative Analysis," in *Sage Handbook of Qualitative Data Analysis,* ed. Uwe Flick, 277–96 (Los Angeles, Calif.: Sage, 2014); "Choosing an Appropriate CAQDAS Package," CAQDAS Networking Project, 2014, http://www.surrey.ac.uk/sociology/research/researchcentres /caqdas/support/choosing/.

25. LINDAT/CLARIN, https://lindat.mff.cuni.cz/en/.

26. DiRT: Digital Research Tools, http://dirtdirectory.org/.

27. Visual Media Resources, http://dariah-it.isti.cnr.it/browse.

28. Our final list is integrated into the Visual Media Resources website, http://dariah-it.isti.cnr.it/browse, using the category "Annotation and Semantification" as a filter in the category tab. We invite scholars to keep this list updated. Ongoing work inventorying video annotation tools is being conducted by the DARIAH working group on digital annotation, http://dariah .eu/activities/working-groups.html.

29. Peter Enser, "The Evolution of Visual Information Retrieval," *Journal of Information Science* 34, no. 4 (2008): 531–46.

30. Pauline Rafferty and Rob Hidderley, *Indexing Multimedia and Creative Works: The Problems of Meaning and Interpretation,* ed. Pauline Rafferty and Rob Hidderley (Aldershot, U.K.: Ashgate, 2005).

31. R. H. van Leuken, "Content-Based Multimedia Retrieval: Indexing and Diversification," PhD thesis, Utrecht University, 2009.

32. James M. Turner, Michele Hudon, and Yves Devin, "Organizing Moving Image Collections for the Digital Era," *Information Outlook* 6, no. 8 (2002): 14–25.

33. Nixon and Troncy, "Survey of Semantic Media Annotation Tools."

34. Billy Wilder, *Menschen am Sonntag,* dir. Robert Siodmak, Edgar G.

Ulmer, Rochus Gliese, Curt Siodmak, and Fred Zinnemann (Germany, 1930; restored in 1997 by EYE Filmmuseum in collaboration with Martin Koerber from the Deutsche Kinemathek).

35. Siegfried Kracauer, *From Caligari to Hitler: A Psychological History of the German Film*, rev. ed. (Princeton, N.J.: Princeton University Press, 2004).

36. Description based on Noah Isenberg, "*People on Sunday*: Young People Like Us," Criterion Collection, https://www.criterion.com/current /posts/1904-people-on-sunday-young-people-like-us; and Peter Bosma, "Enjoy: People on Sunday (1930)," http://www.peterbosma.info/downloads/files /PB_PeopleOnSunday.pdf.

37. This time stamp refers to the version available on YouTube: https://youtu .be/2D9W2zfZPps.

38. Cinemetrics measurement software includes the "classic tool" (the authors' designation) and the "frame accurate tool" (FACT). The latter is under development and in beta testing. See "Cinemetrics Software," Cinemetrics, http://www.cinemetrics.lv/cinemetrics.php.

39. See Barbara Flueckiger's article "A Digital Humanities Approach to Film Colors" in this issue of *The Moving Image* for more information. See also Barbara Flueckiger, "FilmColors: Bridging the Gap between Technology and Aesthetics," ERC Advanced Grant, http://www.research-projects.uzh.ch /p21207.htm. They intended to use ELAN for annotating a big corpus (approximately four hundred films) but experienced important drawbacks. This experience is discussed in the CLARIAH Annotation Symposium, Amsterdam, May 11–12, 2017, http://www.clariah.nl/.

40. The current development status and future projects related to this tool are not clear at the time of writing this article. A web-based version of the application (http://ldt.iri.centrepompidou.fr/ldtplatform/ldt/) has maintained some of the original tool's core functionalities. It allows users to upload up to five videos.

41. Adelheid Heftberger, Michael Loebenstein, and Georg Wasner, "Auf Spurensuche im Archiv. Ein Arbeitsbericht," *Maske und Kothurn* 55, no. 3 (2009): 137–48. See also Olesen, "Formalising Digital Formalism."

42. However, it is possible to do an automatic segmentation for audio. ELAN currently incorporates fourteen recognizers suitable for audio and linguistic analyses. Even though these are not relevant for our analysis of a silent film, it would be interesting to explore this option for automatically segmenting sound films. See Han Sloetjes, "ELAN: Multimedia Annotation Application," in *The Oxford Handbook of Corpus Phonology*, ed. Jacques Durand, Ulrike Gut, and Gjert Kristoffersen, 305–20 (Oxford: Oxford University Press, 2014).

43. Sloetjes, "ELAN," 317.

44. This glossary is available through Onomy.org (http://onomy.org/), one of the services provided by the Media Ecology Project (http://sites.dartmouth .edu/mediaecology/).

45. Patricia Bazeley and Kristi Jackson, eds., *Qualitative Data Analysis with NVIVO*, 2nd ed. (Los Angeles, Calif.: Sage, 2013).

46. There is a significant body of knowledge about content analysis–grounded theory and coding. See, e.g., Margrit Schreier, "Qualitative Content Analysis," in Flick, *Sage Handbook of Qualitative Data Analysis*, 170–83. At least forty coding methods are identified in Johnny Saldaña, *The Coding Manual* *for Qualitative Researchers*, 3rd ed. (Los Angeles, Calif.: Sage, 2016), 291–98.

47. We used version 11.3.2 for Mac. Liliana Melgar, "A Comparison of CAQDAS Support for Coding and Annotating Audio-Visual Media," presented at the Kwalon Conference: Reflecting on the Future of QDA Software, Rotterdam, August 2016.

48. The data structure of Transana is problematic for compatibility with other QDA software because it is quite idiosyncratic. This was discussed at the Kwalon Conference (Rotterdam, August 2016). It is important to note, though, that Transana, in comparison to NVivo, offers the possibility of simultaneous "transcripts" or content fields for the same segment, which are displayed synchronously when the video is played. Also, it offers the option of having up to four videos in the same synchronized display, which is useful for analyzing scenes recorded with multiple cameras. See Liliana Melgar and Marijn Koolen, "Audiovisual Media Annotation Using Qualitative Data Analysis Software: A Comparative Analysis," *The Qualitative Report* (forthcoming).

49. Raymond Bellour, *The Analysis of Film*, ed. Constance Penley (Bloomington: Indiana University Press, 2000), 97.

50. Since ELAN was not specifically made for video analysis, an obvious limitation in comparing it to other professional tools developed specifically for annotating video is that certain functionalities associated with granularity at the visual level are lacking, such as the annotation of still regions within a frame (as offered by the tools VIA, VideoAnnEx, or SVAT, described in Dasiopoulou et al., "A Survey of Semantic Image and Video Annotation Tools").

51. Referring to the philological requirements for critical editions of texts, Kurt Gärner expressed his concern about the "inherent dangers of this flexible medium, particularly its great capacity, which tempts to ambitiously and inexhaustibly stockpile materials at the expense of critical analysis," further indicating that only critical analysis will assure the usefulness of a critical edition. Quoted in Loiperdinger, *Celluloid Goes Digital*, 49. Applied to the annotation tasks, because both groups of tools widen the possibilities, these dangers are equally present.

52. For example, the two tools offered by the Cinemetrics project (Classic and Frame Accurate) also allow for free segmentation, because the system works as a "stopwatch" that records the beginning and end times of a segment. However, most metrics assume that these segments correspond to shots. See further discussion in Christian Gosvig Olesen, "Towards a 'Humanistic Cinemetrics,'" in *The Datafied Society: Studying Culture through Data*, ed. Karin van Es and Mirko Tobias Schäfer, 39–54 (Amsterdam: Amsterdam University Press, 2017).

53. Miriam Posner, "How Is a Digital Project Like a Film?," in Acland and Hoyt, *Arclight Guidebook*, 185.

54. Sloetjes, "ELAN: Multimedia Annotation," indicates that, depending on the accuracy level, annotating can take between 1:1 and 1:100 hours (one hundred hours of annotation work for one hour of audio/video). In archival/cataloging settings, creating shot lists for one hour of transmission (in this case, for a television broadcast) may take between sixteen and thirty hours. Christine Sandom and P. G. B. Enser, *VIRAMI: Visual Information Retrieval* *for Archival Moving Imagery,* Library and Information Commission Research Report 129 (London: Resource: The Council for Museums, Archives and Libraries, 2002). One of the authors of this article spent approximately forty hours manually segmenting a single film of approximately one hour.

55. Sloetjes, "ELAN," 14.

56. Videana offered automatic software for shot boundary detection, superimposed texts, and face recognition. It integrated programs that gave recognition rates of 80 percent to 97 percent for cut detection, similar to scores achieved via manual human segmentation. See Ralph Ewerth, Markus Mühling, Thilo Stadelmann, Julinda Gllavata, Manfred Grauer, and Bernd Freisleben, "Videana: A Software Toolkit for Scientific Film Studies," in Ross et al., *Digital Tools,* 101–16.

57. See the project page at http://aum.dartmouth.edu/~action/index.html.

58. See Stefan Hahn, "Filmprotokoll Revisited: Ground Truth in Digital Formalism," *Maske und Kothurn* 55, no. 3 (2009): 129–35. Olesen's 2017 interview with Adelheid Heftberger also includes some details about the use of protocols in the ANVIL annotation tool used in this project. See Olesen, "Formalising Digital Formalism." Humanities scholars are also reflecting on finding ways of encoding content that facilitate interpretation. For a description of one workshop, see Thomas Bögel, Evelyn Gius, Marco Petris, and Jannik Strötgen, "A Collaborative, Indeterministic and Partly Automatized Approach to Text Annotation," presented at Digital Humanities, Lausanne, Switzerland, 2014, http://dharchive.org/paper/DH2014/Workshops-802 .xml.

59. For a detailed reflection about analytic frameworks, and a proposal for a semiotic framework for film analysis, see John Bateman and Karl-Heinrich Schmidt, *Multimodal Film Analysis: How Films Mean* (London: Routledge, 2013). See also David Bordwell's concept of "text schemata" and "semantic fields" in his *Making Meaning: Inference and Rhetoric in the Interpretation of Cinema,* reprint ed. (Cambridge, Mass.: Harvard University Press, 1991).

60. Transcription can be defined at various levels. The most common meaning is the transcoding of speech into text. However, transcripts are also used to represent, via textual summaries, the most significant events or aspects of a moving image segment (e.g., in dance). Speech-to-text transcription, or automatic extraction of speaker-related information, is a common wish among researchers who use audiovisual media: "Many researchers make some kind of transcription of materials, and would value tools to automate this process." Marsden et al., "Tools for Searching," 469.

61. Both ELAN and NVivo—as well as most QDA software—support "memoing," which in qualitative analysis means adding comments of different types as part of the interpretation and writing process.

62. Sloetjes, "ELAN."

63. We checked the options of simulating a tiered approach in NVivo, Atlas.ti, Transana, and MaxQDA. They offer coding stripes to observe code density but not an easy way to type the segments.

64. This has been illustrated in the previous section. To summarize, a shot description written in a natural way may look like this: "*Taxi and introduction of Erwin. Erwin is introduced first by the number plate of his taxi,* *introduction of taxi driver Erwin via a close-up of Erwin looking at customer, then a medium panning shot of taxi driving away."* In a tier-based segmentation, selected elements would be separated according to a category, for instance, persons and types of shots.

65. Gregory Waller, "Search and Re-search: Digital Print Archives and the History of Multi-sited Cinema," in Acland and Hoyt, *Arclight Guidebook,* 45–64. Gérard Genette's concept of transtextuality applied to film studies is discussed by several authors. For a synthesis, see Liliana Melgar, "From Social Tagging to Polyrepresentation," PhD thesis, University Carlos III of Madrid, 2016, especially appendix L.

66. Marsden et al., "Tools for Searching."

67. Christina Silver and Jennifer Patashnick, "Finding Fidelity: Advancing Audiovisual Analysis Using Software," *Forum Qualitative Sozialforschung/ Forum: Qualitative Social Research* 12, no. 1 (2011): Article 37.

68. Information retrieval researcher Jaap Kamps has used the term *incunabula* to refer to the tools that mimic analog practices. This corresponds to the stages of technological development explained by Besser, in which the first conceptual steps typically try to "replicate core activities that functioned in the analogue environment," lately "implementing new functions that did not exist within this." See Jaap Kamps, "MuSeUM: Multiple-Collection Searching Using Metadata," presented at Multimedial Information Retrieval, Utrecht, Netherlands, January 12, 2009, and Howard Besser, "The Past, Present, and Future of Digital Libraries," in *Companion to Digital Humanities,* ed. Susan Schreibman, Ray Siemens, and John Unsworth, 557–75 (Oxford: Blackwell Professional, 2004).

69. See Tony Tran, "Coding and Visualizing the Beauty in Hating Michelle Phan: Exploratory Experiments with YouTube, Images, and Discussion Boards," in Acland and Hoyt, *Arclight Guidebook,* 196–215; Giunti, "L'analyse du film"; and Olesen, "Towards a More 'Humanistic Cinemetrics.'"

70. Ross et al., *Digital Tools,* 178.

71. For further discussion about this topic of writing styles in the context of digital humanities, for instance, about "reflective essays," see Eric Hoyt, "Curating, Coding, Writing: Expanded Forms of Scholarly Production," in Acland and Hoyt, *Arclight Guidebook,* 347–73.

72. An example of how to use chains of tools is offered by the Digital Formalism project: the annotations in ANVIL could be used as input for Cinemetrics to perform the measures and visualizations, as explained by Heftberger in Olesen, "Formalising Digital Formalism." In the DVD release, the two— ANVIL and ImageJ—are used in combination, showing the annotated segments in color-coded ImageJ visualizations of Vertov films.

73. Stephen Ramsay indicates that what is proper of digital humanists is the "moving from reading and critiquing to building and making" and that "building" is a new kind of hermeneutic. See Ramsay, "On Building," November 1, 2011, http://stephenramsay.us/text/2011/01/11/on-building/.

74. See Liliana Melgar Estrada and Marijn Koolen, "Audiovisual Media Annotation Using Qualitative Data Analysis Software: A Comparative Analysis," unpublished manuscript.

A DIGITAL HUMANITIES APPROACH TO FILM COLORS

BARBARA FLUECKIGER

And much of the data mining that leads to visualization...is based on a flawed method that conflates literal discourse and symbolic/ interpreted reference. In an art-historical context, this would be the equivalent of counting instances of the color red across a collection of images without discriminating between symbolic and representational functions. The reds are not the same, and cannot be counted the same way, put into the same category, or re-represented as data for visualization in a graph or chart, without monstrous distortion.

JOANNA DRUCKER, "GRAPHICAL APPROACHES TO THE DIGITAL HUMANITIES," *A NEW COMPANION TO DIGITAL HUMANITIES*

There are strong and justifiable objections to the measurement or, more broadly, the computer-assisted analysis of aesthetic phenomena—as Johanna Drucker makes clear.[1] One pitfall of quantitative analysis is its potential to disregard the meaningful context of data occurrences across the body of works studied. In fact, any quantitative approach to aesthetics that aims to reduce the inherently ambiguous quality of works of art into measurable units runs the risk of engaging in positivist reductionism and of fundamentally ignoring philosophical aesthetics and its analytical tradition. Given these reservations, it may seem extremely bold to investigate one of the most intangible aspects of film aesthetics, namely, film colors, by computer-assisted tools in the emerging field of digital humanities.

Colors are elusive. Our perception of them is deeply influenced by the context of their appearance, their material presentation, the given cultural framework, and each individual spectator's subjective response. However, it was precisely this challenge that led to the development of the projects elaborated and reflected in the digital humanities platform Timeline of Historical Film Colors and, most importantly, the research project FilmColors, which was funded by an Advanced Grant from the European Research Council (ERC). By their very definition, ERC Advanced Grants are meant to be "high risk, high gain" projects that "are designed to allow outstanding research leaders of any nationality and any age to pursue ground-breaking, high-risk projects in Europe."[2] This article offers insight into the current state of research in computer-assisted film color analysis and applications that are either available or in development.

FilmColors is closely linked to the interactive Timeline of Historical Film Colors, which started in 2012. The platform consists of a comprehensive web resource and online database for all topics related to film colors, with a special focus on their technology, aesthetics, analysis, and restoration. Thus the Timeline is a collection, an archive, a documentation process, and, increasingly, an annotated system for the investigation of the topic, which offers access to a curated body of information to researchers, archivists, film historians, and a broader audience of users from different backgrounds. Four different interdisciplinary approaches investigate the relationship between aesthetics and technical innovation as applied to film colors.

First, the database-driven analysis of film color aesthetics, their affective qualities, and their narrative functions aim to identify diachronic aesthetic patterns. Based on this offline database, the research team is developing a computer-assisted tool with a web interface that will allow the crowdsourcing of film color analyses applying recent advancements in digital humanities and custom-made visualizations. Then these aesthetic analyses are connected to the study of film color technology in combination with chemicophysical analyses of historical color films to understand the influence of film stocks and color processes on films' aesthetic appearance. Third, the team will apply insights gained during the digitization and restoration of historical films by taking into account the requirements of restoration ethics while improving workflows. Finally, three PhD theses in progress will provide case studies from three periods: the emergence of film colors from early applied colors to so-called natural colors (1896–1930), the development of standards in film color technology and aesthetics (1930–55), and the dominance of chromogenic processes (1955–95).

The project features a truly interdisciplinary approach to consider and connect all the relevant factors—from technology to perception and aesthetics—because they are closely intertwined. The focus remains firmly rooted in the humanities.

METHODOLOGY: STYLISTIC ANALYSIS AND DIGITAL HUMANITIES

The planned computer-assisted tool for analyzing film colors derives from the widespread positivist notions of measurable entities in perception proposed in the second half of the nineteenth century by Gustav Theodor Fechner,[3] which had descended from the psychophysicists Hermann von Helmholtz, Ernst Heinrich Weber, and the many other researchers of the stimulus–response relationship. Fechner's approach was shaped by normative assumptions about universal laws on the concept of beauty, expressed most notably in the principle of the golden mean.

In the 1920s, with the advent of abstraction in the visual arts and in film, artists sought to elaborate universal principles for nonrepresentational art. With nonreferential modes of representation, compositional patterns were analyzed with analogies to harmonics in music and the rigorous notational systems that governed their creation and performance. Wassily Kandinsky, in his theoretical writings, *Über das Geistige in der Kunst (Concerning the Spiritual in Art)* and *Punkt und Linie zu Fläche (Point and Line to Plane)*,[4] analyzed minute elements of composition to hypothesize universal structural formations of art. In a similar vein, we find analytical investigations in the writings of Bauhaus representatives, such as Paul Klee, Josef Albers, Johannes Itten, and Ludwig Hirschfeld-Mack. Similar attempts were made within avant-garde filmmaking movements, for instance, Soviet filmmaker Dziga Vertov's strict diagrammatic tools for structuring utopian art.[5] These approaches are role models for analytical classification systems with a strong commitment to qualitative research.

In the 1980s, David Bordwell, Kristin Thompson, and Janet Staiger, in their famous 1985 study *The Classical Hollywood Cinema*, elaborated a triadic model that combined neoformalist analysis, historical poetics, and cognitivist investigation.[6] Historical poetics and neoformalist analysis remain the most important methodological foundations for contemporary film style analysis. Bordwell and Thompson's neoformalist analysis follows methodologies introduced by formalist approaches in art history and the Russian Formalist school that attempted to extract and organize patterns of style *(poetics)* from larger groups of artworks. This method allows for the identification of personal, group, or period styles by applying specific parameters to the corpus of work under examination. Historical poetics connects the observation of these patterns to foundational economical, technological, and institutional frameworks. As Bordwell puts it,

> a historical poetics of cinema produces knowledge in answer to two broad questions:
>
> 1.   What are the principles according to which films are constructed and by means of which they achieve particular effects?
> 2.   How and why have these principles arisen and changed in particular empirical circumstances? . . .
>
> In place of a bottom-up analysis of a large group of films, historical poetics aims at a broader understanding of "*what* happened, *how* it happened and *why* it happened."[7]

Another strand of this methodology is statistical style analysis, first applied by Vlada Petrić in 1974, and notably by Barry Salt[8] in his seminal investigation into the relationship between technological innovation and stylistic features in film. This approach was then redeveloped and transformed by Yuri Tsivian and Gunars Civjans into a web-based tool, Cinemetrics, to statistically measure average shot lengths (ASL). A crowdsourcing interface has collected measurements on hundreds of films. Both in Salt's analysis and in the Cinemetrics interface, the obvious shortcomings of a purely statistical method become apparent. Such analyses fail to consider, for example, the effects of a certain camera movement or framing. In contrast to Cinemetrics, the tool proposed in FilmColors is decidedly multidimensional and includes human interpretation to produce significant results that connect the various parameters and observations, as is demonstrated later.

FilmColors is typical of the emerging field of digital humanities, which is not a methodology but rather a set of tools encompassing diverse technologies: from database analysis, textual analysis, and corpus linguistics to the annotation of data, all of which are essentially verbal methods of investigation. These methods are extended visually by video annotation, diagrams, and visualizations or by 3-D mappings and animated computer simulations. Big data processing and evaluation—scraping, crowdsourcing, or geographic information system mapping, to name a few—are inherently digital methods that require access to larger bodies of data collection.

While digital humanities have developed rapidly since the early 2000s—especially in the fields of textual analysis in literary studies, or the historical study of primary and secondary sources—they have not yet been widely implemented in film studies. As Adelheid Heftberger noted, one reason is the sheer complexity of the task.[9] Audiovisual representations consist of many layers of information and are time-based media, which makes the task even more daunting.[10] Several researchers working in the fields of artificial intelligence (AI) and computer vision have stressed the high-level requirements of such tools to extract meaningful entities out of the complex arrangements present in films.

DATABASE-DRIVEN AESTHETIC AND NARRATIVE ANALYSIS

The research project focuses on material properties of film and the resulting aesthetics—as expressed in the concept of *material aesthetics*. Therefore great care must be given to the source material. The FilmColors research team aims to focus on the aesthetic and narrative functions of colors in film by analyzing a large group of films. The titles chosen are widely regarded as landmarks of film color aesthetics. They were selected from the results of an online poll featuring more than one hundred canonical films. The poll was completed with a meta study of online listicles that focused on film colors and focused on the study of monographs on film colors. The resulting canon was then counterbalanced by comparative groups of films that were identified by the study of primary and secondary sources; the works of national film productions, individual filmmakers, or cinematographers; and specific genres, such as musicals, science fiction films, melodramas, and horror films. For practical reasons, the first step of computer-assisted analysis has been executed mainly on films available on DVD or Blu-ray. The results will be checked through photographic documentation with a calibrated camera setup based on the extensive examination of analog film prints in archives around the world.[11]

Researchers initiating a computer-assisted workflow for analyzing film colors must establish parameters defining a consistent grid applicable to a very large corpus of films. Seen from the perspective of theories of representation, film colors can shift between stylization and verisimilitude, structural patterns of pure abstraction, or the

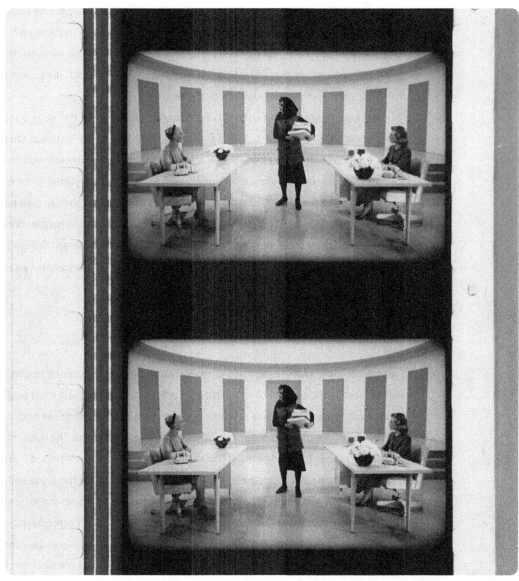

Figure 1a. Restrictive color scheme in *Funny Face* (Stanley Donen, 1957). Image courtesy of the Academy Film Archive. Photograph of the Technicolor dye-transfer safety print by Barbara Flueckiger.

Figure 1b. Hyperchrome color scheme in *Gentlemen Prefer Blondes* (Howard Hawks, 1953). Library of Congress. Photograph of the Technicolor dye-transfer safety print by Barbara Flueckiger.

Figure 2a. Central deep staging in *The Red Shoes* (Michael Powell and Emeric Pressburger, 1948). British Film Institute. Photograph of the dye-transfer nitrate print by Barbara Flueckiger.

Figure 2b. Flat ornamental image composition in *Les Chrysanthèmes* (Segundo de Chomón, 1907). Library of Congress. Photograph of the stencil-colored nitrate print by Barbara Flueckiger.

suppression of ostentatious modes of expression to achieve a realistic mode of representation. Stylized or emphasized uses of colors—such as in *The Wizard of Oz* (Victor Fleming et al., 1939)—enhance the narrative with sensual richness. These color schemes can be arranged on a continuum ranging from restrictive to gaudy to hyperchrome palettes, based on the relationship, the numbers of hues in a given shot or sequence, and their saturation (Figures 1a and 1b).

Color contrasts and harmonies are discussed with existing frameworks, first and foremost with the seven types of color contrasts outlined by Bauhaus theoretician Johannes Itten.[12] After identification of the basic color scheme, the compositional arrangement of the colors in patches, lines, or shapes and their dynamics and planar structuring principles are scrutinized on the two-dimensional level of image formation (Figures 2a and 2b).

The colors of the mise-en-scène (set design, environment, costumes) and lighting colors have to be taken into consideration. We follow Philipp Otto Runge's distinction between surface colors *(Körperfarben)* and luminous colors *(Lichtfarben)*.[13] Lighting greatly affects color appearance, because the colors we see are a result of object colors and their interaction with light, their color temperature, and spectral properties. Colored lights are often associated with the moods and psychological states of characters.[14] High-key, low-key, and chiaroscuro lighting schemes were adapted to color cinematography beginning in the late 1920s with the Technicolor Process 3, as in *The King of Jazz* (John Murray Anderson, 1930) and *Doctor X* (Michael Curtiz, 1932).

Object colors, on the other hand—often in conjunction with colors attributed to characters, their costumes, their hair and skin tones—establish relationships or conflicts.[15] The dominant object worlds in melodramas reflect the *conditio humana* of the protagonists as an immediate aesthetic experience of their emotions suppressed by bourgeois conventions.[16] Furthermore, color appearance and aesthetics are closely connected to the surface properties of objects and scenes depicted, such as shiny or glossy, tarnished or dull materials, or textures with small-scale variations or coarse patterns. Similarly, the optical transformation by the cinematic apparatus affects the appearance of colors through variations in depth of field or deep focus, lens diffusion, or optical resolution. And the film material influences the appearance of colors with specific shifts in hue, graininess, and flatness versus three-dimensionality. Motion and montage analysis identifies successive patterns of temporal structures and *visual rhyming*—a term proposed by avant-garde filmmaker Hans Richter.[17] For our offline database currently in operation, we developed a detailed system that allows for careful analyses that identify aesthetic developments in certain historical, cultural, or national contexts, considering the associated technical systems.

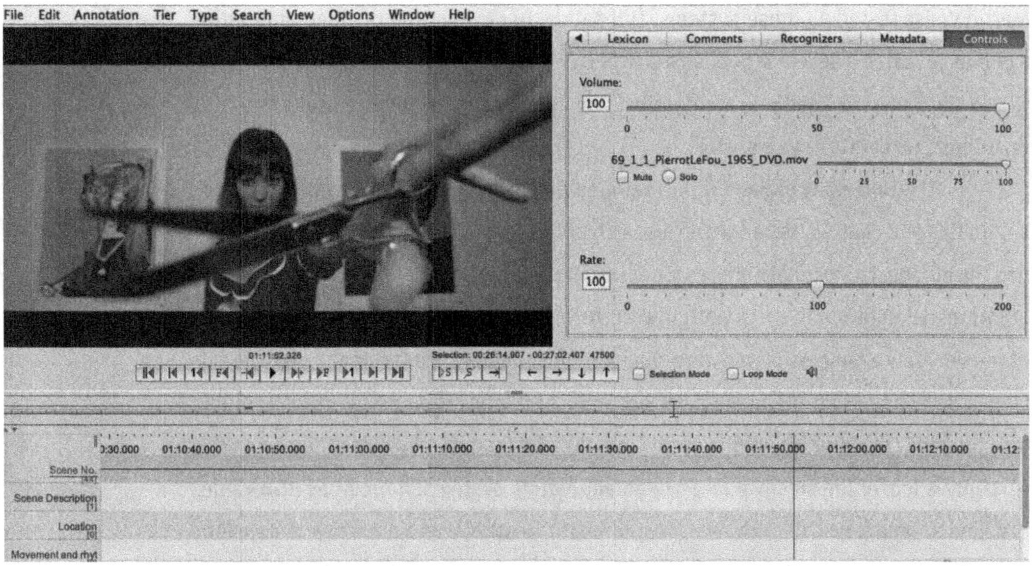

File Edit Annotation Tier Type Search View Options Window Help

Figure 3. Screenshot video annotation tool ELAN, template used in the research project ERC Advanced Grant FilmColors. Screenshot by Barbara Flueckiger.

On the basis of the huge data set that is being collected, the insights will be contextualized with questions about historical, cultural, societal, or technical aspects of colors useful in interpretation and discussion. How did production design reflect trends in consumer culture? How was color cinematography limited or advanced by the technologies? What are the differences in film color aesthetics when we compare, for instance, Technicolor to Agfacolor or Gasparcolor? What were professional discourses and practices within a given production context?

DEVELOPMENT AND APPLICATION OF A COMPUTER-ASSISTED TOOL FOR ANALYZING COLORS

The tools planned and applied in the FilmColors project require human intervention to produce significant results. Since fall 2016, the platform has utilized a video annotation system called ELAN that enables segmentation of film content and provides several tracks of annotation (Figure 3). Next, the team exports the data from the video annotations into a custom-designed FileMaker database, which includes all the different concepts presented in the previous section. We settled on ELAN after investigating the many video annotation tools that have been developed during the last decade. We based our choice on a survey published by Harvard University[18] and on a lively discussion about users' experiences we initiated in the Facebook group Filmwissenschaft/Film Studies. The four most promising tools were ANVIL, Advene, ELAN, and Lignes de temps. Team member

Martin Weiss tested all these systems. Ultimately, our evaluation of video annotation systems revealed a severe lack of sustainability. Most of the tools had been developed within third-party-funded research projects and abandoned when the projects ended or, at best, two or three years later.

The University of Saarland developed the ANVIL[19] software as a tool for video annotation and analysis as part of the research project called Digital Formalism. Advene[20] had the broadest number of features for our purposes, such as shot detection and region of interest annotation in combination with the automatic creation of thumbnails. One of the very few examples of software that contains an interface for analyzing colors is Lignes de temps, from the Institut de recherche et d'innovation du Centre Pompidou, developed for film studies with support from the film historian Sylvie Lindeperg.[21] This certainly is one of the most valuable video annotation systems. It provides RGB values distributed on a time axis. However, it ignores the aesthetic and narrative dimensions (as outlined earlier) and thus does not provide valid results indicating audience perceptions. It also does not consider the complex relationships between the colors present in differing proportions on the two-dimensional image plane and the sequential unfolding on the time axis. Like most of the other systems, recently it has been abandoned in its initial offline version. A new online version is simplified and requires staff to upload films, which reduces the number to only a few more feature-length films.[22]

For these reasons, we decided to work with ELAN.[23] It was developed for analyzing spoken language but boasts an elaborate user interface and many features. For instance, we take screenshots during the analysis that later may be extracted and inspected with a semiautomatic color scheme extraction tool (discussed shortly). A student assistant developed a template based on our main concepts. One of the most useful functions is the possibility of detaching the video being analyzed from the interface and screening it independently on a second screen. To this end, we installed color-calibrated 4K monitors that allowed working in parallel with ELAN, the FileMaker database, and GraphicConverter software to process the extracted screenshots. However, ELAN also has several serious drawbacks. Most significantly, it was not designed for the aesthetic analysis of feature-length films. Consequently, it has a very limited range of annotation selections in its timeline. It does not offer any of the more sophisticated features present in other systems, such as shot or motion detection, let alone a tool for analyzing color schemes. For these reasons, we decided to have an additional video annotation tool, VIAN, developed by Gaudenz Halter, that communicates with ELAN and amends its drawbacks with improved visual and analytical annotation tools.[24] The main advantages of ELAN are its stability, the openness of the system to ingest many different types of video codecs, an easy-to-operate segmentation mode, and the ability to create screenshots and to export the data in many different formats.

For the human-operated, computer-assisted analyses, the team applies a FileMaker database that is easy to customize by project leader and, in the case of any more difficult tasks, allows for instant troubleshooting by in-house advisor Simon Spiegel. After approximately seven months' experience with the tool, however, we have to admit that the analyses are very labor intensive and time consuming. We reevaluate the tool on a regular basis to reduce its complexity or offer different layers of detail with varying complexity for different users, such as PhD students, the student assistants, or external test users.

SEMIAUTOMATIC COLOR ANALYSIS AND VISUAL REPRESENTATION OF RESULTS

The next step in the development of FilmColors will be the semiautomatic extraction of color schemes. This tool's aim is to deliver objective results that complement the other analyses by extending them, either on the macro or meso level. The macro level connects observations made on larger numbers of films; the meso level focuses on whole individual films; and on the micro level, the researchers investigate individual shots or short sequences.

Approaches recently have been developed to detect color schemes or color distributions in films and artworks.[25] For instance, in Data-Driven Film History, the analyses integrated each frame of the film under study into a large picture that, read from left to right and from top to bottom, summarizes the color scheme in one view.[26]

The resulting comprehensive overview renders the color distribution and its temporal unfolding into a plot that provides synchronic information about the entire film at a glance. This approach is especially fruitful for early cinema, which was usually monochrome with tinted and/or toned segments. Other films, however, have very pronounced temporal or structural patterns, such as the ones that assign color codes to different narrative strands or levels of subjective point of view.[27] *Hero* (Yang Zhou, 2002) and *Traffic* (Steven Soderbergh, 2000) are good examples.

Kevin L. Ferguson applied yet another method to his study of Westerns employing the code ZProjector.java. He created visual summaries that layer all the images on top of each other. "Each image in the montage," Ferguson explains, "is a sum image of every 10th second of each film (that is, one frame from every 10 seconds was extracted and summed with the others to create a real image."[28] This method produces a color

Inception (2010)

Figure 4. Color scheme of *Inception* (Christopher Nolan, 2010) depicts the levels of narration. From James Cutting et al., "Perception, Attention, and the Structure of Hollywood Film," http://people.psych.cornell.edu/~jec7/curresearch.htm.

fingerprint for each film and comparison of the color palettes of Western films.

These images are not only beautiful to view but also useful. By projecting them onto a grid that distinguishes between saturation on the y axis and hue on the x axis (using the software ImagePlot), distribution patterns become obvious. Ferguson has applied the technique to demonstrate the different color schemes in Disney films, Westerns, *gialli* (Italian horror films), and Zatoichi films (a series of samurai action films).[29]

Movie bar codes are the most widely used visualization tools and have been presented online for some time (see, e.g., the Tumblr blog created by an unknown cinephile[30]). They apply a sampling method that compresses each individual image or a sequence of images into one pixel on a grid of vertical lines chronologically from left to right. In contrast to ImageJ's method, this averaging completely obscures the visual impression. The movie bar coding process for *The Red Shoes* (Michael Powell, Emeric Pressburger, 1948) elides the eponymous shoes. *The Wizard of Oz,* in contrast, is revelatory when certain segments—most prominently the green associated with the wizard—become instantly visible. James E. Cutting, in collaboration with Kaitlin L.

Brunick and Ayse Candan, chose a more sophisticated approach by creating a line for each individual color scheme, arranged from red to blue, for an exemplary analysis of *Inception* (Christopher Nolan, 2010) (Figure 4).[31]

While it might be valuable to apply all these tools to the corpus investigated in FilmColors, we use our video annotation tool for a more ambitious solution to extract color schemes, similar to Adobe's Color CC. It has a user interface allowing manual adjustments when extracting colors from screenshots or video files. However, as becomes instantly evident in a comparison of different films, Color CC does not do justice to three main requirements. It does not consider the quantitative distribution of hues identified; it does not make a distinction between foreground and background, which is one of the most important types of expressive means in color film aesthetics;[32] and it completely disregards the textures of colors by projecting them onto uniformly colored patches. This is unfortunate, because, as can be seen in films such as *Gate of Hell* (Teinosuke Kinugasa, 1953), *Red Desert* (Michelangelo Antonioni, 1964), and *A Single Man* (Tom Ford, 2009), textures are of utmost importance to film aesthetics. They greatly affect our color perception and convey the protagonist's psychological experiences.[33] As one observer noted in an online forum, color schemes that do not take into account the spatial distribution are like a cooking recipe in which all spices are listed with no idea of the quantities.[34]

The ideal tool thus must apply spatial filtering; that is, it must divide images into patches of similar colors that identify the quantitative distribution of dominant hues. Such tools do exist. There is the Cinemetrics tool by Frederic Brodbeck[35] (not to be confused with Tsivian's Cinemetrics) and the tool by TinEye, which identifies patches of similar hues, measures the percentage of their occurrence, and assigns them color names and a hex code.[36] TinEye, however, defines the constraints for individual hues quite coarsely. In *The Umbrellas of Cherbourg* (Jacques Demy, 1964), for example, although different shades of red play an important role in characterizing the complicated mother–daughter relationship in the film, the tool collapses them all into one red hue (Figure 5). Hence the tool should be used cautiously regarding different expressive and narrative systems that are connected to individual films' aesthetic repertoires.

Color saturation and saliency are other noteworthy concepts. The latter, according to Laurent Itti, "is the distinct subjective perceptual quality which makes some items in the world stand out from their neighbors and immediately grab our attention."[37] Similar to Itten's definition of color contrasts, this concept is often tied to both a quantitative and qualitative contrast, drawing attention to a figure, an object, or a part of the environment that may or may not be of narrative importance. The related so-called pop-out effect describes a stimulus-driven bottom-up perception defined by the

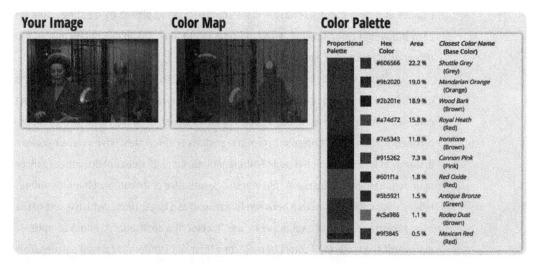

Proportional Palette	Hex Color	Area	Closest Color Name (Base Color)
	#606566	22.2 %	Shuttle Grey (Grey)
	#9b2020	19.0 %	Mandarian Orange (Orange)
	#2b201e	18.9 %	Wood Bark (Brown)
	#a74d72	15.8 %	Royal Heath (Red)
	#7e5343	11.8 %	Ironstone (Brown)
	#915262	7.3 %	Cannon Pink (Pink)
	#601f1a	1.8 %	Red Oxide (Red)
	#5b5921	1.5 %	Antique Bronze (Green)
	#c5a986	1.1 %	Rodeo Dust (Brown)
	#9f3845	0.5 %	Mexican Red (Red)

Figure 5. Color scheme extraction from one still of *The Umbrellas of Cherbourg* (Jacques Demy, 1964) with the online tool TinEye (https://www.tineye.com/).

opposition of a stimulus to its surroundings, be it a regular pattern that is broken or a difference in quality, such as saturation. Regardless of their narrative significance, saturation and saliency direct the viewers' attention to an area in the frame and charges it with a specific aesthetic value. A smart algorithm that models the human response to such stimuli is needed to scrutinize it.[38] The findings could be verified by empirical eye-tracking studies and by human interpretation afforded by the offline analysis tool.

Texture analysis is the next factor to be evaluated. We can apply a concept that Kandinsky and the Russian Formalists referred to as *faktura*.[39] On the level of representation and image formation, textures result from the profilmic arrangement of environments, objects, or costumes in framing, lighting, and movement. On the levels of film stock and color process, each material is also characterized by its own graininess. Different material properties of film stocks' graininess may be expressive in their own right.[40] The FilmColors analysis of the first batch of samples (approximately 150 out of the 400 planned) indicates that the legibility of the filmic composition, the surface properties, and textures is highly significant for colors' aesthetic and affective dimensions.

A sophisticated system ideally should integrate recent deep learning tools related to computer vision. AI motion detection devices that have been developed for use in image processing and visual effects could be adapted as filmic tracking systems to annotate temporal unfolding, distinguishing, for example, between character movement and camera movement.[41] In March 2017, we began developing computer vision software for the investigation of the figure–ground relationship mentioned earlier, in collaboration with the Visualization and MultiMedia Lab of Renato Pajarola at the University of Zurich (Figure 6).[42]

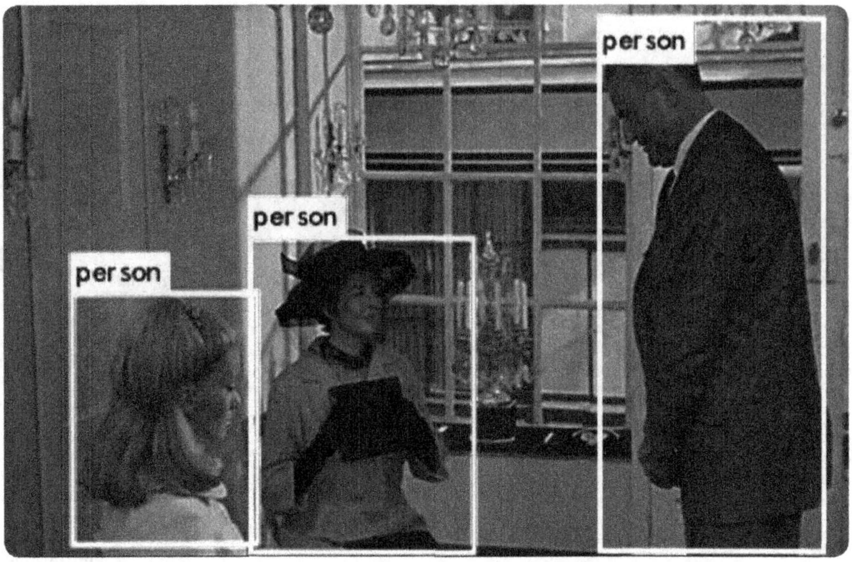

Figure 6. Foreground–background extraction using computer vision. Noyan Evirgen, ERC Advanced Grant FilmColors, in collaboration with the Visualization and MultiMedia Lab of Renato Pajarola at the University of Zurich. As of November 2017, this visualization is outdated. Owing to the production process of *The Moving Image*, it was not possible to include the current state. Please check updates on the blog https://filmcolors.org/.

The visualization tool in FilmColors will project color schemes and color contrasts into a perceptually uniform color space that contains all the relevant color and space data similar to the one in the CIE LAB, developed by the Commission internationale de l'éclairage.[43] This color space provides data dimensions, hue, saturation, and brightness that are objective, referring to measurable unities, and perceptually uniform, adjusted to the properties of human vision.

The FilmColors tool will select from these several types of visualizations that compare temporal and spatial color structures for micro-, macro-, and meso-level analyses: single frames, segments, and the entire work (see Figure 7).

INTEGRATION AND CRITICAL DISCUSSION OF RESULTS

FilmColors's significance lies in its ability to connect the analyses of the formal aesthetic features to semantic, historical, and technological aspects. Because most analyses of film colors are organized by starting with a semantic and narrative investigation, or by confining their history to technical or institutional perspectives, they often neglect the aesthetic level completely. Once the hermeneutic mode of interpretation sets in, aesthetic features become functionalized and lose their primary sensory qualities. In fact,

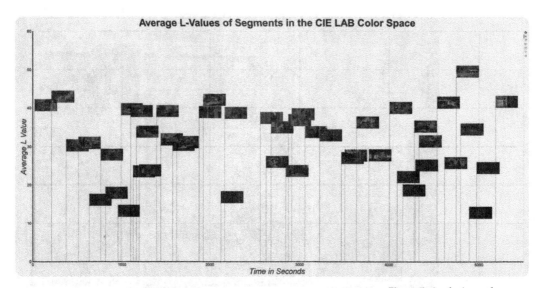

Figure 7. Analysis on the meso level: segmentation and average lightness of *All That Heaven Allows* (Douglas Sirk, 1955). Gaudenz Halter, ERC Advanced Grant FilmColors, in collaboration with the Visualization and MultiMedia Lab of Renato Pajarola at the University of Zurich. As of November 2017, this visualization is outdated. Owing to the production process of *The Moving Image,* it was not possible to include the current state. Please check updates on the blog https://filmcolors.org/.

the dominant mode in color film production and in professional discourses on color in film has always subordinated color to narrative principles. Normative and ideologically charged notions of taste called for the restrictive use of colors in accordance with traditions in visual arts and culturally established conventions.

Symbolic uses of colors referred to such traditions, most prominently following Natalie Kalmus.[44] However, upon closer examination, these second-order meanings are seldom stable. Except for the color red, with its widespread associations of love, blood, passion, and aggression, every other color has different and contradictory meanings depending on contextual, cultural, and historical uses.[45] These meanings must therefore be investigated and questioned, based on studies on the meaning of color in art history, design, and the culture of everyday life.[46] In the silent era, with its applied colors, tinting, and toning, symbolic and stereotypical uses of colors were common. As many scholars have elaborated,[47] except for a few rather stable stereotypical associations like red for fire, blue for night scenes, or amber for interiors, every film should be analyzed carefully to extract the structural functions and narrative meanings of colors.

As mentioned in the introduction, there are valid and strong objections to the reduction of complex aesthetic phenomena to preconceived and rigid data grids. Conversely, there is also a considerable advantage to being able to translate visual impressions into visually accessible diagrams. Drucker's skepticism does not do justice to one of the biggest problems in analyzing audiovisual representations, which is the severe limitations of language when it comes to investigating and communicating sensory spatial and temporal phenomena. As David Rodowick has commented, every description of moving images lags behind the object of its analysis: "The solid ontological anchoring of a worked substance is grasped only with difficulty, yielding an art that, so far, leans, more than any other, on an experience of the Imaginary."[48]

Visual and diagrammatic representations can be significant epistemological instruments to compensate for the shortcomings of language. While they are never neutral—as critics of such instruments continue to emphasize—they offer important insights not otherwise attainable in the purely linguistic realm. Diagrammatic methods have been a rising topic of scholarly debate, especially within the theory and history of art. Drucker notes that their logic, epistemological underpinnings, and functions have been investigated as "visual forms of knowledge production."[49] Dating back to Charles Sanders Peirce's notion of graphs as operations of reasoning, the productive contribution of diagrams has been a subject of semiotic and philosophical theories of symbolic representation.[50] Sybille Krämer notes, following Peirce, that relationships depicted by diagrammatic iconicity create evidence. They do not show the objects themselves but rather the relationships between the objects and the insights derived from their analysis.[51]

Nelson Goodman underlines the abstract nature of diagrams and schemata, referring specifically to colors to illustrate his position:

> We categorize by sets of alternatives. Even constancy of literal application is usually relative to a set of labels: what counts as red, for example, will vary somewhat depending upon whether objects are being classified as red or nonred, or as red or orange or yellow or green or blue or violet. What the admitted alternatives are is of course less often determined by declaration than by custom and context.[52]

Visualizations thus depend fundamentally on the underlying classification systems that define them as well as on the corresponding reference system. Each tool should critically reflect its own built-in biases and basic assumptions. Or, as Patrick Vonderau puts it, there is a difference between a soufflé and a muffin tin, regarding not only their specific purposes and functions but also their respective cultural traditions.[53]

The double purpose of diagrams to both visualize and structure knowledge is at the core of FilmColors. We identify patterns by researching perceptual, colorimetric, and aesthetic properties of colors as well as their history in art, consumer culture, and design. Along with their narrative functions, we analyze and contextualize their expressive and affective or emotional values.

The evidence created by computer-assisted analysis and its subsequent visualizations will answer—in Bordwell's words—the question of "why it happened." What were the epistemological assumptions that guided inventions in the realm of film colors? What were the guiding discursive notions in professional practices and in the marketing of film colors' added value? How did the color systems and technical solutions respond to cultural norms of taste in a given period and geographical location? How are color schemes and aesthetic patterns connected to chemical and physical properties of film stocks? As research progresses on an ever-growing group of films, we will get closer to the answers.

Barbara Flueckiger has been a professor for film studies at the University of Zurich since 2007. She is the author of two textbooks about sound design and visual effects. Her recent research projects investigate the digitization and restoration of archival film, in collaboration with archives and the film industry. In 2015, she was awarded the prestigious Advanced Grant by the European Research Council for a research project that investigates the relationship between the technology and aesthetics of film colors (http://www.zauberklang.ch/).

NOTES

Special thanks to my ERC Advanced Grant FilmColors team members, especially Olivia Kristina Stutz for her in-depth research into visualizations of film colors in the framework of her master's thesis, Bregt Lameris for fundamental discussions about the topic, and Martin Weiss for his investigations into video annotation systems.

This article is based in part on my essay "Die Vermessung ästhetischer Erscheinungen," *Zeitschrift für Medienwissenschaft* 2, no. 5 (2011): 44–60.

The illustrations may be viewed in color in the online edition of *The Moving Image*, accessible via JSTOR.

1. Joanna Drucker, "Graphical Approaches to the Digital Humanities," in *A New Companion to Digital Humanities*, 2nd ed., ed. Susan Schreibman, Ray Siemens, and John Unsworth (Malden, Mass.: John Wiley, 2016), 247.

2. "Advanced Grants," November 12, 2016, https://erc.europa.eu/funding-and-grants/funding-schemes/advanced-grants.

3. Gustav Theodor Fechner, *Vorschule der Aesthetik* (Hildesheim: Olms, 1871).

4. Wassily Kandinsky, *Über das Geistige in der Kunst, insbesondere in der Malerei* (Munich: R. Piper, 1912), and Wassily Kandinsky, *Punkt und Linie zu Fläche* (Bern: Benteli, 1926).

5. Adelheid Heftberger, *Kollision der Kader: Dziga Vertovs Filme, Die Visualisierung ihrer Strukturen und die Digital Humanities* (Munich: Edition Text + Kritik, 2016).

6. David Bordwell, Janet Staiger, and Kristin Thompson, *The Classical Hollywood Cinema: Film Style and Mode of Production to 1960* (London: Routledge, 1985).

7. David Bordwell, "Historical Poetics of Cinema," in *The Cinematic Text: Methods and Approaches* (New York: ASM Press, 1989), 371–73.

8. Vladimir Petrić, "From a Written Film History to a Visual Film History," *Cinema Journal* 14, no. 2 (1974): 20–24; Barry Salt, *Film Style and Technology: History and Analysis*, 2nd ed. (London: Starword, 1983).

9. Adelheid Heftberger, *Materiality and Montage: Film Archives and the Visualization of Time-Based Media*, 2016, https://www.youtube.com/watch?v=pXqpGTPT-6A.

10. Patrick Vonderau, "Quantitative Werkzeuge," in *Handbuch Filmanalyse*, ed. Malte Hagener and Volker Pantenburg, 1–15 (Wiesbaden, Germany: Springer, 2017); Charles R. Acland and Eric Hoyt, eds., *The Arclight Guidebook to Media History and the Digital Humanities* (Falmer, U.K.: REFRAME Books, 2016).

11. See Barbara Flueckiger, "Color Analysis for the Digital Restoration of *Das Cabinet des Dr. Caligari*," *The Moving Image* 15, no. 1 (2015): 22–43.

12. Johannes Itten, *Art of Color* (Ravensburg, Germany: Ravensburger Verlag, 1970); Faber Birren, *Principles of Color: A Review of Past Traditions and Modern Theories of Color Harmony* (New York: Van Nostrand Reinhold, 1969); Josef Albers, *Interaction of Color: Grundlegung einer Didaktik des Sehens* (Cologne: DuMont Schauberg, 1970); Albert Henry Munsell, *A Color Notation* (New York: Munsell Color Co., 1919); and Wilhelm Ostwald, *Die Harmonie der Farben* (Leipzig: Verlag Unesma, 1918). For a comprehensive overview of color systems, see Narciso Silvestrini and Ernst Peter Fischer, *Farbsysteme in Kunst und Wissenschaft* (Cologne: DuMont, 1998).

13. Philipp Otto Runge, *Farben-Kugel oder, Construction des Verhältnisses aller Mischungen der Farben zu einander, und ihrer vollständigen Affinität, mit angehängtem Versuch einer Ableitung der Harmonie in den Zusammenstellungen der Farben* (Hamburg: F. Perthes, 1810).

14. Barbara Flueckiger, "Color and Subjectivity in Film," in *Subjectivity across Media: Interdisciplinary and Transmedial Perspectives*, ed. Maike Sarah Reinerth and Jan-Noël Thon (New York: Routledge, 2016), 217.

15. Christine N. Brinckmann, *Color and Empathy* (Amsterdam: Amsterdam University Press, 2015).

16. Thomas Elsaesser, "Tales of Sound and Fury," in *Movies and Methods*, vol. 2, ed. Bill Nichols, 166–89 (Berkeley: University of California Press, 1985).

17. Pascal Vimenet, "Poésie et animation, affinités électives?," *FOCAL*, http://www.focal.ch/doc/vimenet/poesie.htm.

18. "Harvard Video Annotation Survey," May 20, 2016, http://annotations.harvard.edu/video, inactive May 19, 2017.

19. http://www.anvil-software.org/. Barbara Wurm, Klemens Gruber, and Vera Kropf, eds., *Digital Formalism: Die kalkulierten Bilder des Dziga Vertov* (Vienna: Böhlau, 2009); Adelheid Heftberger, "Film Archives and Digital Humanities: An Impossible Match? New Job Descriptions and the Challenges of the Digital Era," *MedieKultur: Journal of Media and Communication Research* 30, no. 57 (2014): 135–53; Heftberger, *Kollision der Kader*.

20. http://liris.cnrs.fr/advene/index.html.

21. http://www.iri.centrepompidou.fr/outils/lignes-de-temps-2/. Sylvie Lindeperg, presentation, Moving Image Analytics: Research Infrastructure for Film Heritage, Stockholm, October 16, 2015.

22. For a critical discussion of video annotation systems, see Livia Giunti, "Problemi dell'analisi del testo di finzione audiovisivo: Verifica e sviluppo di un modello analitico e interpretativo con strumenti digitali," PhD thesis, Università degli Studi di Pisa, 2010; Livia Giunti, "L'analyse du film a l'ère numérique: Annotation, geste analytique et lecture active," *Cinéma & Cie* 14, no. 22/23 (2014): 127–43.

23. https://tla.mpi.nl/tools/tla-tools/elan/.

24. See update on the blog https://filmcolors.org/.

25. Heftberger, "Film Archives and Digital Humanities"; Heftberger, *Kollision der Kader*; Kevin L. Ferguson, "The Slices of Cinema: Digital Surrealism as Research Strategy," in Acland and Hoyt, *Arclight Guidebook*, 270–99. Some have worked with ImageJ, which was initially developed for medical image analysis. The scholars created a plot of entire films. See Jacqui Ross, "Colour Analysis Tools in ImageJ," https://www.unige.ch/medecine/bio imaging/files/3814/1208/6041/ColourAnalysis.pdf. For a description of the project Data-Driven Film History: A Demonstrator of EYE's Jean Desmet Collection (2014–15) for analyzing cinema programs shown in the 1910s, see Christian Gosvig Olesen, Eef Masson, Jasmijn van Gorp, Giovanna Fossati, and Julia Noordegraaf, "Data-Driven Research for Film History: Exploring the Jean Desmet Collection," *The Moving Image* 16, no. 1 (2016): 82–105.

26. Ibid.

27. Lev Manovich, "Data Science and Digital Art History," *International Journal for Digital Art History* 1 (2015): 12–35.

28. Kevin L. Ferguson, "Western Roundup," *Typecast: How Can Film Speak of Writing* (blog), October 7, 2013, http://typecast.qwriting.qc.cuny .edu/2013/10/07/western-roundup. He follows the approach outlined in *Colour Study (Top Gun)* by Baden Pailthorpe in 2012: see http://kotaku.com /the-entire-film-top-gun-squashed-into-a-single-paintin-673789502.

29. Ferguson, "Slices of Cinema."

30. http://moviebarcode.tumblr.com/?og=1.

31. James E. Cutting, Kaitlin L. Brunick, and Ayse Candan, "Perceiving Event Dynamics and Parsing Hollywood Films," *Journal of Experimental Psychology* 38, no. 6 (2012): 1476–90, http://psycnet.apa.org/doiLanding?doi=10.1037% 2Fa0027737.

32. Brinckmann, *Color and Empathy*; Hans J. Wulff, "Die Unnatürlichkeit der Filmfarben: Neue Überlegungen zur Signifikation und Dramaturgie der Farben im Film," *European Journal for Semiotic Studies* 2, no. 1 (1990): 2–25.

33. David Katz, *The World of Colour* (London: Kegan Paul, Trench, Trubner, 1935); Anya Hurlbert, "The Perceptual Quality of Color," in *Handbook of Ex-*

perimental Phenomenology: Visual Perception of Shape, Space, and Appearance, ed. Liliana Albertazzi (New York: John Wiley, 2013), 380; Flueckiger, "Color and Subjectivity in Film."

34. http://liftgammagain.com/forum/index.php?threads/visually-satisfying-project-shares-the-color-palettes-of-iconic-film-scenes.6812/#post-64672.

35. http://cinemetrics.fredericbrodbeck.de/.

36. http://labs.tineye.com/color/. The question of color nomenclature is an additional, very fundamental one, omitted in the present article. For an introduction, see Umberto Eco, "How Culture Conditions the Colours We See," in *On Signs: A Semiotics Reader,* ed. Marshall Blonsky, 157–75 (Oxford: Basil Blackwell, 1985); Heinrich Zollinger, *Color: A Multidisciplinary Approach* (Zurich: Verlag Helvetica Chimica Acta, 1999).

37. Laurent Itti, "Visual Salience," *Scholarpedia* 2, no. 9 (2007): 3327.

38. Itti, "Visual Salience"; Neil D. B. Bruce and John K. Tsotsos, "Saliency, Attention, and Visual Search: An Information Theoretic Approach," *Journal of Vision* 9, no. 3 (2009), http://jov.arvojournals.org/article.aspx?articleid =2193531.

39. Kandinsky, *Über das Geistige in der Kunst*; Wolfgang Beilenhoff and Christoph Hesse, eds., *Poetika Kino: Theorie und Praxis des Films im russischen Formalismus* (Frankfurt am Main, Germany: Suhrkamp, 2005).

40. Barbara Flueckiger, "Materialmix als ästhetisches und expressives Konzept," in *Filmische Atmosphären,* ed. Margrit Tröhler, Jörg Schweinitz, and Philipp Brunner, 73–90 (Marburg, Germany: Schüren, 2012); Flueckiger, "Photorealism, Nostalgia, and Style," in *Special Effects: New Histories, Theories, Contexts,* ed. Michael Duffy, Dan North, and Bob Rehak, 8–96 (Basingstoke, U.K.: Palgrave Macmillan, 2015).

41. Barbara Flueckiger, *Visual Effects: Filmbilder aus dem Computer* (Marburg, Germany: Schüren, 2008), 239ff.

42. Barbara Flueckiger, Noyan Evirgen, Enrique G. Paredes, Rafael Ballester-Ripoll, and Renato Pajarola, "Deep Learning Tools for Foreground-Aware Analysis of Film Colors," https://avindhsig.wordpress.com/deep-learning -tools-for-foreground-aware-analysis-of-film-colors/.

43. http://www.cie.co.at/.

44. Natalie M. Kalmus, "Color Consciousness," *Journal of the Society of Motion Picture Engineers* 25, no. 2 (1935): 139–47.

45. Eco, "How Culture Conditions the Colours We See"; Zollinger, *Color.*

46. John Gage, *Color and Culture: Practice and Meaning from Antiquity to Abstraction* (Berkeley: University of California Press, 1993); Charles A. Riley, *Color Codes: Modern Theories of Color in Philosophy, Painting and Architecture, Literature, Music, and Psychology* (Hanover, N.H.: University Press of New England, 1995); Zollinger, *Color.* For a bibliography on the cultural history of film, see Noemi Daugaard and Josephine Diecke, "SNSF Film Colors: Technologies, Cultures, Institutions," http://zauberklang.ch/film colors/timeline-entry/10544/.

47. Nicola Mazzanti, "Colours, Audiences, and (Dis)Continuity in the 'Cinema of the Second Period,'" *Film History* 21, no. 1 (2009): 67–93; Elfriede Ledig and Gerhard Ullmann, "Rot wie Feuer, Leidenschaft, Genie, Wahnsinn: Zu einigen Aspekten der Farbe im Stummfilm," in *Der Stummfilm: Konstruktion und Rekonstruktion,* 89–116 (Munich: Schaudig, Bauer, Ledig,

1988); Monica Dall'Asta, Guglielmo Pescatore, and Leonardo Quaresima, eds., *Il colore nel cinema muto* (Bologna: Clueb, 1996); Daan Hertogs and Nico de Klerk, eds., *Disorderly Order: Colours in Silent Film* (Amsterdam: Stichting Nederlands Filmmuseum, 1996); Luciano Berriatúa et al., *Tutti i colori del mondo: Il Colore nei mass media tra 1900 e 1930 = All the Colours of the World: Colours in Early Mass Media 1900–1930* (Reggio Emilia, Italy: Diabasis, 1998).

48. David N. Rodowick, commenting on Raymond Bellour's essay "The Unattainable Text," in *The Virtual Life of Film* (Cambridge, Mass.: Harvard University Press, 2007), 21.

49. Johanna Drucker, *Graphesis: Visual Forms of Knowledge Production* (Cambridge, Mass.: Harvard University Press, 2014).

50. Charles Sanders Peirce, *The Collected Papers of Charles Sanders Peirce: Electronic Edition*, ed. Charles Hartshorne, Paul Weiss, and Arthur W. Burks (Charlottesville, Va.: InteLex Corp., 1994); Matthias Bauer and Christoph Ernst, *Diagrammatik. Einführung in ein Kultur-und Medienwissenschaftliches Forschungsfeld* (Bielefeld, Germany: Transcript Verlag, 2010).

51. Sybille Krämer, "Operative Bildlichkeit: Von der 'Grammatologie' zu einer 'Diagrammatologie'? Reflexionen über erkennendes Sehen," in *Logik des Bildlichen: Zur Kritik der ikonischen Vernunft*, ed. Martina Hessler and Dieter Mersch (Bielefeld, Germany: Transcript Verlag, 2009), 100.

52. Nelson Goodman, *Languages of Art: An Approach to a Theory of Symbols* (Indianapolis, Ind.: Hackett, 1968), 71ff.

53. Patrick Vonderau, "Quantitative Werkzeuge," in *Handbuch Filmanalyse*, ed. Malte Hagener and Volker Pantenburg, 1–15 (Wiesbaden, Germany: Springer, 2017), http://link.springer.com/referenceworkentry/10.1007/978-3-658-13352-8_28-1.

FORUM

FORUM

(Micro)film Studies

MARÍA ANTONIA VÉLEZ-SERNA

I live and work far from the place where I was born, so the past I research is a country twice foreign. When people ask why I research Scottish cinema history rather than Colombian, I confess that the reason is not an intense passion for this rainy corner of Europe but because I am here. I wanted to do archive work, and so my topic would need to be local. It is easy to underestimate the degree to which simple availability and access can determine entire research paths. And therefore it is easy to misunderstand the significance of the transformations brought about by digitization and online access to sources.

Like many people, I like archives. What I like even more is traveling to archives. They give you a hidden purpose, both in tourist-thronged cities and unprepossessing industrial outskirts. The quest takes you on slow train lines, gets you lost, makes you hitch rides and despair in snow blizzards—all much more enticing than spending another day in front of the computer. Having the choice speaks of privilege: I can travel easily (as long as no visa is required), and I have the right credentials—for now—to pass as a bona fide researcher in the eyes of the gatekeepers. These conditions are contingent on institutional status, political climate, physical mobility, and how society parses class and race markers. Whatever its limitations, the internet has removed barriers to curiosity and has challenged the geographical exclusivity of postcode-lottery access to knowledge.

The online database and the archive reading room are different vectors of experi-ence, but they are complementary rather than opposed. Any archive visit is preceded and followed by many more hours of looking at a screen. Remote access to archive catalogs motivates travel to an archive in the first place. We tend to take them for granted, but online catalogs are extraordinary resources. Aggregation portals that bring together the holdings of many different institutions, such as Scottish Archive Network[1] and the Archives Hub,[2] are astonishing achievements. This infrastructure enables new forms of discovery. For instance, in Australia, the Humanities Networked Infrastructure project allows researchers to document relationships between different archival entities, offering ways to represent and share the expertise involved in discovering these connections.[3]

It is really the ability to make these connections—as much as access to original materials—that facilitates good research. Carolyn Steedman, in *Dust,* articulates this archival passion. She writes that the historian's authority "comes from *having been there* (the train to the distant city, the call number, the bundle opened, the dust . . .)."[4] While such "dirty," "dusty" archival work is seen as a professional rite of passage, this really annoys the archivists who work very hard at making archives clean, bright, easy to use, and accessible.[5] It also installs a specific professional practice as a kind of moral imperative. And yet, archive work is not always necessary or morally superior. What it is, often, is moving and beautiful. There is the aura of the original as an emotional connection to the past but also as material evidence—not only about the moment of its creation but also about the unbroken series of events that have allowed this object to travel from the past to now, leaving traces all over it. The archival document, in Arlette Farge's words, "is a tear in the fabric of time" that produces in the reader an "insistent and stubborn" feeling of being in contact with the real.[6]

In the spirit of generosity, let us believe that it is this feeling, rather than professional defensiveness and a Calvinist work ethic, that makes many historians wary of mechanical and electronic reproduction of sources. This is not new; Farge, for instance, writes that "an archival manuscript is a living document; microfilm reproduction, while sometimes unavoidable, can drain the life out of it."[7] Microfilm: a technology that has been around since the 1920s. A reel of microfilm is the thing most similar to a movie reel and also the most alien to it. Like an exhibition print, the microfilm reel is an access copy produced to be transported and stored easily. Durability and portability are key to its appeal, so its adoption by academic libraries was founded on ideas that resonate with current digital optimism. The technology was to ensure long-term preservation of fragile materials, enable long-distance research and exchange, and become a tool for the individual scholar. Decades before the World Wide Web, microfilm and microfiche allowed thousands of newspapers, periodicals, and primary sources to be used, copied, and circulated widely. Its convenience as a format, however, was not matched by sufficient attention to the actual practices of use, so that, as Susan A. Cady argued in 1990, "scholars continue to dislike microfilm."[8] Perhaps not all. Richard Abel claims he has "a nostalgic fondness for running through microfilm reels of newspapers."[9] But really, reading newspapers on microfilm hurts your eyes and makes you dizzy, and there is never space to set down your notebook or laptop, so you end up alternatively hunched and stretched over miniature, low-contrast newsprint. Instead of living in quaint or imposing reading rooms, microfilm readers are in the cold backrooms of big libraries, where the Wi-Fi does not reach. Instead of being scarce and unique, there is drawer after drawer full of little boxes with their identical reels. Microfilm is not glamorous, and yet, when it was introduced, the rhetoric around it matched the optimism of current paeans to digitization: eternal preservation, global knowledge interchange, convenience, and portability.

In practice, there is rather more friction.

Let me illustrate. A few years ago, while working on my PhD thesis, I probably annoyed the staff at the National Library of Scotland by requesting more than a hundred different microfilmed newspapers and printing a page off each one. It was an attempt to understand how films circulated around Scotland before the end of World War I. There were not many archival sources. The film distributors left almost no records for that era, and the few records for individual cinemas were not enough to support the weight of the argument. So, I decided to look for the effects of distribution, namely, to look at what cinemas were showing and then work backward to figure out how the patterns worked. One way of doing this was to look at the ads for cinemas that appeared in newspapers. But I did not just want to look at the main cities; I was interested in nonmetropolitan perspectives. Inspired by Robert C. Allen's calls to abandon "Gothamcentrism," I was determined to give Leuchars or Lochgelly the same importance as Glasgow and Edinburgh.[10] At the time, however, the only Scottish newspaper that had been extensively digitized was the *Scotsman,* which is Edinburgh's paper of record; but that only carried tiny classified ads for a few cinemas in the capital and generally did not bother much with film. Meanwhile, mass digitization projects were gaining significant traction. For instance, the 19th Century British Library Newspapers database carried a few Scottish titles, but only up to 1900, which was frustrating but enough to demonstrate to me that local papers would be a crucial asset.[11]

In the period I was studying, there were more than five hundred different newspaper titles in Scotland. I was obviously not planning to read them all. The first filter, then, was to find out which ones were accessible, using the Newsplan catalog as a baseline. The Newsplan project was a preservation initiative that transferred 618 Scottish newspaper titles to microfilm.[12] For the dates I was considering, more than a hundred titles were available in this format at the National Library of Scotland. A further dozen or so were available in local libraries to which I could travel easily. That was still too large a number to read in any detail. My goal, however, was not to read them but to mine them, and to build a data set from them documenting the cinemas and films they advertised. So instead of looking at a fixed place over a long time, I decided to look at as many places as possible, over a very short time. The two synchronic samples were one week in 1913 and one week in 1918. Because I did this at the National Library before it installed the new digital microfilm readers, I had to print each cinema ad from microfilm to paper and then scan it. All the time, I was very aware that this is exactly the kind of work that digitized newspaper archives were making obsolete, and rightly so. Four years later, out of the hundred newspapers I consulted, fifteen have been scanned by the British Newspaper Archive.[13]

Having scanned the ads, the individual details that localized the expansion of cinema could be observed by anyone browsing a simple map.[14] To enable more systematic analysis, however, the collection had to be converted into a data set by typing up the information contained in the ads into a relational database. Other sources allowed me to triangulate and enrich this resource. For instance, to map the cinemas and understand their surroundings, I could use historical maps through the Edina Digimap service.[15] I also used digitized town directories from the National Library of Scotland.[16] I could learn about demographic context through Vision of Britain.[17] When it came to the films, the resources were fewer. Checking UK release dates, which I needed to do to understand distribution patterns, required me to look at the lists on the trade papers for months before. Apart from *The Era,* there seemed to be little hope of finding digitized trade periodicals. And then, just after I submitted my thesis, the Media History Project put online the *Cinema News and Property Gazette,* a less well-known British film trade journal, which contains film lists and reviews. It was searchable, downloadable, and scanned beautifully to the Internet Archive.[18]

The project I worked on after finishing the PhD started, then, in a changed environment. The Media History Digital Library (hereafter MHDL) had a profound influence on the work carried out by the Early Cinema in Scotland project team.[19] It transformed our access to the trade press and therefore the way we used it as a source. For the silent period, the major British trade journals were *The Bioscope* and *The Kinematograph Weekly,* which were the main sources for the still unsurpassed history of British cinema that Rachael Low wrote in the 1940s. Historians have combed the microfilm copies of these two publications thoroughly, so most British cinema historiography comes from them. This narrow focus is unavoidable, because a user must choose if she is going to spend a long time with a single source. This is where digitization, coupled with optical character recognition (OCR) and information retrieval algorithms, has been transformative. As Jim Mussell argues, "search can disrupt existing hierarchies" and canons of sources.[20] Franco Moretti pointed out when outlining his influential concept of "distant reading" how such disruptions allow us to go beyond the exceptional event and to analyze the repetitive, the unremarkable, the noncanonical.[21] For a project like ours, that means being able to trace traveling exhibitions or the construction of new cinemas, items that do not make it into the industry yearbooks but get a solitary mention in the local news column. These snippets of information can then be integrated into the weave of a broader story or brought together to restore a glimpse of the individual lives of those who never wrote autobiographies.[22]

Eric Hoyt, in relation to the Media History Project, cites Moretti when discussing how citation patterns in academic articles tend to perpetuate the dominance of a few trade journal sources.[23] Digitization is challenging those traditional hierarchies, while illustrating how access creates canonicity. Importantly, this is not just a question of providing access to images of primary sources—you could do that with microfilm. Beyond the scope of the collections and the inherent richness of the material, three things made the Media History Digital Library immensely useful for the Early Cinema in Scotland project: first, its powerful and intuitive search engine, Lantern; second, its deliberate attempt to address scholarly concerns about the loss of context by designing forms of display that preserve some of the item's surroundings; and third, the availability of the raw OCR text on the Internet Archive repository.

After having spent so many hours trying to chance upon a fact through endless microfilm reels, using Lantern is a revelation. The disruptive mechanics of "search" are deployed here to great effect. A film title or name might pop up in a completely unexpected publication from across the world.[24] This experience can also be replicated when simply Googling a film title and obtaining hits from the digitized newspaper archives of Australia (Trove),[25] New Zealand (Papers Past),[26] and Singapore (NewspaperSG).[27] This is how Caroline Merz, a researcher in the team, found screenings of *Rob Roy*, the first Scottish feature film, advertised in Adelaide and Auckland. The Early Cinema in Scotland project leader, John Caughie, extended his exploration of Scottish-themed films by reference to the digitized US trade press, adding many new titles to the canon of Scottish representation. The links to *Moving Picture World* and *Motion Picture News* included alongside the film notes give convenient access to contemporary reviews, thus enriching our empirical understanding of how Scotland and the Scots were represented and addressed. Allowing us to engage with sources that we never would have dreamed of using, digitized collections bring into focus the international scope of the film trade, giving new meaning to our local investigations.

This does not mean that reading sources is a thing of the past. The seriality of the press, emphasized by the linear medium of microfilm, is helpful as a device for historical writing. Caughie read on microfilm twenty years of *The Bioscope*, plus whole runs of several small-town weeklies.[28] The same sense of time unspooling is harder to get from a list of search results. Julia Bohlmann based much of her thesis on exciting archival finds and read volume upon volume of council minutes.[29] That experience of surprise punctuating tedium comes closer to lived history. Trevor Griffiths sifted through bundles of business records and court cases carefully tied with cotton ribbon, plus the odd souvenir handkerchief or postcard found on eBay.[30] However, these quiet thrills of discovery can now routinely be followed up with a quick search on Lantern or the British Newspaper Archive. Digitized primary sources started working for us as reference tools, as efficient triangulation points.

Some researchers find this way of querying sources too disruptive and feel that it sacrifices context. A similar critique can be made of black-box text-mining tools. To counter

that, Arclight, the first major application built to mine and analyze the MHDL collections, is engineered to retain the principle of "continual back-and-forth movement between close and distant scales of reading."[31] This is enabled by how the MHDL's search engine, Lantern, takes care to foreground context. Referring to her own work with those and similar tools, Haidee Wasson has written about the eclectic nature of historical research, which picks up evidence and methods where it can, from the weight of a projector case to the algorithmically generated data table. Wasson argues that the apparently banal process of searching can enable "nimble and playful" strategies that cut across disciplinary and national borders.[32] Through critical and creative use, search and data mining can decontextualize, but also recontextualize. This is a fluid situation in which the same source can provide the anecdote and the background, shifting from primary document to reference material and back again.

Returning to the preceding cinema programs example, digitized resources that I could access remotely proved invaluable for constructing the analytical context for the data set. In particular, when it comes to places or periods that are poorly represented in generalist or survey histories, digitization has turned primary sources into reference tools. As Mussell argues, we need to go beyond static conceptions of the primary source, and of digitized material as secondary, as an access copy, by opening up the metadata and full-text contents as well as the scanned images.[33] Recognizing digitized sources *as* sources in their own right demands critical thinking and transparency about metadata, OCR, and keyword searching.[34] Institutionally, we need to understand and challenge the restrictions imposed by the commercial imperatives of some digitization projects but also to build our projects with deliberate openness.

From a practical and scholarly point of view, Arclight's inventive approach to topic modeling for its subject-specific collection relies on the MHDL's location within the Internet Archive, which means the content is freely available in a variety of formats, including plain text. The responsive and inclusive model that the MHDL has adopted keeps the path open for the addition of more regional and local cinema trade periodicals, but it is also part of, it is hoped, a greater trend for open scholarship. Cinema historians have been wishing for more comparative approaches for a long time, after the limiting paradigm of national cinemas stopped seeming obvious.[35] International collaboration is still, I think, the most desirable model for comparisons, but access to global primary sources would be an excellent way to combat both parochialism and Gothamcentrism. A good example is Laura Isabel Serna's use of the MHDL's Cine Mundial Collection on Mexican cinema.[36]

In the merciless waters of contemporary tech capitalism, "disruption" is both a utopian promise and a neoliberal threat. As digitization transforms the meaning and practice of archive research, we need to be watchful about what sort of new canons are being created in the wake of the old ones and to be concerned about what we can do to make open access resources effective in challenging inequalities. It is no surprise that Colombian archives and libraries, untroubled by the Anglo-American baby boomer appetite for family history, have less money to carry out digitization. But it is being done.[37] In any case, remote access should not only mean that someone based in a big British or American university now can write the histories of all peripheral and nonmetropolitan cinemas without leaving his desk. It should mean that access to the necessary reference points to write any history should not be restricted to those with the right passport, the right academic status, and enough money to get to the archive.

Since I researched my PhD at the beginning of this decade, much has changed. Digitization has continued. The use of digitized sources has become entrenched and naturalized in writing histories. The mixed approach described herein resulted from pragmatic choices at a time of transformation. Documenting it is a way to acknowledge that we write about the past from a contested present, with the tools and perspectives of our fleeting moment.

María Antonia Vélez-Serna is a Leverhulme Early Career Fellow at the University of Stirling. She is coeditor and coauthor of the Early Cinema in Scotland website and forthcoming book of the same title.

NOTES

A first version of this article was presented at the University of St. Andrews in February 2015, as part of a postgraduate training workshop titled Remote Access: Conducting Archival Research from a Distance. The workshop was organized by Dr. Grazia Ingravalle and Dr. Tom Rice. I thank Grazia and the workshop participants for their interest in and comments on the presentation.

1. http://www.scan.org.uk/.

2. http://archiveshub.ac.uk/.

3. http://huni.net.au/.

4. Carolyn Steedman, *Dust: The Archive and Cultural History* (New Brunswick, N.J.: Rutgers University Press, 2001), 145, qtd. in Richard Abel, "The Pleasures and Perils of Big Data in Digitized Newspapers," *Film History* 25, no. 1–2 (2013): 6.

5. Examples of the offending trope are collected in a Tumblr blog, *Dusty Archive Kitten Deaths*, http://dustyarchivekittendeaths.tumblr.com/.

6. Arlette Farge, *The Allure of the Archives* (New Haven, Conn.: Yale University Press, 2013), 6, 9.

7. Ibid., 15.

8. Susan A. Cady, "The Electronic Revolution in Libraries: Microfilm Déjà Vu?," *College and Research Libraries*, July 1990, 379, http://crl.acrl.org/index.php/crl/article/view/14565.

9. Abel, "Pleasures and Perils," 7.

10. Robert C. Allen, "Decentering Historical Audience Studies: A Modest Proposal," in *Hollywood in the Neighborhood: Historical Case Studies of Local Moviegoing*, ed. Kathryn Fuller-Seeley, 20–33 (Berkeley: University of California Press, 2008), 20.

11. http://find.galegroup.com/bncn.

12. http://www.nls.uk/about-us/working-with-others.

13. http://britishnewspaperarchive.co.uk/.

14. The original version of the map with the scanned ads can be viewed at http://early cinema.gla.ac.uk/blog/maria/scotlandcine maps.html.

15. http://digimap.edina.ac.uk/.

16. http://digital.nls.uk/directories/index .html.

17. http://www.visionofbritain.org.uk/.

18. http://mediahistoryproject.org/.

19. To access the Early Cinema in Scotland database and find out more about the project, completed in 2015, visit http://earlycinema .gla.ac.uk/.

20. Jim Mussell, "Doing and Making: History as Digital Practice," in *History in the Digital Age*, ed. Tony Weller, 79–93 (London: Routledge, 2013), 80.

21. Franco Moretti, *Distant Reading* (London: Verso, 2013).

22. The value of digitized sources for "history from below" is best demonstrated by projects like London Lives (https://www.londonlives .org/), which connects the digitized collections of eight archives with fifteen additional data sets to piece together individual histories of eighteenth-century plebeian Londoners. Their online availability also implies and invites a broader, nonacademic audience for these projects. Tim Hitchcock and Robert Shoemaker, "Making History Online," *Transactions of the Royal Historical Society* 25 (December 2015): 75–93.

23. Eric Hoyt, "Lenses for Lantern: Data Mining, Visualization, and Excavating Film History's Neglected Sources," *Film History* 26, no. 2 (2014): 146–68.

24. More recently, Project Arclight has enhanced Lantern's capabilities through scaled entity search. As Long et al. argue, Arclight results further "highlight the unexpected and the marginal in ways that our human perception may want to disregard." Derek Long, Eric Hoyt, Kevin Ponto, Tony Tran, and Kit Hughes, "Who's Trending in 1910s American Cinema? Exploring ECHO and MHDL at Scale with Arclight," *The Moving Image* 16, no. 1 (2016): 73.

25. http://trove.nla.gov.au/newspaper.

26. http://paperspast.natlib.govt.nz/cgi-bin /paperspast.

27. http://eresources.nlb.gov.sg/newspapers/.

28. John Caughie, "Small Town Cinema in Scotland: The Particularity of Place," in *Cin-ema beyond the City*, ed. Judith Thissen and Clemens Zimmermann, 23–37 (London: British Film Institute/Palgrave, 2016), 25.

29. Julia Bohlmann, "Regulating and Mediating the Social Role of Cinema in Scotland, 1896–1933," PhD thesis, University of Glasgow, 2016, http://theses.gla.ac.uk/7198/.

30. Trevor Griffiths, *The Cinema and Cinemagoing in Scotland, 1896–1950* (Edinburgh: Edinburgh University Press, 2012).

31. Eric Hoyt, Kit Hughes, and Charles R. Acland, "A Guide to the Arclight Guidebook," in *The Arclight Guidebook to Media History and the Digital Humanities*, ed. Charles R. Acland and Eric Hoyt, 1–29 (Falmer, U.K.: REFRAME Books, 2016), 18.

32. Haidee Wasson, "The Quick Search and Slow Scholarship: Researching Film Formats," ibid., 40.

33. Mussell, "Doing and Making," 88.

34. Tim Hitchcock, "Confronting the Digital," *Cultural and Social History* 10, no. 1 (2013): 9–23.

35. This has been, for instance, a key driver of "New Cinema History" and the History of Moviegoing, Exhibition, and Reception (HoMER) network. See http://homernetwork.org/.

36. Laura Isabel Serna, *Making Cinelandia: American Films and Mexican Film Culture before the Golden Age* (Durham, N.C.: Duke University Press, 2014).

37. The Colombian National Library (Biblioteca Nacional) and the Luis Angel Árango library have digitized more than three hundred press titles from the nineteenth century, most of them only running to a few issues. To my knowledge, none of the major national newspapers has been digitized for public access. See http:// bibliotecanacional.gov.co/ and http://www .banrepcultural.org/blaavirtual/hemeroteca-digital-historica/all. Readers may also enjoy the digitized photograph and document collections at Biblioteca Pública Piloto, which contain cinema architecture, advertisement slides, and both published and unpublished film criticism, at http://www.bibliotecapiloto .gov.co/buscadores/bpp-digital.

Tracing a Community of Practice: A Database of Early African American Race Film

MARIKA CIFOR, HANNA GIRMA,
WILLIAM LAM, SHANYA NORMAN,
AND MIRIAM POSNER, WITH
KARLA CONTRERAS AND
AYA GRACE YOSHIOKA

The definition of "race film," as many scholars have noted, is notoriously elusive. Any proposed criterion—an all-black cast, for example, or a black director, or an exclusively black audience—ultimately will fail as a singular defining factor, because, in reality, the race film industry was multifaceted, contentious, and ever changing. Filmmakers and audiences defined race film not by pronouncing criteria but by actively creating and negotiating the community. Historians of the race film industry have dealt with the difficulty of defining race film by discussing the problem at length, acknowledging that many films sit uneasily within any classification system.

We discuss in this article the methodological, historical, and epistemological questions we faced as a research team in building a comprehensive database of the early African American race film industry, 1905–30. The database seeks to reconstruct a detailed history of silent films made for and by African Americans in the early twentieth century. Because of widespread racial discrimination, silent-era productions that fit the description of "race films"—that is, films designed for African American audiences—could be shown only in certain theaters or at certain times or in nontheatrical settings and were exhibited to racially segregated audiences. For these and other reasons, most of these race films received scant attention in the mainstream media. The actual film reels were not preserved in any systematic way, so few of these early race films have survived.[1] Though scholarship on early race film thrives,[2] until our project, a filmography of these early silent films had not been publicly available. Moreover, various spelling and orthographical errors have propagated through scholarship on early race film, so the creation of our database was an opportunity to verify the original spellings, dates, and—as far as possible—casts and production companies of these films.

Race, as Stuart Hall and many others have shown, is a category that is both exceedingly fluid and unforgivingly rigid:[3] fluid, because race functions in different ways in different places and times, and rigid, because, once applied, the label of a race ramifies through a person's life in infinite ways. The example of filmmaking in the first half of the twentieth century is no exception. Early-twentieth-century filmmakers experienced and articulated race in myriad ways, but the stark categories of *black* and *white* nevertheless had an undeniable role in shaping the film industry. This article demonstrates how a data-driven project should hold both realities in tension: the truth, on one hand, of people's varied and disparate lived experiences and the equal truth, on the other, of the real political, social, and legal implications of the way a person is classified. A database, no matter how well conceived, tolerates relatively little ambiguity. Therefore the media scholar who wishes to encode race must make and adhere to difficult, carefully considered decisions about how to classify people's lives.

This project team, however, did not have this luxury. Because we were setting out to build the first publicly available, downloadable database of the race film industry, we had to decide if any given film was, in stark binary terms, simply *in* or *out* of our data set. The team discusses here how we dealt with this daunting challenge, linking our efforts to the broader question of how moving image data might be created and used with nuance and rigor by scholars, archivists, librarians, and students.

In addition to the complexities of the subject matter itself, we faced a number of practical questions in our creation of this digital humanities (DH) project. We begin by discussing the details of the project and its specifications. In the next section, we turn to the difficulties posed by defining and classifying race films. Through film studies scholarship, we develop a definition of race film for the project and consider how that definition shaped our project. Finally, we turn to the many practical concerns we faced, including the selection of an appropriate platform, modeling the database, the process of tracing sources through archival materials and secondary works, and creating a data set designed for reuse and augmentation. We also focus on the challenges and opportunities posed by working collaboratively. While we hope the project stands on its own as a work of scholarship, it is also an experiment in DH pedagogy, because the team is composed of five undergraduate students, one graduate student, and a faculty member, all of whom worked together to complete the project during an academic quarter. Our goal is to suggest ways other scholars and archivists might partner with students to build digital work that honors every collaborator's skills and expertise.

DEFINING RACE FILM

At the center of the methodological, historical, and epistemological questions we faced was the difficulty of bounding the category of a "race film." Race films are notoriously challenging to define. Various scholars working at the intersections of film history and African American studies give markedly different criteria for the definition. In addition, a film's connotations frequently change depending on its exhibition context. Indeed, scholarly consensus on race filmmaking is that its personnel constitute not a rigidly bound club but rather "a circle—a loose federation of production companies and producers who competed with and depended on each other."[4] And yet, for the purpose of this project, we had to solidify the ambiguity of the term *race film*; to refine in toto an extensive survey of primary and secondary literature on race film, the team settled on a definition of a race film as *a film with African American cast members, produced by an independent production company, and discussed or advertised as a race film in the African American press.* Although this definition seemed to our team to come closest to approaching the generally understood meaning of the term, it also left us with a great deal of work to do, because no existing filmography currently defines race film in exactly these terms.

We began our work in composing the data set by casting a very wide net and then gradually pared down our data. We drew on our primary source research and also recorded the majority of the films before 1930 that are captured in the secondary literature on African American film, particularly those contained in Larry Richards's *African American Films through 1959* and Henry Sampson's *Blacks in Black and White.*[5] However, both filmographies are more capacious than our own data set because they contain not only race films per se but also films produced by mainstream production houses featuring African American actors in prominent roles. The secondary literature also sometimes includes films containing white actors performing in blackface designed for white audiences within the history of African American film. Following our definition of a race film, ultimately, we discarded such films from our data set. In order that other scholars can evaluate our decisions, however, the films and people we discarded from the database are themselves captured in our data set, as three linked Excel files in a folder labeled "Discarded Data." For an annotated list of the archival and secondary sources we employed, see http://dhbasecamp.humanities.ucla.edu/afamfilm/sources-further-reading/.

THE DATA SET

The data set we created contains information on every race film produced prior to 1930 that we could verify. It also presents information in separate tables about actors and other film personnel as well as the production companies involved in the race filmmaking industry prior to 1930. The database currently contains 303 silent titles, linked to 759 actors and personnel and 176 race film companies. Each record is augmented with descriptive and archival information. The project's website (http://dhbasecamp.humanities.ucla.edu/afamfilm/) also contains maps and visualizations designed to show how these data might be used, along with a set of beginner-friendly tutorials.

We began our research by entering data we derived in the course of our work with the newspaper clipping and note files contained in the George P. Johnson Negro Film Collection, a collection held within the UCLA Library Special Collections at the Charles E. Young Research Library. Johnson was a key figure in the Lincoln Motion Picture Company, one of the most active race film production companies, who assembled these files during his time working in the race film industry and for many decades afterward.[6] We quickly discovered, however, that while the materials within the Johnson Collection are an invaluable resource, they also contain discrepancies and omissions, including misremembered names and titles. Therefore we expanded our scope to consider secondary sources, such as scholarly books and articles, and primary sources, chiefly African American newspapers from the period.[7]

Databases can take many forms, from "flat" spreadsheets to sophisticated linked data tables. We opted for a relational database, a time-tested solution that arranges data in multiple, linked tables. This arrangement allows for relatively complex queries—for example, "all films produced by companies based in Texas during the 1920s"—and yet is simple enough for inexpert users to manage and query. As the research team gathered information about films and people from the period, we collaboratively entered that information by using the relational database software Airtable (http://www.airtable.com/), relatively new web-based software that allows for the creation of easy-to-use, versioned, collaborative relational databases. The data themselves are contained within four linked spreadsheets: "People," "Film," "Companies," and "Sources." In determining whether a film or person met our criteria for inclusion in the data set, our policy was to err on the side of comprehensiveness and then to confirm the record's appropriateness for inclusion after the fact, generally by checking primary sources to see if the film circulated among African American audiences as a "race film."

The project exists as a perusable database on Airtable and as raw comma-separated value (CSV) files on the code-sharing site Github. This enables others to use, build upon, and correct the data. All entries contain a citation or a link to the primary and/or secondary source where the data were obtained for anyone needing to validate specific entries. The data could be combined with other similar sets or could be mashed up with data sets that draw related variables together. For example, the History of Moviegoing, Exhibition, and Reception (HoMER) network might combine our film titles with its list of film exhibitions, thus helping to shed light on where these important works were actually shown.[8] The data also might be combined with information about the locations of existing films, thus allowing film viewers to discover copies of race films. The data also have potential for reuse and augmentation by archivists and librarians who hold collections related to the race film industry or film history more broadly. The data may also provide the basis for more complete descriptions of existing archival materials and collections and for building new relationships between archival institutions collecting in these areas. We believe, therefore, that these data, in addition to their value for scholarly research on race films and filmmaking, and African American history, have far-reaching potential in the digital humanities for film studies of the silent era, and for general knowledge.

While this data set represents our best effort to capture the people, companies, and films active in the race film industry, no data set can perfectly capture the complexity and dynamism of this period. For example, some people—but not others—might consider films that were produced by the Ebony Company to be race films.[9] Similarly, the ownership and personnel of race film companies changed a great deal during the period, a dynamism not captured in the data. However, this is the first publicly available data set of the industry, and we are confident that other scholars will use it as a starting point.

We have made every effort to adhere to current best practices in curating and publishing humanities data. While these practices are evolving quickly, they entail, at a minimum, documenting the decisions that were made when assembling and fine-tuning data. Once the data set was complete, we chose an archiving solution that is both lightweight and consistent with current thinking about sustainability. We created a repository for it on Github and then linked it to the data repository Zenodo, a widely respected archive associated with CERN, the European Organization for Nuclear Research. Zenodo issued our data set a stable digital object identifier (DOI; a unique, citable identifying number) as well as citation instructions. Within the data package, we included a data dictionary, a Creative Commons license, and other documentation important to understanding the data set.[10]

DH PEDAGOGY

Our project is both a work of scholarship and the product of an experiment in DH pedagogy. Other scholars and archivists might use it as a model for partnering with students to build digital work that honors the collaborators' diverse academic and personal backgrounds and individual skills. In every step of the project, we adhered to the "Student Collaborators' Bill of Rights," a document coauthored by UCLA DH students and faculty that codifies the responsibilities and expectations for all members of DH project teams.[11] In particular, the "Student Collaborators' Bill of Rights" requires that in faculty–student collaborations in which students are unpaid, students should have intellectual oversight of their portions of the project, should feel authorized to publish and present on the work, and should be recognized for their contributions in all subsequent publications.

All research team members shared some expertise in the digital humanities. The students on this project shared an academic background through the UCLA DH program. The graduate student on the team was completing course work for the DH graduate certificate. The undergraduates had project experience through course work completed for a minor in DH. With primary training from various disciplines across the humanities, arts, and social sciences, the students did not bring a great deal of subject expertise on early African American film. They thus gained subject knowledge in the process of completing this digital project through primary and secondary research, including new and canonical scholarship on the subject, through viewings of films and exposure to other archival materials.

The data set's accompanying visualizations are valuable as a teaching and learning tool for students. The project's website features tutorials on how to utilize the data set and to create visualizations and analyses regardless of the user's experience level. For example, because the data set includes locations for production companies, the tutorials provide the basics of mapping using the data set.

We are gratified that the project has re-ceived favorable notices from other scholars and practitioners, including honorable mention for the Garfinkel Prize in Digital Humanities from the American Studies Association. Most valuable for all of us, however, has been the experience of working carefully, methodically, and collaboratively through some of the most pressing questions about race, artistic output, and American history.

Marika Cifor is the Consortium for Faculty Diversity postdoctoral fellow in gender, sexuality, and women's studies at Bowdoin College. Cifor's work has appeared in *The American Archivist, Archival Science, Library Trends, Archivaria, Archives and Records, InterActions,* and *Transgender Studies Quarterly.*

Hanna Girma is studying world arts and cultures at the University of California, Los Angeles, with a minor in digital humanities (DH). As a DH minor, she is interested in the cultural and social impacts of new media and information technologies.

William Lam is a graduate of the University of California, Los Angeles. Born in the San Gabriel Valley and now residing in Los Angeles, he is utilizing skills attained from UCLA's digital humanities program in a career in digital media.

Shanya Norman, a recent UCLA graduate with a BA in sociology and a minor in digital humanities, has a high interest in the intersection between entertainment, popular culture, social awareness, and community engagement.

Miriam Posner is an assistant professor of information studies and digital humanities at the University of California, Los Angeles.

Karla Contreras is a fourth-year applied linguistics and Spanish community and culture double major and digital humanities minor at the University of California, Los Angeles.

Aya Grace Yoshioka graduated from the University of California, Los Angeles, in 2016 with a sociology major and digital humanities minor. She contributed to the research, web design, and publicity for the Early African American Film project.

NOTES

Many thanks to the distinguished scholars, archivists, and librarians who generously provided guidance to the project, including Peggy Alexander, Cara Caddoo, Allyson Field, Brian Graney, Jan-Christopher Horak, Charles Musser, and Thomas Padilla.

1. On the locations of surviving films, see Jan-Christopher Horak, "Preserving Race Films," in *Early Race Filmmaking in America*, ed. Barbara Lupack, 199–230 (New York: Routledge, 2016).

2. See, e.g., Cara Caddoo, *Envisioning Freedom: Cinema and the Building of Modern Black Life* (Cambridge, Mass.: Harvard University Press, 2014); Thomas Cripps, *Slow Fade to Black: The Negro in American Film, 1900–42* (New York: Oxford University Press, 1977); Allyson Nadia Field, *Uplift Cinema: The Emergence of African American Film and the Possibility of Black Modernity* (Durham, N.C.: Duke University Press, 2015); Jane Gaines, *Fire and Desire: Mixed-Race Movies in the Silent Era* (Chicago: University of Chicago Press, 2001); Phyllis R. Klotman, *Frame by Frame: A Black Filmography* (Bloomington: Indiana University Press, 1979); Barbara Lupack, *Richard E. Norman and Race Filmmaking* (Bloomington: Indiana University Press, 2013); Charlene Regester, *African American Actresses: The Struggle for Visibility, 1900–1960* (Bloomington: Indiana University Press, 2010); Mark Reid, *Redefining Black Film* (Berkeley: University of California Press, 1993); and Cedric Robinson, *Forgeries of Memory and Meaning: Blacks and the Regimes of Race in American Theater and Film before World War II* (Chapel Hill: University of North Carolina Press, 2007). The project's website contains a complete list of secondary sources.

3. Stuart Hall and Media Education Foundation, *Race: The Floating Signifier* (Northampton, Mass.: Media Education Foundation, 2002).

4. Pearl Bowser, Jane Gaines, and Charles Musser, "Introduction: Oscar Micheaux and Race Movies of the Silent Period," in *Oscar Micheaux and His Circle: African American Filmmaking and Race Cinema of the Silent Era*, ed. Pearl Bowser, Jane Gaines, and Charles Musser (Bloomington: Indiana University Press, 2001), xvii–xxx, xx.

5. Larry Richards, *African American Films through 1959: A Comprehensive, Illustrated Filmography* (Jefferson, N.C.: McFarland, 1998); Henry Sampson, *Blacks in Black and White: A Source Book on Black Films*, 2nd ed. (Metuchen, N.J.: Scarecrow Press, 1995).

6. George P. Johnson Negro Film Collection (Collection 1042), UCLA Library Special Collections, Charles E. Young Research Library, University of California, Los Angeles.

7. These papers were accessed in digital form through the Readex database African American Newspapers, 1827–1998.

8. For more on the HoMER project, see the project's website at http://homernetwork.org/.

9. Films made by the Ebony Company contained some of most negative stereotypes in their depiction of African Americans, yet these films were widely shown in "race" theaters. Film historian Jacqueline Stewart wrote, "Perhaps Ebony films speak in two voices," one for white audiences and one for African American audiences. See Stewart, *Migrating to the Movies: Cinema and Black Urban Modernity* (Berkeley: University of California Press, 2005), 201.

10. See, e.g., Trevor Muñoz et al., *DHDC: Digital Humanities Data Curation*, http://www.dhcuration.org/.

11. Haley Di Pressi et al., "A Student Collaborators' Bill of Rights," UCLA Digital Humanities, 2015, http://www.cdh.ucla.edu/news-events/a-student-collaborators-bill-of-rights/.

The Amateur Movie Database: Archives, Publics, Digital Platforms

CHARLES TEPPERMAN

I have a confession to make: I am a digital humanities (DH) amateur. After reading about new digital approaches to film scholarship and developing my own project, I quickly discovered that, while imagining a DH project is an exciting proposition, building one is another thing altogether.[1] The Amateur Movie Database (AMDB) began with a rather straightforward goal in mind: to collect information about significant amateur films in one place so that researchers, archivists, and the interested public can investigate this category of filmmaking. Now the AMDB (http://www.amateurcinema.org/) faces a range of challenges around *refining* what the information collected should contain, *specifying* which groups are most likely to use the database and how, and *selecting* the most appropriate digital tools for the task from the wide array of available DH tools and methods.

In terms of refining the information our project might collect, Acland and Hoyt's recent *Arclight Guidebook to Media History and the Digital Humanities* provides a valuable introduction to the broad categories of DH projects. These include ones that transform information into data sets, digitize materials for wider dissemination (typically via the internet), use digital technologies for new kinds of multimedia publication and interactive presentation, and employ social media and networked communities to help build a DH project in progress.[2] The AMDB project employs—or could potentially employ—each of these elements to some degree.

The goals of the AMDB are closely aligned with the first kind of DH project, that which transforms information into a new data set. We begin with a selection of significant North American amateur films produced between 1928 and 1971. This corpus includes winners of amateur movie contests as well as films that are determined by project collaborators to be otherwise significant (having gained scholarly or archival recognition, such as National Film Preservation Foundation preservation grants, or representing works from marginalized communities). This corpus consists of approximately thirteen hundred films, including relatively well known works like *The Fall of the House of Usher* (Watson and Webber, 1928) and *Multiple Sidosis* (Laverents, 1970). But there are many more unheralded films. These film data are already a productive set for analysis, but there is still room for additional future contributions, such as winners of other movie contests or films that are discovered in archives. An area for future expansion is the geographical range of the project, widening the focus from North American filmmakers to include more information about international films.

The AMDB is unlike typical library or archival databases in that the films included are not ones that we possess. In fact, one of the goals of the project is to compile a large list to use for locating extant films and evaluating the proportion of films that have been lost. In this sense, the project is like the *AFI Catalog of Feature Films* and the Library of Congress's (LOC) American Silent Feature Film Database, which include both extant and lost films.[3] The AMDB resembles a catalog in that it compiles information about the films (and filmmakers) into discrete fields, making the data more "granular" and available for metadata searching and analysis. Like the AFI resource, the AMDB mines textual documentation to provide content summaries and production details. Like the LOC database, we are interested in identifying which films have survived, and where.

The Amateur Movie Database was designed (by our technical guru Jack Brighton) with PBCore metadata standards in mind so that the data could be shareable in the future. The data that we collect come from a variety of sources, including textual documentation in published sources (such as amateur movie magazines), archives, online sources (especially the Media History Digital Library and the Internet Archive), and (when possible) the films themselves. The challenge here is to find and enter pertinent information about the films, a task that progressively is more research intensive. After basic information (title, filmmaker, and year) is entered, finding more information about the films (descriptions, images, locations, etc.) requires item-by-item research.

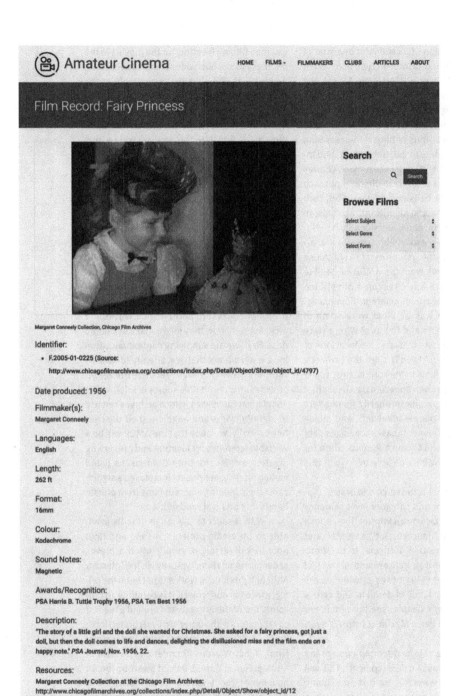

Figure 1. AMDB record for *Fairy Princess* (Margaret Conneely, 1956). Conneely Collection, Chicago Film Archives, http://www.amateurcinema.org /index.php/film/fairy-princess.

While the creation of a catalog of one kind of films is a fairly old-fashioned type of research with its basis in print—think the AFI catalog or the more recent *Field Guide to Sponsored Films*—making use of a digital platform creates new opportunities for analyzing the data and exploring this corpus of films.[4] In describing his Canadian Educational, Sponsored, and Industrial Films (CESIF) database project, Charles Acland calls this a "low-tech digital" approach that eschews the bells and whistles of DH, such as visualizations and algorithmic analysis, in favor of simple research functionality.[5]

Because we expect film scholars and archivists will be the groups most likely to use the database, we want the AMDB to be able to answer some basic research questions: What was the scope of amateur filmmaking? How extensive was it? What were some of the main subjects and themes? Where were they filmed (or what were some locations of focused activity)? Even though the project's focus is on the films in the corpus, the project is actually three interconnected databases that include films, people (primarily filmmakers but also other people involved), and movie clubs. Each of these databases organizes data distinctly and will produce granular data for analysis. What will we be able to do with this database?

We will be able to *search and browse* (operational). Item- and category-level searches allow users to track down information about a specific film or filmmaker, let's say, Margaret Conneely (Figure 1); a particular form (short, animation, feature); genres; and high-level subject headings. Tag boxes provide access to more specific kinds of detail in and across the records. For example, see the filmmaker entry for Hiram Percy Maxim at http://tinyurl .com/lez9q3k.

We will be able to *filter and analyze* the data in visual ways (in development). This will provide useful ways for, for instance, using word clouds to see how widespread genres or subjects are within the corpus. Filtering a search according to specific criteria (such as filmmaker gender or properties of the film itself) can shed light on the social and aesthetic dimensions of amateur moviemaking.

We will be able to *map* (operational at item level; in development for aggregate). We can map filming locations of the movies in the database to see how widespread amateur filmmaking was. This is already available at the item level and in the future will be searchable by an interactive map. Similarly, we are entering information about the exhibition of amateur films as we find it. In this way, we will be able to map the circulation of specific amateur movies, for example, *The Fall of the House of Usher* (http://tinyurl.com/mpvdxpr) (Figure 2).

Our data set will eventually be deposited at the University of Calgary's digital repository, achieving one goal of the project, which is to create data that other researchers will be able to work with. Scholars will be able to download the database and analyze it in new, unforeseen ways. And while researchers and film historians might be the primary users of the AMDB, no less important are archives and archivists and how they might make use of the data. First, we are supplying contextualization for amateur films that are already identified within archival holdings. Second, the AMDB provides an authoritative source of information about amateur movies, which archives can use to identify works and augment their descriptions. Finally, we hope that the AMDB will be a valuable reference for locating and preserving amateur movies, for both the reasons listed earlier. Already, our project has played a significant role in guiding amateur films from private hands into archival repositories.

With respect to the range of tools available to DH media projects, Acland and Hoyt note that digitizing materials often achieves wider dissemination, typically via the internet. Although this kind of work has not been the primary focus of our project, it is certainly an outcome. The AMDB is organized around a team of collaborators with strong archival connections: Karan Sheldon (cofounder of Northeast Historic Film), Nancy Watrous (founder and director of Chicago Film Archives), Dwight Swanson (board member of the Center for Home Movies), and Dan Streible (NYU and the Orphan Film Symposium). These collaborators bring to the project their expertise in archiving nontheatrical and amateur films. They also have worked on projects that digitize amateur films from their holdings, to which we can link the database. Given that the AMDB does not hold its own collection of amateur movies, we welcome other

Figure 2. AMDB screening map for *The Fall of the House of Usher* (Watson and Webber, 1928). http://tinyurl.com/mpvdxpr. Map data copyright 2017 Google, INEGI.

archives as digitizing partners to increase the visibility of amateur films. Since the website's launch in March 2017, we have been contacted by archives that hold films listed in our database but that aren't currently accessible via their own websites or catalogs. Our database can help enhance the discoverability of these archival holdings by directing viewers from the topic-focused AMDB portal to the archives where these films reside.

Typical of DH projects that use digital tools for new kinds of multimedia publication and interactive presentations, the AMDB includes an "Articles" section with short, informative pieces by our project members and other researchers. There are, for example, web-based blog posts with text and images, as in our article about the Amateur Cinema League (http://tinyurl.com/mmwxvdn). We invite authors to use the forum to experiment with platforms, such as SCALAR, that provide opportunities to annotate and link together visual materials provocatively. The data that our project contains are available for scholars

interested in presenting innovative kinds of analyses and visualizations.

DH projects appeal in their ability to employ social media and networked communities to help build a project in progress. In contrast to traditional scholarship, which might produce an outcome like an article or book, DH endeavors are iterative. They can, indeed, should, change over time as new materials are added, new technologies and techniques are developed, and approaches are refined and revised. A corollary of this is that the life span and sustainability of DH projects can be variable. Often they require continued attention in ways that published works do not. Networked communities can contribute to this process by updating information about items in the database and helping to locate films included in it. In fact, a primary motivation for this project was to use the power of the internet to crowdsource—or, better, *crowd-locate*—amateur films that haven't yet found their way into archives. We have discovered caches of amateur films that aren't held by archives but have shown up on YouTube channels or other websites, having been posted by movie clubs and other interested individuals. As N. Katherine Hayles notes, in digital (and especially online) projects, "worldwide collaboration can arise between expert scholars and expert amateurs."[6] The amateurs to whom she refers may be the "history buffs" long dismissed by academics but who are often the keepers of histories and artifacts that can enrich our account of amateur film history. If, as Hayles suggests, collaboration can "leap across academic walls," perhaps it can leap across archival ones as well. Social media can link the AMDB with these films (and others not yet posted online) and more generally help discover these works online and facilitate their preservation.

Developing the AMDB project has not made me feel less like a DH amateur, but it has led me to understand that this isn't such a terrible thing. Like amateur moviemaking, some of the best DH media projects involve pragmatic and creative approaches that are nearly always in some stage of (re)development: *refining* information that is never complete, *specifying* which groups are most likely to use the database (and how), and *selecting* the most appropriate digital tools for the task from the wide array of available DH tools and methods. These processes need not be a zero-sum proposition so long as the data can be made available to other scholars (and amateurs) who want to take them in whatever new directions they can imagine. And none of this detracts from our original, and still straightforward, goal of creating a source of information about amateur films that is comprehensive and accessible.

Charles Tepperman is associate professor in the Department of Communication, Media, and Film at the University of Calgary. Tepperman has published articles on early cinema in Canada and on nontheatrical film culture and technology. He is the author of *Amateur Cinema: The Rise of North American Moviemak-* *ing, 1923–1960* (2015) and director of the Amateur Movie Database Project (http://amateur cinema.org/).

NOTES

1. The Amateur Movie Database Project is supported by a grant from the Social Sciences and Humanities Research Council of Canada and the Faculty of Arts at the University of Calgary. The author acknowledges the many contributions of Karan Sheldon, Dan Streible, Dwight Swanson, and Nancy Watrous that have shaped and advanced the project; Jack Brighton, for his crucial role as designer of the database and website; and Sheena Manabat, Andrew Watts, Lucas Anderson, and Isabel Lara, for their research assistance on the project.

2. Charles R. Acland and Eric Hoyt, eds., *The Arclight Guidebook to Media History and the Digital Humanities* (Falmer, U.K.: REFRAME Books, 2016), 4–6.

3. The *AFI Catalog of Feature Films* is located at http://www.afi.com/members/catalog/default.aspx. The LOC American Silent Feature Film Database, with an accompanying report about extant American silent feature films by David Pierce, *The Survival of American Silent Feature Films: 1912–1929* (Washington, DC: Library of Congress, 2013), is available at http://lcweb2.loc.gov:8081/diglib/ihas/html/silent films/silentfilms-home.html.

4. Rick Prelinger, *The Field Guide to Sponsored Films* (San Francisco: National Film Preservation Foundation, 2006).

5. Charles R. Acland, "Low-Tech Digital," in Acland and Hoyt, *Arclight Guidebook,* 133.

6. N. Katherine Hayles, *How We Think: Digital Media and Contemporary Technogenesis* (Chicago: University of Chicago Press, 2012), 36.

The Amateur City: Digital Platforms and Tools for Research and Dissemination of Films Representing the Italian Urban Landscape

PAOLO SIMONI

Geodatabases are tools that can help viewers to reread landscapes through media, especially when applied to distinct collections, such as in home movies. In Italy, archival activities and projects concerned with home movies and amateur cinema are relatively recent, mostly carried out by the Archivio Nazionale del Film di Famiglia (Italian Amateur Film Archive), founded in 2002 in Bologna. The archive is managed by the Home Movies Association, a group of film archivists, historians, restorers, and curators. The team often works together with other scholars and professionals from different fields toward the dissemination of the archive's material.[1]

The mission of the archive is to recover amateur film material from the twentieth century, which increasingly is acknowledged as a significant cultural heritage. This archival work necessarily includes the description, classification, publication, and valorization of private and family memories through a multidisciplinary approach involving experts in cultural heritage, databases, and management and storage of multimedia files. Audiovisual records produced by individuals are part of a wider collective memory; through this perspective, home movies and amateur films acquire a new "public" status and, at the same time, are recycled within new filmic texts and media and disseminated through innovative methodologies. In addition to providing direct access to these amateur moving images to scholars, filmmakers, and students in digital formats, the Italian Amateur Film Archive is developing tools to diffuse (and open) amateur materials to a wide and varied audience. This is facilitated by the database of the project Una città per gli archivi, by publishing film collections on the web portal archIVI,[2] and by using an interactive platform to explore the stories of families through their private film archives, Vite filmate.[3] In these and other cases, new media and digital technologies allow users to present and rework amateur footage in a variety of ways. By means of exhibitions, installations, screen-based live performances, and local projects involving film, the heritage of amateur movies is recirculated within the community to which the films belong.[4]

Geodatabase tools can help viewers reread the diverse views of filmed landscapes, especially the urban ones. The findings are the result of a four-year research project conducted across film archives holding amateur material on past urban landscapes, specifically the cities of Bologna and Reggio Emilia. I will concentrate on the issue central to my work, as researcher and curator, of better understanding how new media technology helps to connect images with the places where they were shot in new and unconventional ways. We analyzed and resituated the movies in a new digital environment. Clips originally in 8mm, Super 8mm, 16mm, and 9.5mm formats representing visual fragments of the city or single shots located in urban settings were identified and selected for digitization. Once "remediated," edited, and geolocalized, amateur footage may be embedded into apps, platforms, and installations that allow users and visitors to use them as their guide into (historical) maps of the city.

Endeavors including the Play the City RE project (2015)[5] and on-site installations and videos produced for exhibitions such as *Cinematic Bologna* (2012–13)[6] transformed amateur footage into geographical experiences. They were based on the reuse of amateur film materials collected in Bologna and Reggio Emilia and provide users or visitors with a "time machine" showing changes in those landscapes over time. They also document how these urban transformations have been perceived by amateur filmmakers and citizens. While anyone may explore the urban locations where the amateur films originally were shot, our research work shifts the focus from media archaeology to something that we could dub *media stratigraphy*, wherein the archival footage could be used not only to take a sentimental journey through the individual gaze of past inhabitants but also as an interpretative and operative device for the analysis of urban development. As Penz and Lu stated, "crucially, the processes involved in cinematic urban archaeology exhume, unlock and preserve memories. And, as an applied concept, it may have far-reaching implications for planning and urban regeneration purposes as well as for heritage and conservation."[7]

THE IMAGE OF THE CITY AND THE AMATEUR FILM ARCHIVE

The combination of geodatabases[8] that plot latitude and longitude coordinates for each individual film sequence using web cartography and dissemination platforms provides users, visitors, and researchers with a "bottom-up" diachronic representation of twentieth-century urban landscape (since the views initially were through the eyes of amateur filmmakers). This "unexpected" function recalls Kevin Lynch's description of the city's image as being determined by its inhabitants' perception of urban space, interpreted and read through a set of identifiable physical elements.[9] Mental maps produce visual and geographic representations derived from city dwellers' descriptions of the locations of everyday life, collected as primary sources. Lynch specifies combinations of common elements and patterns that shape the individual perception of urban space and create these urban mental maps. Physical elements are *paths* (streets, walkways, transit lines, canals, railroads), *edges* (boundaries, linear breaks such as shores, railroad cuts, edges of development, walls), *districts* (sections of the city), *nodes* (junctions, mobility hubs), and *landmarks* (buildings, signs, stores, physical elements linked to the urban identity). Lynch's discourse is crucial in analyzing the amateur footage, conceiving the idea of a collective gaze made by many fragments and using the visual recordings as a reflection of the way people see and live day by day the physical elements of the urban landscape.

Paths, edges, districts, nodes, and landmarks are the basis of the concepts of *legibility* (how people understand the layout of a place) and *imageability* (the evocation of a strong image in any observer). Lynch's theory was a stimulus for trying to reconstruct a cinematic image of the city that begins with the gazes of amateur filmmakers, with figures moving in and

traversing the urban space, thereby measuring it with the camera. Such footage constitutes cognitive maps of the urban environment.

Let's consider the image of the city of Bologna after World War II, in the years of the so-called economic boom, as amateur filmmakers recorded it. These images were recombined, fragment by fragment, in the *Cinematic Bologna* exhibition.[10] The films are concentrated in the city center, where *landmarks* consist of conspicuous buildings and/or monuments, well-known symbols of the urban identity: the Asinelli Tower (Figure 1),[11] the uplands of San Luca,[12] San Michele in Bosco, the church of San Petronio, the Palazzo d'Accursio. There are also the train station and the central gas station that mark the northern limits of the city. Border signs *(edges)* are the ancient city gates, physical marks dividing the city center from the outskirts, and the ring-road boulevards. The *paths* of amateur cities are the main streets that determine the urban shape (via Rizzoli, via Ugo Bassi, and the intersection with via dell'Indipendenza). Some amateur filmmakers are interested in tram and bus routes and their *nodes*, points of departure, arrival, and exchange. Particularly crowded (and represented) locations are the stadium, the racecourse, and the public parks, such as Giardini Margherita (Figure 2).[13] Montagnola was a park that had been the site of exhibitions and political events, but when these moved to the suburbs later, it was less frequently filmed. Other filmmakers represent the *district* of their residence. Another keystone of the city image is the metamorphosis that took place over the 1950s and 1960s, when the filmmakers' attention is captured by changes in urban planning, such as the new ring road that redefined the northern borders of the city, new buildings with significant architectural changes, and the transformation of the northern skyline.

EMBODIED VIEWPOINTS

While this might not be an intentional and/or conscious process, amateur movies document the places to which the filmmakers are emotionally tied. These images serve most often as backdrops for scenes involving family, loved ones, and friends. But the city itself often becomes the leading character and emerges

Figure 1. *Cinematic Bologna* (2012), frame from video installation: views of the Asinelli Tower. Copyright Home Movies—Archivio Nazionale del Film di Famiglia, Bologna.

Figure 2. *Cinematic Bologna* (2012), frame from video installation: views of the Giardini Margherita public park. Copyright Home Movies—Archivio Nazionale del Film di Famiglia, Bologna.

into the foreground when the filmmakers shoot places or aspects of the urban space that they inhabit. The images thus become evidence and sources. Julia Hallam observes that, regardless of the intimate reasons behind the films (to document family life, to play with the movie camera as a toy), "the amateur is a member of the urban crowd, a participant observer/ witness who creates an embodied viewpoint of city life."[14] If one looks at the whole picture, it is easy to see that these films repeat gestures with meanings, are the outcome of social practices, evidence shared languages and common social experiences. But the role of the amateur cine-eye in the urban context also is to preserve an overall image of the city, creating an idealized cognitive map of the urban environment. The point of view of the person behind the camera is intimate and unique, as it still belongs to the private, personal act of filming. But if we look carefully at the images shot by various individuals, we find many common views of the same landscape. Taken as an ensemble, they become the vision of a collective gaze, a mosaic of the daily, fragmented reality that surrounded the amateur filmmakers.

The *Cinematic Bologna* installations reconstructed the city through these views. Piazza Maggiore, the city's main square, was a remarkable example of visual stratigraphy, formed by a rich and unequivocal sedimentation of gazes. Countless filmmakers over time have filmed it from similar points of view. Recurring shots of the Renaissance Neptune

Fountain or children playing with the inevitable pigeons identify this place with a constant character that is independent of the numerous different looks (Figure 3). Additionally, in some cases, the same filmmaker has shot the same place from the same point of view during different periods, offering us a mutated visual.[15]

LOOKING FOR (AND FINDING) THE AMATEUR CITY

It is possible, then, to see Bologna, as presented above, as an example of what Les Roberts has called an "archive city."[16] Furthermore, we could call it an *amateur city* that consists of the sum, juxtaposition, layering, comparison, and dynamic assembly of the cinematic gazes of those who filmed it from time to time, driven by their desire to document places and buildings, thereby defining, in moving images, the setting and background of their lives.

The adjective *amateur* refers both to the fact that images were historically produced by nonprofessionals armed with small-gauge film cameras and also to the filmmakers' affectionate feelings toward the subjects they filmed in close surroundings. A fundamental feature

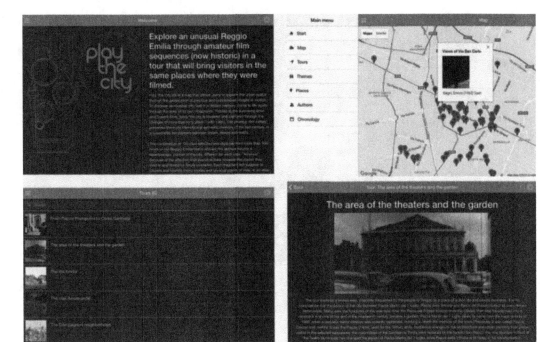

Figure 4. Play the City RE (2015), screenshots from the app. Copyright Home Movies—Archivio Nazionale del Film di Famiglia, Bologna.

of the amateur city's perspective is that it reflects the orientation of its inhabitants rather than the "tourist gaze" of occasional visitors. Examples of amateur filmmakers' inhabitants' view are the films that record formerly habitual places or events when they disappear. In 1963, for instance, many residents filmed the last ever tramway journey in Bologna, almost as a collective ritual. There have been efforts to restore the traces of what already has disappeared, such as the ruins of the ancient buildings destroyed in World War II before postwar reconstruction began, conceiving of the act of filming specifically as an archaeological enterprise.

What shape does the amateur city take? In the pattern that I am developing, the amateur city takes on different forms and dimensions related to each other through connections, contaminations, and intersections. Fundamentally, it is the archive that shapes the amateur city. Its relational databases amount to a "symbolic form" of the type proposed by Lev Manovich.[17] Semantic connections are established among documents. In this case, we consider the different gazes of the filmmakers as elemental. The database is, in fact, the main device through which we can synthesize a mosaic of thousands of fragments that can be reassembled in virtually endless combinations, as in *Cinematic Bologna*. A georeferenced filmed architecture database also is the core of the Play the City RE app, which enables viewers to experience a nonlinear, user-defined sequence of clips. The contents are grouped into categories. The users can browse them as a tour or suggested paths across the urban space. They may explore themes, for example, the city as venue of the everyday life, with its family rituals, leisure and work, public events, sports, and educational activities. The database may be browsed by author, since the clips are selected from films made by forty-four different filmmakers; by chronology according to a timeline that goes from the 1940s to the 1980s; or by selecting specific points of interest (Figure 4).

Play the City RE is built on and presents itself primarily as a map. As such, the amateur city is embodied by many possible cartographic outputs. While, in general, amateur film is "topographical" when it moves across the urban

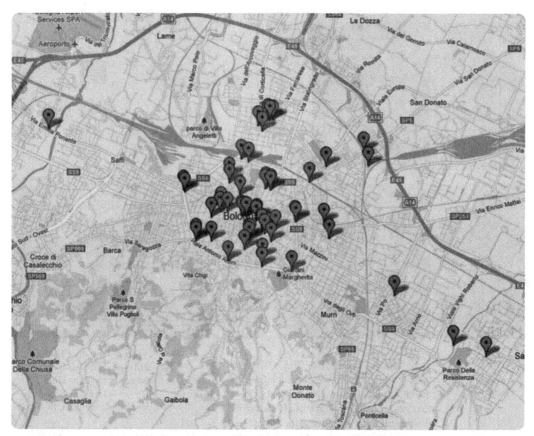

landscape by camera movements or traveling, say, by car, tram, or bicycle, when it describes and measures the space of the route between two places, the filmed topography becomes a metaphorical map (Figure 5). For Teresa Castro, a map is a function and not an object:

> Discussing the mapping impulse in film . . . is therefore not about the (albeit significant or symptomatic) presence of maps in the filmic landscape, but more about the processes that underlie the very conception of images. . . . It can be argued that the coupling of eye and instrument that distinguishes cartography's observa- tion of space is not so distant from the one that determines cinema's careful coding and scaling of the world.[18]

Accordingly, it is useful to consider cinema as a tool for mapping space.

Figure 5. Mapping impulse in amateur films: the case of 8mm *Bologna democratica* by Angelo Marzadori (1951) through its fifty-eight embodied viewpoints on the Google Maps cartographic basis.

For Play the City RE, I locate the images in one or more maps of the city, placing the clips at specific points. That way, every geotagged clip can be read as a locative medium.[19] A tool like Google Street View is essential to compare virtual representations of the same spaces in the amateur city. I used it in combination with old city guides and obsolete maps of tram and bus routes to retrace the physical and cinematic movements of filmmakers. As they depicted their urban spaces, I could follow along virtu- ally, identify places, and highlight the differ- ences between past and present landscapes, shot by shot, frame by frame.

The filmmakers' own stories and narratives, stimulated by their encounter with archival moving images emerged from the past, add a further dimension to the amateur city. The home movie, an open text, needs an integrated oral engagement to be completed and recontextualized. Then filmmakers and their families may contribute recordings of their memories and oral testimonies to create a "city of words." There are several ways in which the stories of actors and witnesses can create a direct relationship between words and images. Each clip in the Play the City RE app relates to a text. In some cases, it is a memory of the filmmakers or one of their relatives; in others, the texts are historical evidence, reflections or anecdotes on the changes in the urban landscapes, and quotations from books and old guides. Historians, writers, artists, musicians, and film editors are often invited to comment on and rework the archival images as a way to stimulate new writing.[20] Following one of the strategies of the Home Movies Archive since its beginning, when the clips are screened, there are live performances and ephemeral but meaningful moments that can be captured. Some of the installations that featured amateur film clips invited participants to associate oral memories with the images.[21] The amateur city archive through such interventions and reorchestrations transforms the archival material. Furthermore, they turn it into a narrative form. The app and the database enrich each visual fragment with texts that contextualize their historical, cultural, and mnemonic value, while altering the original journeys by rerouting them through remixed and/or random paths.

The ability to take advantage of film archives' roam around the amateur city suggests the figure of the *flâneur*. At times, the amateur filmmakers themselves had adopted this strategy of exploring urban spaces, filming according to their fleeting inspirations. Play the City RE turns the visitors of today into virtual flâneurs as they travel in space and time among images of a past that are still active in the present. Archival images play the role of visual testimonies. They also add emotional layering when they transform individual memories into shared experiences. In so doing, technological tools contribute to better understanding the

identity of a community and build an image that renders the past contemporary.

Paolo Simoni has a PhD in cultural heritage from Turin Polytechnic and is a founding member and director of the Italian Amateur Film Archive (Home Movies—Archivio Nazionale del Film di Famiglia, Bologna). As a research fellow currently at the University of Padua and formerly at the University of Modena and Reggio Emilia, he is engaged in projects of recovering and reworking archival film materials. As author, curator, and producer, he has completed a large number of audiovisual archive-based projects, among which are Miss Cinema—Archivio Mossina, Formato Ridotto, Expanded Archive, *Cinematic Bologna,* and Play the City Reggio Emilia.

NOTES

1. Still from *Play the Stories-Cinematic Bologna,* Parmeggiani (https://www.youtube.com /watch?v=Y91iG3NVp2E&t=141s) and Calanchi (https://youtu.be/5x5olHxHeAw).
2. http://www.cittadegliarchivi.it/soggetti -conservatori/it-cpa-sc-home-movies.
3. Five recontextualized film collections are accessible on the web portal of the Italian Ministry of Cultural Heritage and Tourism: http:// www.antenati.san.beniculturali.it/home movies.
4. Paolo Simoni, "Der öffentliche Raum des Archivs. Strategien und Praktiken der Aufwertung," in *Abenteuer Alltag: Zur Archäologie des Amateurfilms,* ed. Siegfried Mattl, Carina Lesky, Vrääth Öhner, and Ingo Zechner, 150–60 (Vienna: Austrian Film Museum, 2015).
5. Play the City RE (http://playthecity.home movies.it/index_en.html) is an app that allows users to explore the urban space through geolocated amateur film materials. It brings an invisible city, lost in distant memories, back to life through the eyes of its own inhabitants.
6. *Cinematic Bologna* (Urban Center-Biblioteca Salaborsa, Bologna) presents different installations for mapping the city as it was filmed by the amateurs. For an interesting interpretation of the exhibition, see Les Roberts, "The Archive City: Film as Critical Spatial Practice," in *Marxism and Urban Culture,* ed. Benjamin Fraser, 3–22 (Lanham, Md.: Lexington Books, 2014). For a virtual tour of the exhibition, visit https://

www.youtube.com/watch?v=83nSpvxrjzE.

7. François Penz and Andong Lu, "Introduction: What Is Urban Cinematics?," in *Urban Cinematics: Understanding Urban Phenomena through the Moving Image,* ed. François Penz and Andong Lu (Bristol, U.K.: Intellect, 2011), 12. From this point of view, the public use of archival amateur sources, mapped on cartographic and interactive platforms, can be opened to the public bodies (superintendencies, municipalities, etc.) directly involved in the preservation and enhancement of the territory and promotion of sustainable development.

8. Guidelines for the construction of the geodatabase imply specific descriptive and metadata tools designed to contextualize archive contents from historical, cultural, and geographic perspectives. Based on open-source software (DB engine and interface, distributed under the MIT license) and compatible with the main online archives systems around the world, specific attention is paid to sustainability and portability. The core of the BraDypUS database (http://bradypus.net/bdus-system) is built on a MySQL engine, providing a multilevel and multiuser collaborative archive structure managing a broad range of data types (audio-video multimedia files, images, texts, bibliographical resources such as PDF files, etc.). The administration and user interfaces are fully customizable and based on PHP language. It is possible to reciprocally link all the data in the various tables of the database, according to patterns of more or less complex user-defined relations. Individual records can thus be browsed in a fully contextual environment. See Julian Bogdani, "Un archivio digitale multidisciplinare per la gestione e la conservazione di un patrimonio culturale a rischio: il progetto Ghazni (Afghanistan)," *Archeologia e Calcolatori,* suppl. 8 (2016): 236–45.

9. Kevin Lynch, *The Image of the City* (Cambridge, Mass.: MIT Press, 1960).

10. As it was displayed also in the installations for the *Cinematic Bologna* exhibition, one of them was intended to edit and compare different shots of the most filmed locations, on a split screen to obtain a collective gaze as an assemble of individual gazes.

11. Views of the Asinelli Tower (*Cinematic Bologna* video installation): https://www.youtube.com/watch?v=ejcKlW-Cuw4.

12. Views of the uplands of San Luca (*Cinematic Bologna* video installation): https://www.youtube.com/watch?v=mgM_tw1SiB8.

13. Views of the Giardini Margherita (*Cinematic Bologna* video installation): the lake, https://www.youtube.com/watch?v=7hbl6y4bPGo, and the lions' cage, https://www.youtube.com/watch?v=dJtfeihy5Dg&t=9s.

14. Julia Hallam, "Civic Visions: Mapping the 'City' Film 1900–1960," *Culture, Theory, and Critique* 53, no. 1 (2012): 37–58, particularly 53.

15. Views of the Piazza Maggiore (*Cinematic Bologna* video installation): children and pigeons, https://www.youtube.com/watch?v=hJKJQwRhniE, and the Neptune Fountain, https://www.youtube.com/watch?v=vHaYthwfmhE.

16. "[T]he archive city refers to not just the city excavated from forms of archival imagery—the city 'in' the archive as it were—but the city itself *as* an archive, bearing traces of hidden or repressed spatial formations." Les Roberts, *Film, Mobility, and Urban Space: A Cinematic Geography of Liverpool* (Liverpool, U.K.: Liverpool University Press, 2012), 28.

17. Lev Manovich, *The Language of New Media* (Cambridge, Mass.: MIT Press, 2001).

18. Teresa Castro, "Cinema's Mapping Impulse: Questioning Visual Culture," *The Cartographic Journal* 46, no. 1 (2009): 9–15; Teresa Castro, "Mapping the City through Film: From 'Topophilia' to 'Urban Mapscapes,'" in *The City and the Moving Image,* ed. Richard Koeck and Les Roberts, 144–55 (Basingstoke, U.K.: Palgrave, 2010), 145.

19. An extended approach is to interpret the amateur film archive as a whole or an individual film collection as a conceptual map. In this article, however, I will not follow this interesting perspective, expressed, for example, in the Belgian artist Jasper Rigole's works (http://www.jasperrigole.com/).

20. See the project *Formato Ridotto* (2012), an episodic found footage film by five writers (http://www.formatoridotto.com/).

21. http://homemovies.it/.

Mapping the Traces of the Media Arts Center Movement

LINDSAY KISTLER MATTOCK

Allen and Gomery's seminal text *Film History: Theory and Practice* encouraged film scholars to move beyond the filmic object and consider the archives as an object of inquiry. The archives contain not only moving images encoded on film and video but also the traces of the activities of the makers, distributors, exhibitors, and audiences that are part of the ecology of media production and viewership.[1] The methodologies of new cinema history encourage the exploration of the archives, deemphasizing the focus on the film-as-text and opening new lines of historical inquiry. The distant reading practices of digital humanities open additional opportunities to explore the archival record and provide a deeper understanding of film and video production and consumption. Building from the archives of the Film Section of Pittsburgh's Carnegie Museum of Art, Mapping the Independent Media Community (MIMC)—an ongoing digital humanities project—builds from these practices to historicize the Media Arts Center Movement of the 1970s and its impact on independent film and video production, distribution, exhibition, and preservation throughout the 1970s and 1980s.

Histories of independent media production center on the efforts of artists, exploring each work of film or video as the personal product of an individual.[2] In reality, the growth of independent media production throughout the mid- to late twentieth century was supported by a network of organizations, including museums, archives, artist collectives and cooperatives, and equipment access centers designated as Media Arts Centers. MIMC uses the *Film and Video Makers Travel Sheet,* a monthly publication produced by the Film Section of the Carnegie Museum of Art from 1973 to 1987, as the starting point for the project. The *Travel Sheet* aimed to "encourage and facilitate wider use of exhibition and lecture tours by film and video makers" by advertising the scheduled screenings and tentative travel plans of film and video makers and publishing the contact information for organizations that were willing to host makers and screen independent media. The *Film and Video Makers Directory,* published as a supplement to the *Travel Sheet* in 1978 and 1979, provides additional data points, listing the organizations and makers highlighted in the subsequent issues of the *Travel Sheet* as well as other subscribers to the publication. MIMC uses the *Travel Sheet* and *Directory* to analyze the network of organizations and individuals supporting the production, distribution, exhibition, preservation, and study of independent film and video during the formative years of the Media Arts Center Movement.

Currently the first stage of development is entry of data from the *Travel Sheet* and *Directory* into a database application. Over the next year, the MIMC project team anticipates launching a web application that will allow researchers to query the MIMC database and generate visualizations of the data using network diagrams and mapping tools. This article outlines the development of the project over the last three years and its future direction as it aims to become a research tool for scholars and archivists concerned with independent media production in the United States and abroad.

MEDIA ARTS CENTERS AND THE TRAVEL SHEET

MIMC grew out of an interrogation of the history of the Media Arts Center Movement and an exploration of the role of Media Arts Centers in moving image preservation.[3] In 1973, Pacific Film Archive curator Sheldon Renan articulated a plan for the development of regional film centers pushing against the perceived faults of the American Film Institute's centralized structure. At that time, he argued, the Museum of Modern Art (MoMA) in New York City, the Library of Congress, and George Eastman House were the three main centers with exhibition and archives programs, leaving key regions in the United States without representation. Renan points to a "grassroots" movement originating in these underserved regions—the Pacific Northwest, the central states, New England, and the Bay Area—arguing for the establishment of a "network" of "full service film resource centers" with a central facility in each region that would

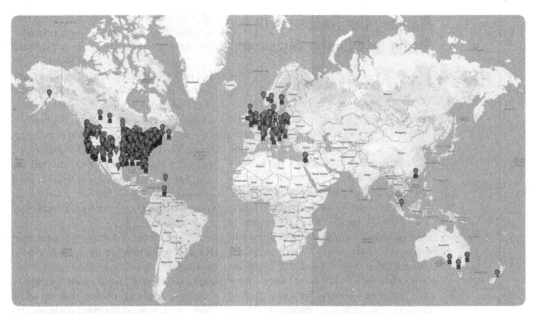

serve as an information center and provide key services for noncommercial media, including supporting research and study, facilitating preservation, coordinating exhibitions and screenings, and providing general assistance to artist and community groups.[4]

Founded in 1970, the Film Section of the Carnegie Institute Museum of Art (now known as Carnegie Museum of Art) served as one of two Media Arts Centers for Pittsburgh, Pennsylvania, and the Mid-Atlantic region. In his 2005 history, Anthology Film Archives's Robert Haller (and former director of Pittsburgh Film-Makers) credits the work of curator Sally Dixon and the Film Section, along with Pittsburgh Film-Makers (founded in 1971), with establishing Pittsburgh as the "third city" for the avant-garde during the 1970s, placing it alongside New York City and San Francisco.[5] Dixon and her successor, Bill Judson, shaped film culture in Pittsburgh, across the United States, and beyond, not only through their efforts to program screenings and lecture tours but also by establishing a standard for honoraria and compensation for visiting film and video makers.

Dixon and Judson's work also supported the efforts of the Media Arts Center Movement. The Film Section jointly hosted one of the Major Media Conferences with Pittsburgh Film-Makers in June 1978.[6] This series of meetings of regional Major Media Centers (a designator

Figure 1. Organizations (squares) and individuals (teardrops) from the 1979 *Film and Video Makers Directory.* **Map generated by the author using Google MyMaps.**

used by the National Endowment of the Arts [NEA] for regional Media Arts Centers) would lead to the establishment of the National Alliance of Media Arts Centers (NAMAC) in 1981.[7] In their efforts to continue to support this growing network of organizations, the Film Section began publishing the *Film and Video Makers Travel Sheet* in 1973. Funded by the NEA, the *Travel Sheet* served as a social networking tool for film and video makers, Media Arts Centers, and other organizations willing to support independent film and video. The editors made no attempt to curate the lists of artists and organizations highlighted in the monthly publication; anyone could contribute his or her information simply by filling out the attached form in each issue. Early iterations included contact information for artists and curators, scheduled events and screenings, and artists' travel itineraries (e.g., "visiting Chicago from March to April"). As the *Travel Sheet* grew, additional sections were added for new works and announcements of general interest (job postings, festivals, and advertisements for distributors and services). The Film Section also

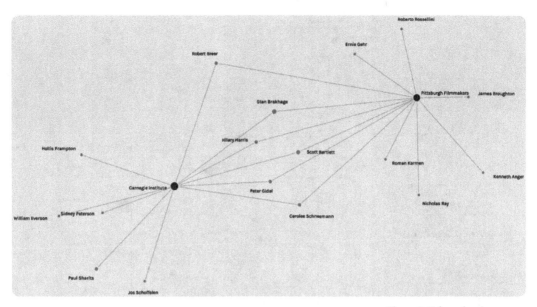

Figure 2. Selected artists presenting in Pittsburgh-based organizations from the *Film and Video Makers Travel Sheet*. Network map generated by the author using Palladio.

published several directories, synthesizing the contact information from the *Travel Sheet*. The supplement first appeared in September 1975. In this version, active artists are separated from institutions and listed by region (East, Midwest, South, West and Southwest, Canada, and overseas). The supplement was followed by the *Film and Video Makers Directory* in 1978 and 1979 and by the *Media Exhibitors' Directory for Independent Artists* (MEDIA) in 1986.

Together these publications generated by the Film Section represent artists and organizations from five continents, as the data from the 1979 *Directory* illustrate (Figure 1). The 1979 *Directory* includes an alphabetical list of the artists and organizations subscribing to and listed in the *Travel Sheet,* separated by country, with the United States further divided by state. Active artists are designated with an asterisk throughout the publication, creating a distinction between entries for those individuals in supporting roles (curators, librarians, and instructors) and the makers who may be interested in booking screenings and tours. The 1979 *Directory* provides additional data self-reported by several organizations regarding formats supported, average honoraria offered, and seating capacity for screening venues, providing an extended accounting of each organization.

MAPPING THE INDEPENDENT MEDIA COMMUNITY

The information contained within the *Travel Sheet* and *Directory* provides a rare opportunity to peer into the network supporting independent media production during the formative decades of the Media Arts Center Movement and the proliferation of independent filmmaking more generally. As a self-contributed publication, there were no criteria for being listed in the *Travel Sheet*—artists now part of the avant-garde canon appear next to film and video makers who are virtually unknown. Similarly, it enumerates influential archives and museums, such as MoMA, alongside community access centers, public libraries, and artist collectives.

This first phase of the MIMC project has focused on building a database of the artists, organizations, individuals, events, and works represented within the *Travel Sheet*. In database form, these data can be queried, analyzed, and visualized to provide a snapshot of the emerging network of support for media

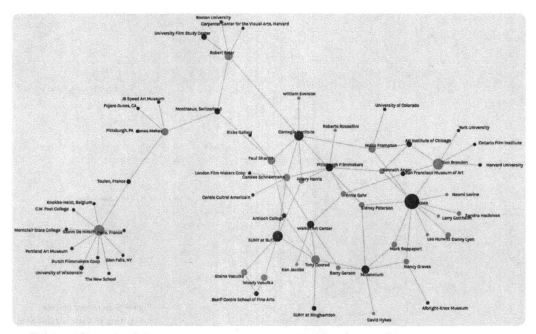

Figure 3. Selected travel data of New York–based artists from the *Film and Video Makers Travel Sheet*. Network map generated by the author using Palladio.

artists during the 1970s and 1980s, including the development of Media Arts Centers across the nation. The database affords opportunities to begin to draw connections between the individual makers and where they were presenting their work over time. Looking at just a small sample of the data from artists presenting in Pittsburgh demonstrates the overlap in artists presenting at the Carnegie Institute and Pittsburgh Film-Makers (Figure 2). In this example, the collaboration between the two organizations is illustrated by the corresponding events centered around individual artists. Looking at selected data from New York–based artists, a different network emerges, extending across the United States from the Carnegie Institute to the West Coast, with San Francisco Museum of Modern Art, north to the Canadian border, with the Ontario Film Institute, and across the Atlantic to the Dutch Filmmakers Coop (Figure 3). These small samples from the *Film and Video Makers Travel Sheet* demonstrate the data's potential to begin visualizing the influence of Media Arts Centers across the United States and abroad. In these examples, the size of the nodes in the diagrams reflects the number of events hosted by specific organizations. This dimension allows us to identify the artists and organizations appearing most frequently in

the *Travel Sheet*. Furthermore, these counts suggest the influence of individual artists or organizations over time and the strength of the ties between individuals and organizations. This dimension of analysis also demonstrates the potential to identify centers of distribution and production outside of the historically celebrated centers, perhaps supporting Robert Haller's arguments about the influence of Pittsburgh and illustrating other locations where film culture had been thriving during these decades. When complete, the MIMC database will hold thousands of data points illustrating the global network of organizations and filmmakers interconnected through the events that each organization hosted featuring the film or video work of artists over time.

Mapping these data geographically allows for analyzing patterns of travel for film and video makers within the United States and abroad. While most of the data reported to the *Travel Sheet* pertain to North America, the publication does include data from across

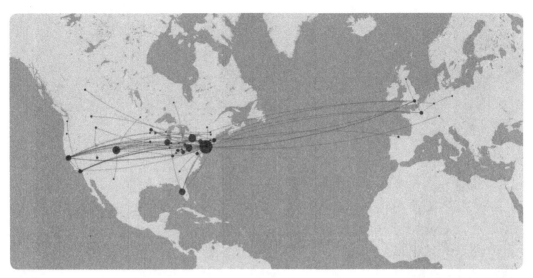

Figure 4. Selected data from the *Film and Video Makers Travel Sheet* representing artists' travels for film and video screenings and events. Map generated by the author using Palladio.

the globe. Not surprisingly, the strongest links demonstrated are between the United States and Europe (Figure 4). In August 1977, the *Travel Sheet* began a collaboration with *Filmmakers Europe*, a similar publication edited by filmmaker William Raban. This open exchange of information about travel dates and newly available works, along with the already established cultural exchanges of cinema across the Atlantic, suggests that the data would demonstrate the strongest international connections between the two continents. Figure 4 shows a small sample of data from artists listed in the *Travel Sheet* between 1978 and 1982. We can see the strongest links between artists and organizations in the United States, Western Europe, and Canada.

While the data may be skewed toward events in North America and Europe, University of Iowa doctoral students Anu Thapa and Chang-Min Yu examined the international network emerging in the 1978 and 1979 *Travel Sheet* as part of a course project. Their findings demonstrate that the data have wider representation than initially thought. Their analysis focused specifically on the international artists appearing in the issues of the *Travel Sheet* and the two *Directory* volumes published during this twenty-four-month period. Mapping the current contact information for artists, along with the reported tour dates from the *Travel Sheet*, Thapa and Yu added one additional data point for each artist: her country of origin. The

resulting geographic visualization of the network demonstrates that the data may represent a broader network when these additional data are added to the database. In Figure 5, the artist's country of origin is represented in purple, while the blue circles represent the organizations where events were scheduled. The size of the nodes represents the number of times that an artist or organization appears in this data sample. While the strongest ties are between the United States and Europe, representing the most frequent exchange of film and video, by mapping the artist's home country, a broader picture of cultural exchange emerges, with representation in South America and Asia. Figure 6 represents an alternative visualization of this same data set in a network map. Here the network is between international artists (in light gray) and organization (dark gray). As with the other visualizations, the size of the node represents the number of events scheduled by a specific artist or at a particular organization. Here we can see that MoMA emerges as one of the predominate nodes, representing the largest number of events scheduled with the greatest diversity of artists. This is

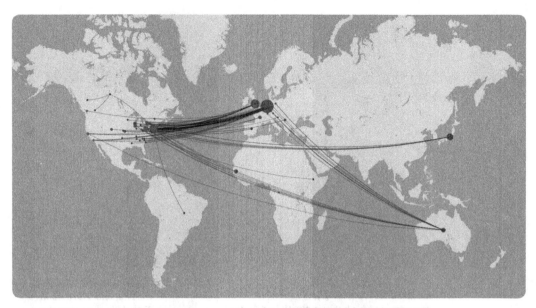

Figure 5. Selected travel of
international artists, 1978–79.
Artists' countries of origin
are shown in blue; travel
destinations are in orange.
Map generated by the author
using Palladio.

unsurprising, given the influence of the museum in the collection and exhibition of moving image media. However, what is interesting is the breadth of other organizations represented in this chart. Public libraries, universities and colleges, artists' collectives, and museums from across the United States and Europe are entangled in this network, demonstrating the potential of these data to illustrate the scope of film and video culture across the United States in known centers of activity, such as New York and San Francisco, as well as areas across the Midwest and southern United States.

It is important to note here that the connections between artists in these network diagrams are not absolutes; rather, they merely indicate common venues. Some relationships between artists, nevertheless, can be inferred from the data through the contact information listed in the *Travel Sheet*. For instance, artists who provided the same contact address—the Chelsea Hotel in New York appears quite frequently in the *Travel Sheet*—imply a personal connection, more than a simple commonality in travel plans. Common event dates, such as those for the Athens International Film Festival in Athens, Ohio, indicate the potentiality for artists to interact at such venues. This is a limitation to the concept of the network. A network presumes endings, nodes, true paths and con-

nections, or ties between static points. But the nodes representing individuals, organizations, and events in the MIMC database are better understood as intersections—where people, places, and materials cross paths over time, but perhaps at different moments in history.

Just as the functions of media production, exhibition, distribution, preservation, and study are entangled, these nodes in the network map represent places of potential investigation as sites supporting the development of film culture. Bounded by time, the *Travel Sheet* provides a limited perspective to the data. As the project builds, though, it will be augmented by information from other published directories, screening schedules and programs, funding data from the NEA and other granting organizations, distribution catalogs, and demographic information such as population density. This additional evidence will support a broader analysis of the data to verify and further contextualize the *Travel Sheet*.

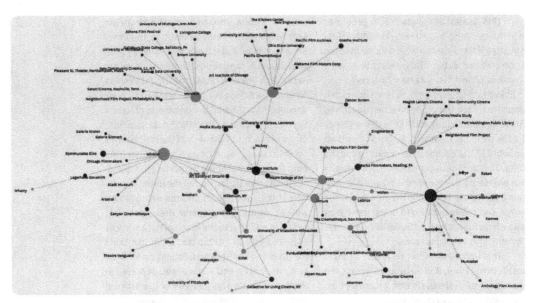

MAPPING THE ARCHIVES

Wendy Duff and Jessica Haskell have explored Deleuze and Guattari's concept of the *rhizome* as a metaphor for generating more open models of the archival finding aid.[8] Pushing against the hierarchical structure of traditional models of archival description, the authors argue for an "open, nonhierarchical, and acentric" engagement with archival materials. MIMC respects these values, providing multiple entry points into the database. Organizations are not privileged over artists, and vice versa. The database affords opportunities to query on an artist, organization, event, film or video work, geographic location, date, or data source. The database's nonhierarchical structure allows users to build different narratives from multiple perspectives.

Deleuze and Guattari further argue that the rhizome is *"a map and not a tracing."*[9] Maps too have multiple entryways and represent multiple narratives. They may be described as performances, whereas traces "always come back 'to the same.'"[10] MIMC, in this sense, is an attempt not to trace historical networks but to generate performances of the data. The static images in this article represent a singular point of view, a tracing of the data. The full MIMC web application will use D3 JavaScript visualizations to visualize dynamically the database, with each query providing a new visualization of the data. Furthermore, although the project in its current state is artificially bounded by the limitations of the *Travel Sheet*, MIMC will eventually include data from other primary and secondary source materials. Historical directories, such as the *Directory of Archival Collections on the History of Film in the United States* and the *Directory of Film Libraries in North America,* provide insight into the archives and libraries providing access to media collections, including organizations represented throughout the *Travel Sheet.*[11] Additional directories generated for media artists, such as the *Citizens Media Directory, 16mm Distribution,* and the *AIVF Guide to Film & Video Distributors,* will also further contextualize the organizations and individuals highlighted in the *Travel Sheet,* representing sites of production and distribution.[12] Archival resources, such as program notes, artist files, correspondence, and moving image material, will also be enfolded into MIMC, further contextualizing the initial data set provided by the *Travel Sheet.*

This rhizomatic approach also generates a performance of the archives. The MIMC data structure links each individual data point to the source of that datum. This means that every instance of an artist's name in a *Travel Sheet* is linked to the corresponding issue in which it appeared. Each *Travel Sheet* is then described in the database along with the archival source for the material. Each archival repository then appears in the database as a source for the data. This approach provides an opportunity not only to explore the exhibition and distribution patterns emerging from the data during the 1970s and 1980s but also to understand how and where the history of the Media Arts Center Movement is being preserved.

This history does not reside in a single institution; rather, it is distributed across the memories of individuals and records of organizations, many represented in the *Travel Sheet*. Some records reside in collections of recognized archives, such as MoMA and the Carnegie Museum of Art, while other materials may still be held by Media Arts Centers, at distribution sites, or in private collections. MIMC therefore not only serves as a finding aid, linking known archival collections to the data, but also illustrates gaps in the archival record and identifies potential sites where those records may be held, where this history may yet be uncovered.

Documentation strategy was originally proposed in the 1980s as a collaborative appraisal methodology, in which multiple archival institutions identify an area that is underrepresented across the collections. The collaborating archives then develop a plan to collect actively records that would fill the gaps across the institutional collections. Criticized for the breadth of resources that it would take to implement such an approach, this strategy only proved successful in a few experimental projects.[13] While MIMC does not aim to build an archives of materials, identifying sites of activity during the Media Arts Center Movement serves the dual purpose of tracing possible leads to collections already accessioned into archives and suggesting other sites where records may be located outside of recognized repositories.

The distribution of the *Travel Sheet* illus-trates this point. Though originating from the Film Section of the Carnegie Institute, the *Travel Sheet* has been collectively preserved by individuals and organizations. Copies of issues are in the archives of NAMAC, the digital Vasulka Archive maintained by artists Steina and Woody Valsuka,[14] MoMA, and the University of Iowa's Special Collections. The MIMC data structure offers the ability to list each of the repositories holding copies of the *Travel Sheet,* illustrating both the active networks supporting independent media production during the initial circulation of the *Travel Sheet* and the archival networks continuing to preserve these materials today. In addition to the archival data sources enfolded into the database, MIMC contains the titles and distribution information for films and videos screened at the events reported in the *Travel Sheet*. This analysis of the archival networks will extend to these titles as well, listing the institutions that have preserved these works over time. In this way, MIMC holds the potential to map both the distribution and preservation networks emerging over time, while further identifying titles and artists that have not been preserved, suggesting further areas of potential collecting for archival institutions and areas of interrogation for historians.

NEXT STEPS

MIMC builds on the legacy of attempts to acknowledge formally the sites where independent, avant-garde, and other orphaned media are preserved. Rick Prelinger's *Footage 89* and *91* and *Field Guide to Sponsored Films* represent other efforts to acknowledge formally the various organizations responsible for collecting, maintaining, and preserving media heritage.[15] These publications bring light to the multitude of archival and nonarchival sites of collection and preservation. Highlighted among these pages are many of the organizations recognized as Media Arts Centers and represented in the pages of the *Travel Sheet*. Unlike MIMC, these resources are static; they are traces rather than maps. But, by representing these data in MIMC, these records are enfolded and entangled in the history of moving image production and preservation, by naming and mapping the many potential sites where collections may continue to be housed or where materials once existed.

MIMC maps the network of artists and organizations that shaped the independent media arts and the records and other traces they left behind. The archival potential of MIMC lies in this enfolding of the archives into the database. Traditional archives are not maps but traces—records bound in the hierarchical structure of the archives and in the order imposed on the collections held within such organizations. MIMC alternatively places these records and traces in conversation with the actors involved: the records creators, the film and video works, the artists, the organizations and institutions, the audiences and local communities, the Media Arts Center Movement, and the independent filmmaker, along with the larger forces at play.

While the project has the potential to impact film history and film studies by providing a comprehensive application that affords opportunities to query and visualize data, MIMC also holds potential for archives. It could be a model for uniting the distributed archives of materials that are disbursed across collections in known institutions. But the project also holds the ability to enfold documentation held within alternative sites of preservation, including community archives and Media Arts Centers.

The archive is always distributed—the moving image archive even more so. With multiple copies and generations of work scattered in collections across the globe, no single archive can hope to contextualize fully the moving image media and records in its collections. MIMC does not aim to institutionalize this history in the archives proper but rather to understand and illustrate the entanglement of the archives and the various other actors—historically and at present. The names, tour dates, and organizations listed in the *Travel Sheet* provide an information resource that illustrates the complexity of the documentary universe surrounding the production of independent and noncommercial media. Much like the *Travel Sheet,* MIMC seeks to be nondiscriminatory; as the project develops, it will incorporate additional records from primary and secondary sources, such as NEA funding data, film pro-

grams, flyers, distribution catalogs, personal papers, and archival records of all kinds. Even a single name or title in the MIMC database could be a potential starting point for exploring this meshwork.

Prelinger's *Field Guide* and *Footage* projects illustrate the myriad sites of audiovisual collection and preservation that contribute to the full ecology of the archival landscape. However, these directories, surveys, guides, catalogs, and the like are all tracings. They are static representations that, when enfolded into the MIMC database, become a map. Like Prelinger's projects, MIMC embraces nontraditional archives, bringing together the collections held by film libraries, Media Arts Centers, distributors, and private collections to unite the sundry repositories that may hold the records not only of established filmmakers in the canon but also of all the media makers whose archives are distributed across the globe. MIMC seeks to map this meshwork and chart the entanglements between artists, distributors, museums, governmental bodies, local communities, and countless other threads in the fabric of the independent media arts.

Lindsay Kistler Mattock is assistant professor of library and information science at the University of Iowa, where she teaches courses in the digital humanities, archives, and digital preservation.

NOTES

1. Robert C. Allen and Douglas Gomery, *Film History: Theory and Practice* (New York: Knopf, 1985).
2. See P. Adams Sitney, *Visionary Film: The American Avant-Garde, 1943–2000,* 3rd ed. (New York: Oxford University Press, 2002); Paul Arthur, *A Line of Sight: American Avant-Garde Film since 1965* (Minneapolis: University of Minnesota Press, 2005); Wheeler Winston Dixon and Gwendolyn Audrey Foster, eds., *Experimental Cinema: The Film Reader* (New York: Routledge, 2002); Erik Barnouw, *Documentary: A History of Non-fiction Film,* 2nd rev. ed. (New York: Oxford University Press, 1993); Chris Meigh-Andrews, *Video Art: The Development of Form and Function* (New York: Berg, 2006); and Kate Horsfield and Lucas Hilderbrand, eds.,

Feedback: The Video Data Bank Catalog of Video Art and Artist Interviews (Philadelphia: Temple University Press, 2006).

3. See Lindsay Kistler Mattock, "Media Arts Centers as Alternative Archival Spaces: Investigating the Development of Archival Practices in Non-profit Media Organizations," PhD thesis, University of Pittsburgh, 2014.

4. Sheldon Renan, "The Concept of Regional Film Centers," *Sightlines* 7, no. 3 (1973–74): 7. See also J. Ronald Green, "Film and Video: An Institutional Paradigm and Some Issues of National Policy," *Journal of Cultural Economics* 8, no. 1 (1984): 61–79, and J. Ronald Green, "Film and Not-for-Profit Media Institutions," in *Film/ Culture: Explorations of Cinema in Its Social Context*, ed. Sari Thomas, 37–59 (Metuchen, N.J.: Scarecrow Press, 1982).

5. Robert A. Haller, *Crossroads: Avant-Garde Film in Pittsburgh in the 1970s* (New York: Anthology Film Archives, 2005).

6. Peter Feinstein, ed., *The Independent Film Community: A Report on the Status of Independent Film in the United States* (New York: Committee on Film and Television Resources and Services, 1972).

7. NAMAC continues to support independent media production, now as the National Alliance of Media Arts and Culture.

8. Wendy M. Duff and Jessica Haskell, "New Uses for Old Records: A Rhizomatic Approach to Archival Access," *American Archivist* 78, no. 1 (2015): 38–58.

9. Gilles Deleuze and Félix Guattari, *A Thousand Plateaus: Capitalism and Schizophrenia* (Minneapolis: University of Minnesota Press, 1987), 12.

10. Ibid., 12–13.

11. Film Library Council, *Directory of Film Libraries in North America* (New York: Film Library Council, 1971); Richard A. Matzek, *Directory of Archival Collections on the History of Film in the United States* (Chicago: Association of College and Research Libraries, 1983).

12. National Citizens Committee for Broadcasting, *Citizens Media Directory* (Chicago: NCCB, 1977); Judith Trojan and Nadine Covert, *16mm Distribution* (New York: Educational Film Library Association, 1977); Kathryn Bowser, *The AIVF Guide to Film and Video Distribution* (New York: FIVF, 1996).

13. Doris J. Malkmus, "Documentation Strategy: Mastodon or Retro-Success?," *American Archivist* 71 (Fall/Winter 2008): 384–409.

14. http://www.vasulka.org/.

15. Richard Prelinger and Celeste R. Hoffnar, eds., *Footage 89: North American Film and Video Sources* (New York: Prelinger Associates, 1989); Richard Prelinger, Cyndy Turnage, and Peter Kors, eds., *Footage 91: North American Film and Video Sources* (New York: Prelinger Associates, 1991); Rick Prelinger, *The Field Guide to Sponsored Films* (San Francisco: National Film Preservation Foundation, 2006).

The Short Film Pool Project: Saving Short Films from Oblivion in the Digital Era

SIMONA MONIZZA

The Short Film Pool[1] is a large-scale digitization and access project initiated in 2013 at the EYE Filmmuseum in Amsterdam. The project is aimed at improving the visibility of short films in the digital age, and as such, it can be an inspiration for others who are pursuing new and fruitful ways to promote collections, specifically short films that do not automatically fall under the standard preservation or presentation policies of archives.

While the project embraces short films without distinction of genre or period, my focus will be on Dutch experimental and artists' short films from the 1970s until recent times. Our archive has developed an active acquisition, preservation, and presentation policy for them, a process accelerated since 2010 as different institutions combined to form the EYE Filmmuseum.

The starting point of the Short Film Pool project was a relatively young distribution collection, assembled in 2003, thanks to the efforts of one of the organizations that merged into EYE in 2010, Filmbank. Its core business was promoting and distributing historical and contemporary Dutch short experimental films by means of curated touring programs, publications, and exhibitions at festivals in Holland and abroad. The organization did a great job of guaranteeing that the life span of the contemporary selected shorts went beyond the normal festival season of just one or two years. Considering that independent short films generally fall out of the main distribution channels, without active promotion, they would fall out of circulation altogether.

When Filmbank merged with EYE, its collection consisted of more than three hundred titles. Most of these were shot on 16mm, but there was also Super 8mm and occasionally 35mm. The collection also encompasses works on video formats like mini DV and Beta SP. The films showcase a variety of styles, genres, do-it-yourself practices, and artistic approaches to filmmaking from young and old practitioners alike. The canon of Dutch experimental cinema—Barbara Meter, Frans Zwartjes, and Paul de Nooijer, among others—is well represented, together with works by contemporary artists, such as Johan Rijpma and Joost Rekveld. The collection is a fine example of how creativity can often flourish under restrictive boundaries like low budgets, limited time, and affordable media types. It is striking that only ten years after this collection was founded, some of the formats used by the filmmakers—not only 16mm but also Beta SP—have become problematic in terms of preservation and access.

Although cinema production was already well on its way to a transition to digital prior to 2012, that year was the tipping point. That was the year that, in the Netherlands, full digitization of cinema distribution was accomplished, financed by the Cinema Digital Project, an initiative of the Dutch Cinema Exhibitors' Association, the Dutch Film Distributors' Association, and EYE.[2] The cinemas' conversion to Digital Cinema Package (DCP) format went hand in hand with the disappearance of almost all analog projectors from the booths. While it is still possible to find a few operating 35mm projectors in some specific cinemas that specialize in art house screenings, it is quite rare, if not impossible, to find well-working 16mm projectors, let alone the projectionists with the knowledge to operate them according to proper archival standards.

One of the direct consequences of this transition to digital was that, all of a sudden, the Filmbank distribution collection of short films, among others, became obsolete. Cinemas equipped only with the new DCP standard could not project them. This resulted in decreased screening requests and, thus, decreased visibility. Considering all the efforts that were necessary to put such a collection together in the first place, to guarantee its circulation in the cinemas, this was a negative turn.

BUSINESS TO BUSINESS

Some of the same people behind Filmbank who are now part of EYE initiated the Short Film Pool project as a response to digital exhibition. The project was born out of an idealistic desire to give short films a second chance in the cinemas of the digital era by embracing the potentials of the new technology. This meant that the films had to be remastered to DCP. That's the point where archival and business practices met—and clashed—and where the challenges of this project arise.

While operating within the boundaries of a film heritage institute, and thus benefitting from its infrastructure and knowledge bases, this project has been devised primarily as a business-to-business model with EYE acting not so much as an archive than as a distributor. The main clients are cinemas in the Netherlands. This initiative, then, is distinct in its nature and scope from typical archival practices of film heritage dissemination. Previously, digitized collections have been published online for academic, artistic, or educational purposes. Such platforms include Open Images,[3] the EYE website, and European Film Gateway,[4] among others.

Other than the aforementioned examples, the Short Film Pool relies on a self-sustaining economical model based upon a yearly subscription fee paid by the cinemas. The revenue is shared equally between the rights holders and EYE. Presently there are approximately twenty-seven active subscribers to this pool. The money EYE makes from the subscription fees helps sustain the costs of digitizing new titles for the pool. The initial costs of setting up the pool and its infrastructure have been covered by external funding, including crucial sponsorship from key partners in the digital field. Among these are Haghefilm Digitaal, the lab that sponsored and mastered the DCPs, and Gofilex, the film transport company that set up the infrastructure to store, deliver, and track the DCPs made for the pool.

The starting goal of this project was the conversion of approximately three hundred short experimental, animation, documentary, and drama films to DCP. From the existing Filmbank/EYE distribution collection, the curatorial team selected as a starting corpus the best 150 titles. The rest of the titles came from outside our collection and were selected from independent producers, TV productions, film academies, and festivals. The idea was to have a collection that offers a variety of short films. The aim is to update this pool with new titles

every year, balancing between films from the archive and more contemporary titles.

The advantages for the pool's subscribers include unlimited access to the supply of short films, which changes every year, with an easy and safe way to order films through the purpose-built website organized by keyword, genre, director, and language. The subscription fee includes exhibition rights and transportation costs. Once they have subscribed, the cinemas can browse the catalog online, preview titles via a secure Vimeo page, and directly order films for their cinemas. They also can choose ready-made programs compiled by our educational or curatorial team for special occasions or for the classroom. One example is the compilation program dedicated to director and editor Johan van der Keuken that the Short Film Pool made available soon after the exhibition on his work at EYE.

Since the official project launch in 2014, there has been an unexpected development in the use of the website and the online catalog. The user-friendly design and easy navigation are attracting users beyond the originally intended market of film bookers. Programmers and curators, as well, who are passionate and curious about short films, are using it. Whether these new users' viewings will lead to actual extra screenings of the titles in the cinemas remains to be seen. Certainly the online presence is enabling a wider audience to get acquainted with a variety of short films that are otherwise hard to see. The collaboration with the Short Circuit Network[5]—the European Network of Short Film and Video Art Distributors—is contributing as well to the cause, with its mission of circulating short films outside of national borders.

It is obvious that the Short Film Pool website, despite never having had a public function, is responding to a need to access online collections. Unfortunately, the site has some limitations. There is not enough technical or contextual information for the works. It would be useful to know if the films have been preserved, how they were scanned, or from which collection they came from. From the distributors' point of view, perhaps providing these data to users is irrelevant. And while this might be true for contemporary works where a plot description and a photo are enough to

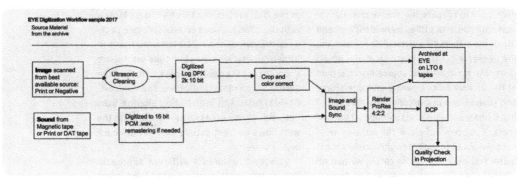

EYE Digitization Workflow sample 2017
Source Material
from the archive

Figure 1. Overview of current digitization workflow.

attract the film bookers, it could have a negative impact on the perception and valuation of the historical titles in the catalog. Additional contextual information could narrow the divide between historical films and contemporary audiences. Currently some improvements have been made to the website, and the original format of the film has been added.

METHODOLOGY: CHOOSING THE RIGHT SOURCE MATERIAL FOR SCANNING

A project like this would not have been possible without the equipment and know-how already available at EYE. We had been using our on-site scanner for preservation and access purposes, but this was the first time that our digitization technology would be used to remaster films to DCPs for cinemas. To meet the cinema standards, a new workflow[6] was required (Figure 1). Among the new parameters were time, budget, copyright clearance, and the number of films we wanted to have available in the pool before its official launch in 2014. We hadn't fully realized how complex the whole process would be. We underestimated, for instance, the technical and logistical challenges we would encounter as we coordinated and managed the selection, digitization, DCP production, and distribution of three hundred films coming from our collection and from outside. The tight schedule forced us to digitize approximately thirty films per month. This basically meant shifting priorities in our scanning calendar to accommodate the project. Because of limited digital storage space, the films were scanned at 2K, then downsized to high definition. Every single DCP produced by the lab was checked for quality control in our cinemas. When it be-

came clear that there were too many errors, we decided to prolong the project by one more year, thus making more time for research and development.

Considering the ambitious plan to produce three hundred distribution DCPs within two years, the decision was made at the beginning to scan only preservation or projection prints instead of going back to the camera originals. Our digital preservation or restoration workflow entails scanning negatives or original reversals. However, the postproduction work necessary to create a projectable digital copy out of this scanned output is much more time consuming and expensive than scanning projection prints. The films must be timed (graded) shot by shot and be digitally restored where necessary. The Short Film Pool project's workflow policy necessitated choosing source material that typically was one or two generations away from the original.

Of course, scanning the originals would have resulted in higher image quality, with care given to timing, repairing damage, stabilizing, and restoring the sound track. Following this path for the pool digitizing films would have taken several years and a massively augmented budget. Besides, the aim of the project was not to undertake full digital restorations but to create good digital copies—"remasters"—of the distribution collection for public screening. The challenge lay in achieving a satisfying quality level while working within the existing limitations.

One of the major difficulties the project encountered was the amount of time and work necessary to prepare the source material for scanning. Once the titles were identified and the rights owners had given their permission, the quest for the best source material would start. We chose the best source material held at the archive by comparing multiple image and sound elements. In some cases, we would use intermediate (master) elements if we had them. If the copies held at the archives were poor, we would contact the rights holders to get better material. In extreme cases, we had no choice but to accept a poorer quality element for scanning or to substitute another title for the project.

The digitization process is very complex, and many hours are spent before and after the film is actually scanned. After selecting the right source material, it must be cleaned and repaired. Then the metadata must be created, managed, and stored, and the files must be migrated. This is the main reason why such large-scale digitization processes are usually externally sponsored rather than implemented by the archives as part of their normal practice, which is still based on an "on-demand" model.[7]

Will the compromises made on choosing a poorer source material cause a backlash in a few years? For example, the rapidly evolving 4K technology is becoming the norm for digitization. Only four years since the start of the project, producers of films in the Short Film Pool are requesting remastered 4K scans from the negatives. The risks of a policy that creates different-quality versions include filling up scarce and expensive digital storage and wasting human resources when an archive has to redo work on titles already in distribution. These are only a couple of the daunting issues to face in the near future.

THE IMPACT OF THE SHORT FILM POOL ON OUR DIGITIZATION WORKFLOW

Even before the Short Film Pool project began, we realized that we would have to deal with the problems of preserving and maintaining uniformity of color and sound. The initial results of our digitization workflow did not achieve the desired goals. There were substantial differences between the look of the files we had approved at our end and how they appeared

in the DCP projection. This had to do largely with the different color control software packages that we and the DCP lab were using. It turned out that we had to fine-tune color space encodings of the delivered files, adjusting the settings for color, saturation, and contrast. Several tests and information sharing from both sides were necessary to synchronize the workflows and get satisfactory results back on the screen.

Sound required a different approach. Prior to starting this project, sound and image were scanned simultaneously from the same print sources. We encountered numerous complications during this stage that originated with the great variety of original sound sources we were using—magnetic masters, original optical and mag files, optical sound tracks copied from prints. There were great differences in quality, speed, and type of mix. The chore was complicated by the fact that the master materials were spread between the archive, the labs, and the filmmakers. We aimed to create a digital sound mix equivalent to the original analog sound. So we went back to the original mix and let the lab remaster the produced sound files to adjust such things as noise level, channel number, and balance. Any mistakes at this stage would alter the way the film was originally intended to be heard.

This project inadvertently proved to be a good learning experience for determining the possibilities and limitations of our digitization workflow when working with different original formats. In fact, there have been many positive consequences. The procedures we innovated for the Short Film Pool project have prompted us to revise and improve our daily digitization workflow. We schedule more time for better color correction and handling of sound. Nowadays, we rarely scan from prints and instead try to go back to the best source material: either the camera original or an intermediate. Thanks to the upgrade of our digital server, we no longer downsize the scanner files to high definition but store them in 2K resolution. We've started implementing 4K scanning, albeit sporadically. Similarly, sound is always processed separately before it is rematched with the image. EYE has recently invested in professional equipment that will permanently change the digital workflow and soon will allow us to digitize sound and perform color timing in-house.

ETHICAL ISSUES

The ethical issues encountered in this project grew out of concerns over the way image and sound were transformed during digitization and over settling on levels of tolerance that we would accept. In the case of experimental and artist-made films, more than other genres, changing the original screening format affects the ways the films are perceived, understood, and appreciated. This becomes even more crucial with those filmmakers who chose the film medium specifically for its inherent aesthetic and technical properties and who expose or manipulate them in their works.

Every source material, whether Super 8mm, 16mm, or 35mm, has its characteristic grain, color, contrast, and density, which digitizing translates differently. Reformatting always results in something different from the analog original. At worst is a loss of picture quality and detail; at best is a different look or experience. I usually compare this translation to applying a magnifying glass to the source material and seeing every detail enhanced, sometimes to an unwanted extreme, as when unnoticed grain becomes visual noise.

In general, learning to recognize what happens during digital remastering is essential in spotting potential prescanning problems. High contrast in original reversals is one of them. Accepting or rejecting the lessons learned from digital translation can depend on a lot of factors, including the value of the experience gained during the process. Our tendency was to be extra strict when dealing with abstract films where the presence of visual noise would visibly alter the perception of the films, as in the case of *Horizontalen* (*Horizontals*, Bart Vegter, 1981). Here the subtle shifting of gray lines turning slowly to black, which constitutes the core of the original 16mm film experience, was disturbed by the artificial movement of grain scanning added to the picture. We took these issues seriously and decided not to include this film in the project.

Accepting the new look of the digital copy derives from the degree of manipulation one tolerates during the process. There is always the temptation, for example, to improve the image in postproduction by applying common image stabilization and dirt removal tools. Yet such intervention could alter the original look of the film. Showing their films on DCP might be a far cry from the original filmmakers' intentions, but most of them already had collaborated with us during the analog restoration of their films. They were well aware that if they didn't embrace the new digital technique, their films were at risk of being forgotten. As such, the project, even with its limitations, opened windows of possibilities that they couldn't refuse.

In terms of access, the benefits of the Short Film Pool project have become evident. Every title we scanned for the pool is part of our digital infrastructure in a collection that EYE stores and now makes available to its users. This means that approximately 150 extra titles from our experimental film collection are now easily viewed and researched online, either at our premises or through access links provided by EYE's curatorial team. The advantages are obvious when access is no longer restricted to the boundaries of the physical archive.

Personally, this is where the double nature of this project becomes clear to me. While it helps solve a visibility problem the short films had, which had been caused by the too-fast and little-thought-out transition to the digital era in the cinemas, the Short Film Pool also feeds the hunger for digital copies without making the case to clients and other users for the importance and unique nature of the analog originals in terms of preservation and of their access. As our senior curator, Mark-Paul Meyer, explains, "the physical archives hold some hundred years of film history enclosed in a large variety of material objects. And many 'stories' that these artifacts contain, may never be 'translated' unto the new formats."[8]

The digital version in common practice has become the analog's surrogate as the chances to show or be exposed to the original version are drastically disappearing. This may be one of the losses created by the digital revolution: the promise of seemingly limitless access does not necessarily preserve what gets lost in translation when collections are transferred from one format to the other. While historical film collections have become more ubiquitous than ever in the digital era, the encounter with the material and technical properties of films is disappearing from the gaze of future generations of film lovers. This loss will influence the way film collections will be studied, researched, and used. It will affect the role of the archive as custodian of such collections.[9]

Archives should engage regularly with new generations of film researchers, students, and practitioners by providing training programs in the research and reuse of both the digital and analog archive. Nonvirtual encounters with the collection—such as film-handling workshops, internships, film lectures, and residencies for artists and researchers—are indeed a welcome antidote to the general tendency of transforming a film heritage into just "images" for the sake of access, detached from their materiality.

WHAT LIES AHEAD

Within the framework in which we operated, we can say that the Short Films Pool project achieved its main goal of bringing short films to wider audiences. Several cinemas throughout the country have been inspired by this initiative and subscribed, thus contributing to the cause of keeping short films visible.

If we focus on the business clients of this project, the exhibitors, then it is also interesting to observe that EYE itself has become a heavy user of the Short Film Pool catalog. There is renewed interest in short films within its premises. Animation films especially are booked several times during the year by the educational department for their own classroom programs or workshops activities. The short films are also used by the programming department to be screened before the new releases in our cinemas, in children's programs, and during museum events.

Users recently responded to a questionnaire. It has mapped the way the short films are used and indicates what challenges lie ahead. One of the limiting issues turns out to be the length of the films. Ninety-eight percent of the cinemas show the short films before the main feature and desire very short films with a maximum length of five minutes, which excludes many of the films in the pool. Showing entire programs made of short films is not a widespread practice among the cinemas, except when hosting festivals or special events. Compiling complete programs for the Short Film Pool has the promise of future interest and growth. EYE occasionally invites filmmakers or festival programmers to compile a personal selection of films using the catalog. These could be made into ready-to-book programs.

The users who requested to have new titles added regularly to the catalog show a preference for animation and documentary. With one hundred screenings in one year, the short animation *Father and Daughter* (Michael Dudok de Wit, 2000) was definitely the box-office hit of 2016. This is explained by the success of the feature-length film *The Red Turtle* by the same director, before which the short film was being shown.

The use of educational programs from the pool is still a concern. While short films are usually suited for this purpose, thanks to their variety and length, we see that schools generally are quite conservative in their choices and tend to show mainly features. This is an area where educators from EYE, in collaboration with other cinemas, could and should take the lead in guiding schools toward the different possibilities short films offer.

Since the start of the project, it is becoming clearer which films work better for various audiences, and in the future, we will be able to provide even more custom-made short film programs to satisfy different needs.

Simona Monizza is a graduate of the L. Jeffrey Selznick School of Film Preservation, class of 1998. After working as a film archivist at the BFI, she joined, in 2000, the Nederlands Filmmuseum, now EYE Filmmuseum, where she has been working as a film restorer and project leader of several restoration projects focused on Dutch experimental films. In 2010, she was appointed curator of experimental film at EYE, where she is responsible for preserving and presenting this collection.

NOTES

1. http://kortefilmpoule.eyefilm.nl.

2. https://www.filmfestival.nl/profs_en/news /dutch-cinemas-100-digital.

3. http://www.openbeelden.nl.

4. http://www.europeanfilmgateway.eu/.

5. http://www.shortcircuitnetwork.org/short -film-pool-catalogue/.

6. The chart illustrates our current digital work-flow.

7. Paolo Cherchi Usai, "The Digital Future of Pre-Digital Film Collections," *Journal of Film Preservation* 88 (Spring 2013): 9.

8. Mark-Paul Meyer, "Care for the Material Ar-chive," https://www.academia.edu/29828464 /Care_for_§_Archive.

9. The exhibition *Celluloid,* organized by EYE in 2016–17, managed to bring the crisis in analog preservation and exhibition to the general pub-lic's attention, albeit only from an artistic point of view.

Conference Report on Transformations I: Cinema and Media Studies Research Meets Digital Humanities Tools (April 15–16, 2016, New York City)

MARINA HASSAPOPOULOU

The Transformations conference series at New York University (NYU) was motivated by the productive convergence of digital humanities (DH) methods and cinema and media studies research as well as the need to further explore the transformative potential of computational methods within the humanities. Transforma-tions I: Cinema and Media Studies Research Meets Digital Humanities Tools launched at NYU's Cinema Studies department on April 15–16, 2016. It was the result of an ongoing collaboration between the department (chaired by Antonia Lant and co-organized by Marina Hassapopoulou) and Columbia University's film studies graduate program (led by Jane Gaines). The conference was supported by NYU's Center for the Humanities.

The conference objective was to provide a cross-disciplinary forum for fostering a col-laborative conversation between humanities scholars, software engineers, computer sci-entists, librarians, and archivists. Film and media studies, often overlooked in overarch-ing discussions of DH practices, was at the forefront. The conference helped connect dis-cussions of theory and practice by proposing various approaches to the historiographical, philosophical, sociocultural, and institutional imperatives that drive the use of digital tools and computational methods in the study of moving images.

Marsha Kinder, professor emerita, Uni-versity of Southern California (USC), keynoted Transformations I. Kinder's pioneering contri-butions to digital studies have been reshaping film and media studies since the 1990s. She was involved in what is considered now to be the first major conference on digital studies and the cinematic arts, Interactive Frictions

(June 1999). Kinder's presence fostered the Transformations conference's twofold aim to expand the definition of DH to include computational experiments in cinematic narrative and to consider alternative and collaborative modes of scholarship. Kinder presented some of the interactive projects created for the Labyrinth Project, a USC-based digital research initiative experimenting with interactive multimedia and database narratives, as well as more recent digital projects.[1] She began by emphasizing the importance of recognizing the nuanced differences between computing and humanities research prior to connecting them. The digital humanities often mask the disparities between the two modes of thinking—machinic and human—to promote an often deceptively seamless, or even intuitive, amalgamation of the two. Kinder's frank acknowledgment of the differences between these two modes of perception was a reminder that conceptual discrepancies can be epistemologically productive when they open new possibilities for knowledge production that stem from incompleteness and incompatibility. In exploring the interplay between linear and modular forms of communication, Kinder's collaborative experiments in database narrative and multimedia scholarship expose and thematize "the dual processes of selection and combination that lie at the heart of all stories."[2] The impulse of making the invisible visible that drives contemporary data visualizations meets its narrative and creative potential in cinematic databases. Kinder's remarks established an understanding of DH practices as inclusive, not precluding artistic innovation and narrative exploration.

Steve Anderson (USC and University of California, Los Angeles), scholar-practitioner and occasional collaborator with Kinder, focused on the ethos of the cinematic humanities and how such inquiry drives the uses of the technology. He juxtaposed this intellectually driven ethos with more typical DH projects (particularly in the field of cultural analytics and software studies) that allow data sets to dictate the research questions. Anderson's critique compared the data-driven logic of certain institutionally funded cultural analytics projects with corporate uses of big data analytics. The Google Brain project (an experiment in machinic intelligence) and Deep Dream (an experiment initially used to help scientists and engineers visualize how deep neural networks respond to images) are examples. Anderson questioned the public sharing of big data for purposes that seem "so trivializing and so reassuring" but conceal the invasive aspects of data surveillance. Digital literacy is a skill for critiquing these algorithmic mass quantification processes and the ideologies that underlie the platforms. It is essential to actively participate in initiatives that provide alternative modes of interacting with such cultural data. Anderson stressed the need for scholars to be involved in designing tools and digital platforms that enable us to continue to expand what Johanna Drucker called "the subjective, inflected, and annotated processes central to humanistic inquiry."[3] Anderson's involvement in open access projects such as *Vectors* (an interdisciplinary online journal for multimedia scholarship), Critical Commons (a public media archive that advocates fair use of copyrighted media for educational and creative purposes), and Scalar (an electronic authoring and publishing platform) exemplifies this commitment to developing new tools and modes of scholarship that take advantage of the affordances of digital media.

The call for humanities scholars to develop their own semantic models and research platforms was reinforced by Mark J. Williams (Dartmouth College) and Eric Hoyt (University of Wisconsin–Madison). Williams stressed the benefits for film preservation and access to media collections across multiple institutions. He focused on the logistics of making archival collections searchable and how scholars ought to become involved in the archival workflow by advocating what materials to digitize next. This would be an expanded concept of archival preservation, because preservation and digitization would become collaborative, discursive processes among media scholars, archivists, preservationists, and curators. The Media Ecology Project (MEP) that Williams directs not only facilitates the online access of archival moving image collections but also encourages researchers to connect with the archiving community by contributing metadata and other information to extend online capabilities.

Eric Hoyt sketched an analytical approach to software development and called not only for building new tools but also for asking questions as to why and how media researchers could find the applications useful. The collaborative initiatives in which he is involved, including the Media History Digital Library (MHDL), have integrated tools that make such vast databases searchable and analyzable. These are Lantern and Project Arclight, which mine the data using keyword searches and can output graphs and data visualizations. The MHDL, according to Hoyt, was the result of "open-*ing* access" and paying closer attention to the nuances and institutional politics involved in making collections available to the public. This intellectual process initiates dialogues among archivists, museums and other cultural institutions, librarians, software engineers, and researchers. Hoyt and Williams promoted both traditional and computationally assisted methodologies to account for the ecologies of media infrastructures. They addressed issues of selective archiving, sustainable online preservation (participatory curation), and the complex relationship between cultural memory and audiovisual heritage.

Hoyt noted the "deformation and transformation" that occur when we compare how we see information and how a computer processes it. Often we take for granted the unpredictable yet productive conceptual shifts that result from the distortion of information inherent in how computers operationally distort data to transform it. Machinic ways of seeing decentralize knowledge to transform the human sensorium. Jane Gaines's talk on "Counting vs. Telling vs. Counting" advanced this argument in the context of digital film historiography. She showcased the Women Film Pioneers Project (WFPP), a collaborative online database of women who worked in the silent film industry. Through a systematic analysis of the practical and methodological challenges involved, Gaines explored the discrepancies between narrative-driven historiography and alternative ways of visualizing sometimes inconclusive clusters of historical data. The WFPP provided a new way of interrogating Wolfgang Ernst's critique of narratological interpretations of archives and the way in which, as he wrote, these story-driven methods "deflect attention from data" and onto "structures of consciousness."[4] For Gaines, this deflection can be positive if it makes us reconsider how we are conditioned to perceive the shape of history, particularly in the context of algorithms, nonnarrativized data, and digital repositories. Gaines further argued, as Ernst and others have, that our understanding of the archive's function has shifted, because of the internet, from thinking of it as storage to thinking of it as transmission. She then applied this reasoning to the disjuncture between the WFPP and the work of the women that it references. Gaines emphasized the deconstructive nature of archives. They endlessly reconfigure data within specific structures of power, as when WFPP reconstructs patriarchal histories of the early film and television industries.

Debashree Mukherjee (Columbia University) elaborated on historiographical issues in "Maps, Microhistories, and Macroanalysis: Digital Futures of Indian Film Historiography." Using Indiancine.ma, a participatory annotated online archive of Indian film, as a case study, she examined the structure, form, and "epistemic valence" of archives rather than the much discussed counterarchival turn. The website's online tools include four film timelines that may be used to visualize narrative information, audio, shot duration, and color saturation. Indiancine.ma, she argued, raises the question of whether all digital film repositories, especially ones, like this, that encourage participatory annotation and multiple forms of film interaction, should be considered inherently preservationist because they must first be digitized to make the materials searchable, annotatable, and interactive. Digitization thereby becomes a means of creating new public commons. That participatory repositories such as Indiancine.ma can only circulate films that are outside copyright (except for scholars' exempt access) brings up inevitable questions regarding the legal status of these materials and the effects of regional copyright restrictions on global access and dissemination.

The macrohistorical turn in DH research involves large-scale historical work based on a massive body of digital data. Yet most of the conference presentations argued for more microhistorical studies and methodological continuities that would bridge the gap between distant and close readings. These would, as Mukherjee stated, enable us to ask different questions and to accommodate the serendipitous discoveries that occur when we are closely reading distant readings. In the same vein, Deb Verhoeven (Deakin University) hoped to end the preoccupation with the dichotomies of close versus distant reading and big versus small data. In place of these debates, it would be better to understand our own spaces and intellectual itineraries when we formulate effective research questions. Verhoeven's work lies at the intersection of cinema studies and the digital humanities in what is now known as new cinema history. This often refers to the methodologies and digital tools being used to study the cultural and social history of cinema and its audiences.[5] The approach encourages collaboration across disciplines, institutions, and social contexts.

Verhoeven argued that the digital humanities have not embraced interdisciplinarity as much as they could. They undervalue, for example, film studies scholars' expertise in analyzing images, space, and time. Her collaborative Kinomatics Project, which studies the "industrial geometry of motion pictures (and music)," operates in the liminal space between close and distant readings. It takes into account cinema's variable distribution and exhibition networks that move across cultural contexts. The project began with an analysis of diasporic cinemas, Greek migrant communities' moviegoing in the 1950s to 1970s in Melbourne and Sydney. Kinomatics incorporated oral histories and archival research to understand the relationship between the movie exhibition circuits and different kinds of distribution arrangements (such as high- vs. low-budget film distribution). Kinomatics's approach had a trial-and-error component, because the available data sets were challenging to quantify and narrativize. The researchers had to use different visualizations to account for all the variants, for instance, animated cartographic charts to diagram patterns of distribution and exhibition. Some applied probability theory and statistics to predict films' movement from their origins to their destinations.

For example, Markov chain analysis and Circos circular visualizations were used to represent a film's movements and repeated screenings in single and multiple venues. This case study demonstrated how researchers can experiment with various data configurations and different modes of representing those data. They also may look at factors beyond the available data, in this case, at travel infrastructures, to understand the movement of films in a global sense. Moreover, these different visualizations suggested that travel and cinema infrastructures are intricately related and that big data studies must explore multidirectional cultural pathways. As Howard Besser (NYU) pointed out, researchers need to question initial assumptions about the data and compensate for their inflexibility once data sets have been entered into automated databases. In questioning the restrictions, power structures, and affordances of digital tools, technical and methodological questions become philosophical ones.

Pedagogy and student projects are frequently marginalized in the DH field, so we wanted to acknowledge the integral role of innovative teaching- and student-initiated research, especially in problem-oriented inquiry, student–teacher collaboration, and playful experimentation. The presenters on the "Teaching as Research" panel, Vito Adriaensens (Columbia University/University of Antwerp), Marina Hassapopoulou (NYU), and Kimon Keramidas (NYU), focused on how process-oriented learning informs their research. Adriaensens's approach invites hands-on "sleuthing" to make discoveries related to early film history. His blended learning techniques "make new media old media again" by tracing connections between early cinema and popular culture. Hassapopoulou considered the archiving potential of social media tools in film reception through a collaborative assignment where students repurposed social media into makeshift archives to document their varying experiences of watching a specific film. They then reflected on the challenges of creating networked film historiographies. Keramidas's teaching encompasses digital and analog ways of engaging with the modularity, nonlinearity, and rhizomatic capacities of digital media. Students produce scholarship that is tailored for online curation and hypertextual and/or nonlinear navigation. All three panelists pointed out that writing through and for digital media platforms consists of more than a straightforward adaptation of traditional modes of academic writing to a digital format.

A panel of NYU Cinema Studies graduate students demonstrated the intricacies of multimedia scholarship projects highlighting particularities of digital media, such as interactivity, modularity, and cross-platform connectivity. These pedagogy panels spoke to a practical and conceptual shift in the way students approach their work. They are no longer studying in isolation, focused solely on the end result of their course work (that dreaded final paper that only the professor has the privilege of reading). This change reflects transformations in the fields of film and media studies and the humanities at large toward collaborative, peer-reviewed, project-based, multimodal forms of scholarship. Although mostly productive, this shift also brings up issues of intellectual property in multiauthored scholarship. Assessing multimedia work, as in the case of interdisciplinary PhD dissertations, exposes the discrepancies between the ethos of expanded scholarship, the rigidity of academic infrastructures, and the vicissitudes of the academic job market.

This first Transformations conference proposed that creating tools, online research initiatives, and multimodal pedagogy should be considered important humanities work in its own right rather than, as Hoyt aptly put it, simply the "precondition" and the "raw materials" for scholarly research. We laid the groundwork for open-ended reflections on—and reassessments of—the identity of the field of film and media studies in the context of the digital humanities. Appropriately, Transformations I contributed to the field by initiating a prototypical collaborative online resource that can be used to identify projects and scholarship that focus on the intersection between the digital humanities and film and media studies. Find it online at https://transformationsconference.net/.

Transformations II is scheduled for spring 2018.

Marina Hassapopoulou is visiting assistant professor of cinema studies at New York University's Tisch School of the Arts. She is currently working on her forthcoming book, *Interactive Cinema: An Alternative History of Moving Images.*

NOTES

1. A hands-on, interactive exhibition of some works from the Labyrinth Project was curated in conjunction with the conference, with the assistance of Professor Kinder, the NYU Cinema Studies department, and the moving image archiving and preservation program.

2. Marsha Kinder, "Narrative Equivocations between Movies and Games," in *The New Media Book,* ed. Dan Harries, 119–32 (London: British Film Institute, 2002), 120.

3. Johanna Drucker, "Blind Spots," *Chronicle of Higher Education,* March 14, 2009, http://www.chronicle.com/article/Blind-Spots/9348.

4. Wolfgang Ernst, *Digital Memory and the Archive,* ed. Jussi Parikka (Minneapolis: University of Minnesota Press, 2013), 151, 213.

5. E.g., Richard Maltby, Daniel Biltereyst, and Philippe Meers, eds., *Explorations in New Cinema History: Approaches and Case Studies* (Malden, Mass.: Wiley-Blackwell, 2011).

REVIEWS

Book

The Arclight Guidebook to Media History and the Digital Humanities
EDITED BY CHARLES R. ACLAND AND ERIC HOYT
REFRAME BOOKS, 2016

Bregt Lameris

From the tremendous video libraries of YouTube and the Internet Archive to the text collections of the HathiTrust and the Media History Digital Library, media historians today confront the challenge of engaging with an abundance of cultural works and archival materials. For those invested in the digital humanities, this abundance presents an opportunity to transform these materials' availability into data to be studied using a variety of methods.

—Eric Hoyt, Kit Hughes, and Charles R. Acland, "A Guide to the Arclight Guidebook," *The Arclight Guidebook to Media History and the Digital Humanities*

This is the opening of the e-book *The Arclight Guidebook to Media History and the Digital Humanities*, edited by Charles R. Acland and

Eric Hoyt. The text sums up the book's subject: scholars' struggle and the hard work they have done over the past years to introduce digital humanities into media history and work with digital tools to expand and broaden their research.

At the same time, various authors also critically evaluate the digital research tools and methods they used for their media historical investigations, making it a very helpful publication for those who need an introduction to digital humanities and media history. Furthermore, it is highly recommended for scholars interested in current developments in the field.

The book answers the following questions: What new skills, competences, and tools are needed when media historians move their research activities into the domain of digital humanities? Toward what new and unanticipated research questions does such a move toward digital humanities lead us? How did this change the workflows in humanities scholarship? And finally, what does that mean?

Project Arclight, from which the book derives, is a collaboration between Concordia University of Montreal in Canada and the University of Wisconsin–Madison in the United States. Its aim is to build new tools to enable media historians to find patterns and trends in media history. This has resulted in the Arclight application that allows scholars to search the Media History Digital Library (MHDL), visualize the search results in several ways, and export the results in various formats, including as an Excel document. This last possibility allows scholars also to use the data for other purposes, as described by Kit Hughes in her article "Field Sketches with Arclight: Mapping the Industrial Film Sector."

The book presents some of Arclight's results and possibilities. Many of its contributors either presented at or chaired the 2015 symposium. Of course, many essays discuss other ongoing projects and research initiatives. This has resulted in an extensive overview of the work done in the United States and Canada in the areas of digital tools in recent media history. It presents a glance into this research practice as well as a good introduction to digital humanities for those media historians who are not (yet) part of this community.

Whereas literary studies, linguistics, and classics have enthusiastically engaged with digital humanities, media history has stayed behind. In their introduction to the book, Hoyt, Hughes, and Acland explain that from the start, "open source technologies for text analysis . . . were faster and more sophisticated than forms of automated moving image and sound analysis" (3). Therefore the adaptation of media history into the field of digital humanities happened relatively late. Most media scholars had already been using, transforming, and developing the already existing digital tools for analyzing written sources. The turn toward audiovisual analysis, however, remained marginal. Projects like Yuri Tsivian's Cinemetrics were more the exception than the rule.

It is, of course, important that written media historical sources are available and searchable. Nevertheless, digital tools and methodologies for analyzing audiovisual sources remain underdeveloped. The project's leaders, as well as the editors of the book, recognize this as a problem. Still, there is a bias toward written materials in the book. Of the seventeen essays, fourteen discuss work done on written sources, whereas only three consider digital humanities as they relate to analyzing audiovisual sources. Over the past decade,

both in Europe and in North America, several annotation and visualization tools have been developed that allow for a digital approach to the moving image. Most of these research projects are not (or only briefly) mentioned in the book. As a result, for scholars who wish to get an introduction to these burgeoning digital humanities and media history initiatives, the book has limitations.

Four parts reflect the diversity of the domains of digital humanities and media history. The first part contains articles discussing how digital humanities have changed the way we search for media historical sources. The second part discusses digital (relational) databases that help ask and answer new and different media historical questions. The third part shows how digital tools help us analyze images, sounds, and words. Finally, the articles in the fourth part evaluate the changes in the research process and the possibilities of and problems with new digital presentation formats.

The articles that discuss how to find written source materials are gathered in the part "Searching and Mapping" and clustered around the topic of nontheatrical film. Remarkably, most traces of this part of media history are to be found outside of the common media historical sources available in the MHDL. This is probably why nontheatrical film is so present as a research topic in this part of the book. However, this is not problematized in an explicit way. That is a pity, because it would have allowed for a more serious consideration of whether and how changing research agendas and interests might be connected to digital humanities. As it stands, this question remains rather implicit. The answers and suggestions that one distills from this series of essays are mostly connected to the increasing availability of a broad range of written source materials, from trade press to newspapers to fan magazines, that can be easily searched thanks to optical character recognition scanning of the material and proper tagging by the archives. Haidee Wasson addresses the situation of audiovisual sources and how "[t]his . . . has changed significantly with digital collections and web-based viewing interfaces where now online moving images are offered up in an unprecedented and resplendent diversity" (36). In all, supplementing written sources with more digitally available audiovisual sources has made the historical investigation of nontheatrical film much easier and probably also more interesting.

One article in this section discusses ways in which mapping software can be particularly helpful in presenting the results of the research in nontheatrical film. This interesting topic, however, might have been more at home in the last section of the book, which discusses how we present our research results. Another option would have been to create a section on visualization technologies that would gather articles describing and criticizing the introduction of the image to present or illustrate research results. This development in digital humanities deserves its own critical attention.

The section "Approaching the Database" is rich, but it is also the least specific for media history, because many digital humanities scholars have been concerned with databases in a broader sense. They have been and are a very important part of our research agenda. Using new digital databases and implementing already existing data sets in new ways in historical research allow us to connect and interrelate them and to find patterns that we did not notice before. Databases have become such an important element of digital humanities that, for example, the humanities faculty of the University of Amsterdam is considering accepting them as academic publishing, comparable to peer-reviewed articles and books. Miriam Posner's article raises serious methodological issues on the use of databases, the belief in objectivity, and in what way an interface constrains how we "read" information in a database. She concludes that databases are constructed following narrative, causal patterns and, as a result, will not and can never be objective, even though they might appear that way. The underlying relational structures of digital databases, though, allow new connections between data and the potential for a new and different understanding of media history.

The third section, "Analyzing Images, Sounds, Words," touches on the use of digital tools to analyze audiovisual sources, the neglected component of digital humanities. With this in mind, it might have been a better choice to leave the analysis of "words" out of this section to focus on digital tools and the analysis of audiovisual sources. The texts discuss in detail concepts such as workflow and methodology, including critical considerations of how the use of these tools influences the way we ask and answer questions. For example, Lea Jacobs and Kaitlin Fyfe explain that investigating audiovisual sources on a more detailed, micro level with the help of digital tools can be "like the microscopic examination of a tissue sample, the close examination of film via digital editing systems opens up a whole new research perspective" (268). Similarly, Kevin L. Ferguson writes that he wants to make the invisible visible by taking "a surrealist view of the hidden in order to imagine what aspects of media texts are literally impossible to see without special computer-assisted techniques" (271). More elaboration on this topic, with a comparative perspective positioning these highly pertinent articles, would have been welcome.

Numerous other research projects are working with audiovisual source materials. Examples are the color visualizations produced in the Mapping Desmet project,[1] for which the open-source software ImagePlot, developed by Lev Manovich, was used.[2] Another example is the work done by Adelheid Heftberger on Vertov's films, which resulted in the book *Kollision der Kader.*[3] And finally, I wish to mention the research project in which I am currently involved, FilmColors, at the University of Zurich. Barbara Flueckiger describes this European Research Council–funded project in this issue of *The Moving Image.*

The last part, "Process, Product, and Publics," is an account of how researchers have seen their workflow change, forcing them to leave their comfort zones. One of the problems discussed is that, with digital tools, larger bodies of data than ever before can be collected. Even though this might not be a problem in itself, the next step is that these data need to be appropriately ordered, described, and analyzed. Another discomfiting element is the need to collaborate with other institutions and other disciplines, as Mark Williams of the Media Ecology Project explains. This implies the need to listen to each other, even if, in some cases, you do not speak the same "language." Finally, Eric Hoyt describes the ways his duties have expanded in the direction of digital collection and of building and developing software, which are needed but not always highly valued in a humanities environment. In all, this last part teaches us that digital humanities increasingly force us to collaborate. This implies that larger projects in digital humanities and media history will need project members and participants with various specialties. Interdisciplinarity is therefore another key to working successfully.

The book is distributed as an open-source e-book by REFRAME Books. It can be downloaded in two different digital formats: PDF, which is optimized for desktops, laptops, and printing, and EPUB, which is unpaginated and optimized for tablets and smartphones. The formats differ in how the pages are presented, which can be confusing for the reader who switches from one to the other. It is highly recommended to read the book while online, because many of the examples contain internet links where one can then immediately see the database, archive, or application referenced. Finally, when reading this book, we should keep in mind that it is focused on the situation in the United States and Canada. Consequently, its perspective on the European research field, including the work done on audiovisual analysis at European universities, is limited.

I recommend that any media historian interested in digital humanities download and read the book. It gives an interesting overview of digital humanities research done over recent years in the United States and Canada. Furthermore, I advise anyone to check out the Arclight application and to start using it for research purposes. In all, Project Arclight, with the application, the symposium, and the book, has provided very important new initiatives and possibilities for the use of digital tools in media historical research.

Bregt Lameris has a PhD in media and culture studies (Utrecht University, Netherlands) and an MA in cinema and theater studies (Radboud University, Netherlands). Her monograph *Film Musealisation and Historiography* appeared in May 2017. She has also worked as a research associate for the Leverhulme Trust–funded project Colour in the 1920s: Cinema and Its Intermedial Contexts, on which she collaborated with Sarah Street, Joshua Yumibe, and Victoria Jackson.

NOTES

1. "Datasets and Colour Visualizations for 'Data-Driven Film History: A Demonstrator of EYE's Jean Desmet Collection,'" Creative Amsterdam: An E-Humanities Perspective, http://www.create.humanities.uva.nl/results/desmet datasets/. Also see his website Film History in the Making, https://filmhistoryinthemak ing.com/.

2. "Image Plot," Software Studies Initiative, http://lab.softwarestudies.com/p/imageplot .html.

3. Adelheid Heftberger, *Kollision der Kader, Dziga Vertovs Filme, die Visualisierung ihrer Strukturen und die Digital Humanities* (Munich: edition text+kritik, 2016).

Blu-ray

3-D Rarities
BLU-RAY DISTRIBUTED BY FLICKER ALLEY, 2015

Jeremy Carr

In an age when 3-D projection (if not actual shooting) is almost a prerequisite for Hollywood's blockbusters, and when the movies from 3-D's previous heyday of the 1950s are greeted with something akin to kitschy amusement, it is easy to forget—or not even to be aware of in the first place—that 3-D films were made decades prior, came in a variety of forms and formats, and were conceived for a multitude of purposes.

This is where *3-D Rarities* enters the picture. Presented by Flicker Alley and the 3-D Film Archive, and produced by Bob Furmanek, Jeffery Masino, and Joshua Morrison, this assortment of twenty-two rare films covers the years 1922 to 1953 and includes color and black-and-white promotional works, feature film trailers, animated shorts, and documentaries, running 147 minutes in all. The disc is supplemented by 3-D photo galleries, a brief snippet from *The Bellboy and the Playgirls* (1962), a "nudie cutie" with 3-D footage directed by Francis Ford Coppola, and commentary tracks by either Thad Komorowski or Jack Theakston on three of the films. An accompanying booklet includes ex-ceptionally informative essays by Komorowski and Theakston as well as by Hillary Hess, Julian Antos, Donald McWilliams, Ted Okuda, and Mary Ann Sell. These articles provide concise detail concerning the exhibition of each film assembled for the set, along with illuminating notes on the context of their production and, in some cases, details about the source print for the respective inclusion.

The films are divided into "Part 1: The Dawn of Stereoscopic Cinematography" and "Part 2: Hollywood Enters the Third Dimension." Following the repeated refrain that stereoscopic cinematography is more lifelike and mimics "natural vision," many of the earliest films tout candid, slice-of-life situations and their authentic representation when seen in depth. Explicitly flaunting the most obvious novelty of 3-D technology, most of the films also showcase an array of off-the-screen effects, with everything from baseball bats and bouncing balls to hot dogs and guns coming toward the camera (the gun image drawing an automatic association with *The Great Train Robbery* [1903], directed by Edwin S. Porter, who, incidentally, presented test footage at the first documented exhibition of a 3-D film on June 10, 1915).

With national landmarks framed by rustling foliage, the aptly titled *Thru' the Trees: Washington D.C.* is part of the *Kelley's Plasticon Pictures* (1922/1923) segment, the "oldest surviving American 3-D film in stereoscopic form," according to Theakston's commentary. Photographed by William T. Crespinel, this portion contains a surprisingly sophisticated use of foreground elements to outline a static image, adding layers to a composition that would otherwise be lacking in markedly perceptible depth. As opposed to the stationary quality of a film like this, the *John Norling/Jacob Leventhal Tests* (1935) and the Pennsylvania Railroad's *Thrills for You* (1940) highlight examples of 3-D's impact on movement along the "Z axis," specifically a roller coaster in the case of the former and a locomotive in the case of the latter (trains being a natural—and early—fit for cinema's dimensional capacity).

Additional titles in this first section include the fully animated films *Now Is the Time* (1951), *Around Is Around* (1951), *O Canada* (1952), and *Twirligig* (1952). Of note, here, is

Figure 1. *Thrills for You* (Pennsylvania Railroad, 1940), from *3-D Rarities*. Courtesy of Flicker Alley.

Around Is Around, which depicts objects rotating in a cylindrical motion, accentuating the receding nature of 3-D, moving against a backdrop that flows from right to left, thus creating a distinct directional contrast. *O Canada*, which incorporates a traveling zoom technique invented by animator Norman McLaren, proved to be an inspiration for Stanley Kubrick, who later developed the process further for the Star Gate sequence of *2001: A Space Odyssey* (1968).

Rounding out the first half of features is *New Dimensions* (1940), an intriguing Chrysler promotion that shows stop-motion animated car parts assembling to music, occasionally popping toward the screen, and eventually forming a new Plymouth, and *Bolex Stereo* (1952), which interestingly promotes the popular consumption and home movie application of stereoscopic technology. The combined 16mm stereo camera/attachment ran about $1,100 at the time, which, as Hess notes, could also purchase a "swell used car back then." This type of device utilized in an average home presumes the appeal of having the generally mundane—farming, family vacations, assorted household activities—rendered more realistic

and, therefore, presumably, more memorable. It is an unglamorous potential of 3-D technology that runs counter to its later and current association with spectacle; it should be noted that this segment does contain underwater scenes, which Hess states were probably the first 3-D movies taken from such a setting.

Part 2 contains several 3-D firsts. Among the pioneering works are the trailer for Jack Arnold's *It Came from Outer Space* (1953), the first trailer actually made in 3-D to promote a 3-D feature, which itself was the first 3-D film to be widely shown in the 1.85:1 widescreen format; the *Rocky Marciano vs. Jersey Joe Walcott* inclusion (1953), the first and only 3-D newsreel; and the ominous *Doom Town* (1953), about atomic bomb testing, the first 3-D documentary. There is also *The Adventures of Sam Space* (1960), "the first in a series of theatrical 3-D puppet cartoons," according to Okuda. Then there is *I'll Sell My Shirt* (1953), a burlesque film unseen in 3-D for more than sixty years, where, as Okuda puts it, "low comedy meets high technology."

An additional animated film is featured in the second section. One of two "Stereotoons" produced by Paramount in the early 1950s, *Boo Moon* (Izzy Sparber and Seymour Kneitel, 1954), featuring Casper the Friendly Ghost, foreshadows the widespread popularity of 3-D cartoon films today, frequently some of the more astounding in the format.

As the "Hollywood Enters the Third Dimension" title suggests, Part 2 also highlights some prominent Hollywood names and their experience with 3-D. Lloyd Nolan guides us through the instructive, if blatantly self-promotional, *M. L. Gunzburg Presents Natural Vision 3-Dimension* (1952), a prologue that ran before Arch Oboler's *Bwana Devil* (1952), and John Ireland is among those featured in the 3-D trailer for *Hannah Lee* (1953), his directorial debut. There is also the trailer for *The Maze* (1953), directed by William Cameron Menzies, and Rita Hayworth sings and loves in radiant 3-D during the *Miss Sadie Thompson* (1953) trailer.

Given its decades-spanning contents, the entire *3-D Rarities* compilation serves as a revealing, sometimes comically quaint time capsule of people, places, and ideas. And several of the films quite accidentally capture moments of historical importance, such as the *John Norling/Jacob Leventhal Tests,* which, as Theakston points out, contains a scene from a baseball game where one can see an African American playing on an integrated team ten years before Jackie Robinson left his indelible stamp on Major League Baseball.

Complementing this collection is a sampling of 3-D photo galleries and examples from a variety of 3-D comic books. The still photos of *The Hunchback of Notre Dame* (1923) highlight the production's lavish sets, while *New York World's Fair* (1939) displays the futuristic design of the event. *3-D Comic Books* (1953) gives a well-rounded sense of what some of the 1950s 3-D English-language comics were like, even if they did have, as Bob Furmanek comments, a notably shorter life span than 3-D movies.

With their emphasis on visual splendor, most of the films collected here seem quite suited to the effects of 3-D photography—the imagery is tantamount. Among the exceptions, however, is a part of the *William T. Crespinel/ Jacob Leventhal Tests* (1924–27) where silhou-

etted individuals partake in various activities. While their actions do flaunt the depth of the format—with lassos, fishing poles, and baseballs coming toward the camera—the flatness of the featureless people results in a curious visual disparity. There is also *Stardust in Your Eyes* (1953), starring comic Slick Slavin (real name Trustin Howard, who, in addition to Leonard Maltin, wrote a brief introductory passage in the booklet). *Stardust* stands out because the entire segment is primarily a Slavin song and comedy routine, something that leaves no real impression as far as its use of 3-D is concerned; he is just standing there.

Tantalizingly discussed by Theakston but unfortunately not presented on the disc is the 3-D fad of "blinkies," whereby viewers could choose the fate of the hero by shutting one eye or the other, therefore only seeing one distinct half of the combined 3-D image. It would take until 2014 for contemporary audiences to see a similar approach toward multivisual 3-D division, with Jean-Luc Godard's *Goodbye to Language,* where two images diverge and the viewer can choose to focus on one or the other (or both at the same time).

Consisting of a combination of random objects and figures with real-world elements, the early demo reels presented here initially were shown at technical conventions, where it was the technology in and of itself that garnered the attention; this was before 3-D aspired toward any sort of narrative integration. In general, in terms of how and why these films were made and presented, as well as how they are perceived today, many of the features are indeed of more interest from a technical rather than artistic standpoint. There is also something of a supposition running through much of this collection that 3-D technology was to be cinema's final major technological innovation, stressing its corresponding potential with, and its influential equivalency to, sound film: "First, we had the silents," states Nolan. "Next, we had the talkies. And third, and last, we have the roundies."

With obviously no way of foreseeing 3-D's rise in popularity during the 1950s, its subsequent gap in appeal, and its recent reemergence, it is fascinating to see how the form was approached and why, and how those interests changed with each passing year. Gone may be the days of flimsy paper and plastic glasses with red/right and green/left designations, but the desired impression of depth in the cinema remains essentially the same. Even in their rudimentary fashion, these early 3-D films give a good indication of what was possible, in some cases proposing uses that have even today been underexplored (sporting events, for example). With all the advances, though, and as one sees how rapidly the aesthetic and the technical potentials developed, still unfulfilled is the widespread realization of 3-D without the necessary "magic glasses." For now, as in 1922, we are left with an invention that takes two images and creates one, and then requires an additional device to view that image properly. Nevertheless, when all works as it should and the end result is a spectacular cinematic presentation, as the *Bolex* narrator declares, "What an image!"

Jeremy Carr teaches film studies at Arizona State University and has written for the publications *Vague Visages, Film International, Cineaste, Senses of Cinema, MUBI/Notebook, Cinema Retro, The Moving Image, CineAction, Movie Mezzanine, Cut Print Film,* and *Fandor/ Keyframe.*